EMPEROR CH'IEN-LUNG RECEIVING TRIBUTARIES. *Enthroned on the Meridia[n]* [...] *Forbidden City, the emperor Ch'ien-lung receives tributaries of a border people, the Ele[...]* [...] *king the honor of Prince of the First Degree. The scene was recorded by the Jesuit Father Attiret toward the end of 1754; a comparison with Photo 4 will show how accurately the setting was here depicted. (Engraving from* Conquêtes des Chinois, *Paris, late 18th century.)*

951.156
C
CAMERON N
PEKING, A TALE OF THREE CITIES   G1750

832155

WILLINGBORO PUBLIC LIBRARY
SALEM ROAD
WILLINGBORO, N.J.   08046

P9-CQM-074

PEKING

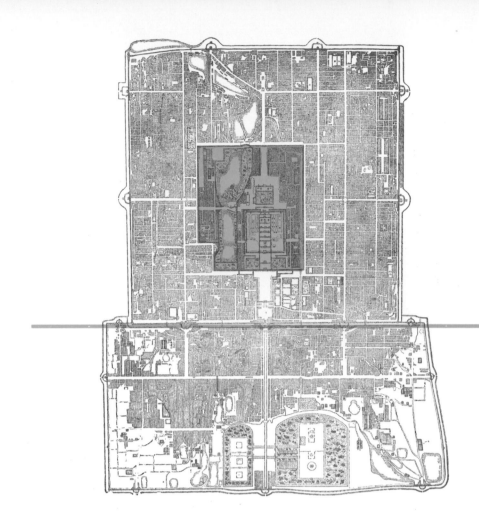

PEKING

A Tale of Three Cities

by Nigel Cameron *&* Brian Brake

foreword by L. Carrington Goodrich

A WEATHERMARK EDITION

HARPER & ROW: *New York & Evanston*

832155

951.156
C

PEKING: A TALE OF THREE CITIES. *Copyright © 1965 by Nigel Cameron and Brian Brake. Produced by John Weatherhill, Inc., Tokyo. Printed in Japan. All rights reserved. No part of this book may be used or reproduced in any manner whatsoever without written permission except in the case of brief quotations in critical articles and reviews. For information address Harper & Row, Publishers, Incorporated, 49 East 33rd Street, New York, New York 10016.*

FIRST EDITION

LIBRARY OF CONGRESS CATALOG CARD NUMBER: 65–22147

To

J. B.

*who has never been to Peking
but would like to go*

Table of Contents

A THIRD BEGINNING

Photographs, Maps, and Charts

Note: Only principal elements are listed here. More detailed references to illustrative material have been included in the index.

Foreword, *by L. Carrington Goodrich*

Mr. Goodrich is the Dean Lung Professor Emeritus of Chinese at Columbia University and the author of A Short History of the Chinese People

As one born in the shadow of the Peking wall and brought up close to the old Drum Tower this reader finds the present account by Nigel Cameron and Brian Brake engrossing from beginning to end. They have brought to life not only the visual aspects but even the tastes and smells and sounds of both the ancient and the modern city and made its past part of the vast panorama of China's history. Peking has been altered markedly by buildings and customs of alien design, but the authors have been able to see beyond these intrusions to what has come down from the days of the northern barbarians and the stately times of the great Ming and Ch'ing emperors.

The Chinese have always believed that both beauty and grandeur for their capital were central; in this they have been followed by their foreign rulers, the Khitan, the Jurchen, and the Mongol. When in the mid-twelfth century the Jurchen conquered the Northern Sung they, like the Khitan two centuries earlier, stripped the capital Pien (Kaifeng) of all its craftsmen—goldsmiths, silversmiths, blacksmiths, and the like—even dismantling the woodwork of the palace buildings to incorporate in structures of their own at the site of today's Peking. Sung envoys to the city marveled at the new capital's magnificence. A century and more later the Mongols had their turn, employing an Arab and his son, Yeh-hei-tieh-er and Ma-ho-ma-sha, as supreme architects.

Here is a translation of the record as it has come down: "In the third year of Chih-yuan [1266] it was decided to locate the national capital at Yen [now Peking]. In the eighth moon Kublai directed the technicians of all the bureaux concerned to assume the duties of constructing the palaces and issued the following command: 'As the Great Enterprise has come to its conclusion, our national influence is in process of expansion. If the palaces and metropolitan adornments are not beautiful and imposing, they will not be able to command the respect of the empire.' Yeh-hei-tieh-er labored ceaselessly at the task until he had drawn up a grand scheme."

The result, as the history of the city records, followed the Grand Khan's wish. Mark these two passages (in renderings by C. Ito): "All the imperial gates had cinnabar doors and vermilion pillars, and the red walls were decorated with a scroll design and green-glazed tiles." As for the decoration of one of the palaces, "the floral base was of blue stone pavement covered with a double fabric; red pillars decorated with gold, surrounded with carvings of dragons. The four walls were red and the windows in emerald green. Between the beams and ceiling it was painted in gold and studded with tiles. The staircase with its balustrade was painted red and covered with gilt-copper. . . ."

All this was swept away by order of the first Ming emperor, but his son erected another great capital, and this, at least in part, is what remains today.

Do I miss anything in Cameron and Brake's graphic and surprisingly full account? Yes, a little, for surely no one book could ever contain all of this many-faceted city nor ever echo all the nostalgic memories of those of us who have had the good fortune to live there. I miss references to the noble speech of Peking, a more beautiful dialect than any other in all China. I miss mention of the sweets sold by traveling vendors to children in the city's byways, sweets shaped on the spot into curious figures and filled with a sugary essence. I miss something about cooks on the main thoroughfares roasting chestnuts in huge ovens, baking sweet potatoes peeled to reveal their golden flesh, and preparing long strips of vermicelli for immediate sale to passers-by. I wonder about the squeaking wheelbarrows with their loads of ordure bound for the fields beyond An-ting-men and the squeals of pigs swinging upside down on carrying poles destined for slaughter for the feasts of the day. Have the fairs all disappeared? Those at the Great Bell monastery, or the shrine of the Fire God, or the temple of the White Cloud—all were memorable occasions both to buy a possible bargain or to be cheated a little. What of the bookshops at Lung-fu-ssu or Liu-li-ch'ang? There was nothing like them in any other Chinese city.

Has modernization done away with all these things? I hope not. But the joy of perusing the present book has made this reader savor the memory of the city once again, and one may hope with Cameron and Brake that the Chinese of today and tomorrow will reshape Peking with a grandeur it has always had.

New York, Spring, 1965

Acknowledgments

Anyone who writes a book about Peking must be deeply indebted to a large number and variety of people whose researches, translations, thoughts, and anecdotes bring perspective to the subject. Throughout the book I have tried in a general way to indicate my principal sources, particularly for quotations, and full bibliographical information will be found in the Bibliography. There is also a further category of material—those many scores of books on a hundred aspects of Chinese life and art and history from which, in part, an author's opinions are formed over a period of years. It is impossible, and would in any case be tedious, to mention them all. But I should like to set down my thanks here, whether I have quoted directly from them or not.

Unless otherwise indicated, all the photographs in this books are by Brian Brake. We traveled together in China, and his work is such an integral part of the subject that this book is in the fullest sense a collaboration. For photographs other than his, we are glad to record our indebtedness to Hedda Morrison, who lived and worked in Peking during the years between the two world wars—her record of that time is an invaluable piece of documentation that might well find its outlet in a volume of its own—and to Dmitri Kessel, of *Life* magazine, whose aerial shots show more clearly than words the unique pattern of palace, temple, and wall which forms the skeleton of Peking.

We are particularly indebted to Professor L. Carrington Goodrich, of Columbia University, both for his kind Foreword, which adds yet another interesting facet to the Peking story, and for a number of valuable suggestions that he made after reading the book in proof.

The following museums, institutions, and private individuals have extended their willing and prompt assistance in the process of assembling the materials, whether works of art, textual matter, or figures: the Rietberg Museum, Zurich; the William Rockhill Nelson Gallery of Art, Atkins Museum, Kansas City; the Seattle Museum; the Smithsonian Institution, Freer Gallery of Art, Washington; the National Geographic Society, Washington; the National Museum, Tokyo; Toyo Bunko, Tokyo; the Palace Museum, Taiwan; the Mansell Collection, London; Dr. Joseph Needham, Cambridge; Dr. James Cahill, Freer Gallery of Art, Washington; Professor F. W. Mote, Princeton University; Mr. Henry McAleavy, London; Mrs. Hope Danby, England; Mr. Fok Po-yuen and Mr. Lam Ka-ping, for certain translations; Frank Eckermann, Hong Kong, for assistance with maps and plans; Mr. Lee Kwok-wing, Hong Kong, for the calligraphy of "Peking" reproduced on both page i and the binding ; Elek Books, Ltd., London, for permission to quote from *Imperial Peking* by Lin Yutang; Geoffrey Bles, Ltd., London, for permission to quote from *The Rise and Splendour of the Chinese Empire* by René Grousset.

The chapter-heading decorations have been adapted from W. M. Hawley's *Chinese*

Folk Design. Those for the chapters on the three Pekings are variants of the much-used dragon-and-pearl design, while that for the Enduring Past chapters shows a fanciful arrangement of three *shou* characters, meaning "longevity."

To friends and acquaintances, to officials and others in Peking who helped on our visits to the city, I must add a word of gratitude. Meredith Weatherby, in Tokyo, has rendered most valuable editorial assistance in the preparation of the manuscript. And finally I would like to mention the facilities granted to me by H. A. Rydings, Librarian of Hong Kong University, and the day-to-day assistance of Geoffrey W. Bonsall, Deputy Librarian. Their help, suggestions, and patience were most valuable.

Needless to say, any mistakes or oversights the book may contain are my own, as are whatever controversial opinions I may have expressed. But the book is better for much help unstintingly given.

NIGEL CAMERON

Hong Kong, Spring, 1965

Introduction

1. Under the Peking Sky

In late March the steely winter of the North China Plain has not long left hold of the city of Peking. Trees in the streets and above the low blank walls of houses are just beginning to bud in a haze of bright green. The sky, laden with the dust that blows in from the west, is between blue and grey, almost pearl colored. You are conscious of the smell of the air, an indefinable smell which is characteristic of Peking.

In the early morning, especially on a weekday, there are few people about in the imperial palaces. Hardly anything contemporary breaks the illusion of walking in courtyards and among buildings which have somehow escaped from the tyranny of time and still belong to the period long ago when they were first constructed. The stillness and the tentative light of daybreak deepen the feeling of the past. And you are extremely aware that this Chinese past is widely different from that of the old cities of Europe and the Western world.

Passing through an arch, you enter one more of the long string of courtyards in the palaces, a vast tranquil space paved with cobbles and bounded by red walls rising thirty or forty feet, topped with ribbed yellow tiles. At first glance it seems as empty as the one you have just left. But a succession of strange high-pitched screams echoes alarmingly in the otherwise peaceful atmosphere—a lunatic, almost animal, sound. In the far corner of this red-walled coffin of a space stands an ordinary-looking man in the usual cloth cap and blue clothes. He is quite motionless except for the head, which wobbles a little as he lets out those strangled cries against the wall. For some reason you know that he is not mad. But it is difficult to imagine the purpose of his cries. Later, when you become more familiar with Peking, you find out that the actors from the Peking opera have an old tradition of exercising their voices as the sun rises, and the corner where two walls meet is considered the ideal place to do this. In Chinese it is called "lifting the throat."

An experience such as this is a good sample of the quality of the city when you first arrive there. Many of the impressions it makes are curious ones. Many things, some trivial, some more important, seem unknowable and unexplainable. The city and its activities raise more questions in your thoughts than can be answered easily, or soon enough. For Peking is still the most remote city of the civilized world. It would be sheer perversity not to notice this.

During much of her long history China has attempted to isolate herself from the rest of the world, and mostly she has succeeded. Inevitably in the course of three thousand years or so a way of life radically different from that of other great civilized peoples has emerged. In Peking, which has been the capital of China for the best part of seven centuries, the results are inescapable. As recently as the 1930's, Peking alone among all the capitals of the world still closed its gates at night, and when one of those gates was destroyed by fire a mere half-century ago, the authorities, in a panic, quickly rebuilt it, not so much for fear of night incursions but because of the danger of the evil spirits which the precise height and position of the structure prevented from flying straight into the city. And somewhat nearer the present, when it was proposed to move two stone lions from their positions inside this same gate (Ch'ienmen) to ease the press of traffic, long deliberations and popular protest eventually solved the problem of the lions' wrath and the resulting evils by performing the operation with the eyes of the beasts blindfolded with blue cloth. In Peking at that time there was nothing comical about such a predicament, nor about its solution. Every facet of living was governed by traditional codes of conduct, and the civilization of China, epitomized by life in the capital, was still at heart unadulterated by the values of the rest of the world.

Since the new regime came to power fifteen years ago, large changes have been made in the unique approach to living which grew up over several thousand years in China and whose quality is still manifest in essence in Peking. A new way of life has been superimposed on the old logic of Chinese living, and new values have been mixed in with the traditional ones. It is as if the civilization of England in the reign of Elizabeth the First had been directly succeeded by the ideas and technology of the present. In a decade and a half complete substitution has not been achieved. But Peking is in the throes of that transformation, its medieval palaces less admired by the populace than its monumental new buildings, its maternity hospitals welcomed, its old curly-dragon life curiously mixed with loudspeakers and the beginnings of industrialization. Two very different kinds of appraisal or appreciation are needed to deal with the ancient and the modern when they are thus abruptly mingled. To admire only the one or only the other, only the Sports Stadium or the Lama Temple, is to miss completely the essence of the city today. However irreconcilable, a frenzy of physical and intellectual change is the very spirit of Peking.

People wake early in the city and most of them also go to bed early, as if it were a village anywhere in Asia. But this is the only resemblance to village life. Never for a moment is there any doubt that this is the capital of China, a metropolis swollen now to a size greater than at any time in its history so that it has spilled, far outside its Ming-dynasty walls, into the dusty miles of the surrounding Peking plain. By dawn the streets are waking from a quiet night, for the hawkers whose cries used to enliven the dark hours have disappeared. The light is pale, yellow, evenly distributed across the sky as people begin to straggle out on their way to work; under its impartial dome the old and the new are hardly distinguishable. The morning faces of the people are blank. Their softly moulded features, lacking the definition of the pronounced noses and mouths of Westerners, are masks suddenly breaking into the odd, almost juvenile innocence of a Chinese smile. Their walk is still the shuffle of the flat-soled Orient. The narrow lanes called *hutung* are still mostly undisturbed by the new living quarters that have risen elsewhere about the city; there, between the blank grey walls of houses, they call their good mornings to each other in the newness of the day: *Ni hao! Ni hao ma!* which means literally "You well, you well!"

Sometimes it is a muffled call. For in spring many people are still wearing a white surgical mask of gauze covering the mouth and looped round the ears. And they are huddled in their clothes, for the air of spring has a definite nip, an almost menacing continental chill, reminding you that cold Central Asian plains influence the Peking weather more than the nearness of the Pacific Ocean. So close to the sea, the capital has the harsh climate of the steppes and deserts of its hinterland, out of which many another influence has come in past centuries. The Chinese, curiously sensitive to a combination of folk beliefs about health and to the pronouncements of their own traditional medicine, are frankly neurotic about changes in the weather. Even on an unseasonably hot day of early summer you can see them in padded clothes, because the date in the Chinese lunar calendar for the discarding of winter garments has not yet arrived. The mask is a new thing, at least in terms of the antiquity of most customs in China, but not so new as foreign visitors think. The sight was common enough in the 1930's, when the Japanese, who are much given to the practice, were already entrenched in numbers in Peking, even before their occupation of North China. And if one requires an indigenous precedent, Marco Polo records that "numerous persons who attend at the sideboard of his majesty [Kublai Khan, the builder of Mongol Peking] and who serve him with meat and drink, are all obliged to cover their noses and mouths with handsome veils or cloths of worked silk, in order that his victuals or his wine may not be affected by their breath."

Nowadays the medical authorities (Western-style public health officers) produce figures to show how the incidence of respiratory infections has declined since the introduction of the mask in the overcrowded city. But the outlandish look of people in the medieval air of Peking, as they pass through the half-light of dawn streets and smile with their eyes over those pads of white, is not reducible to statistics. It is a comical sight, though not to the Chinese themselves, who are lifelong accepters of whatever has been authoritatively decreed.

In Chungshan Park adjacent to the western wall of the Imperial Palace and within the now vanished walls of the Imperial City of old, the dawn-cold trees stand as if conscious of the surrounding air, their branches lightly brush-stroked in against the lightening but featureless sky, the trunks of some wrapped in leggings of straw gone grey with winter frosts. The cold yellow silk of the palace moat is stretched tight between its banks at the base of the great red wall. No bird sings, or at least only an occasional one—somewhere out of sight. For the birds of Peking were exterminated one day a few years back. In one of those mass operations whose thoroughness astonishes, the birds of the city, said to have been consuming a vast amount of grain which the people could ill afford to lose from the surrounding fields, were attacked. On that day the entire populace of

Peking came out in relays to their courtyard gardens, into the streets, and onto the roofs, and beat every kind of noise-making object, from tin cans to Chinese gongs, continuously for well over twenty-four hours. This incessant noise—a remarkable sound it must have been—scared every living bird into the Peking air and kept them there without respite. Correctly fulfilling the scientific prediction, the birds dropped dead from heart failure as they found no rest from hour upon hour of enforced flight. And Peking congratulated itself (quite genuinely) on its popular achievement in safeguarding its food crops. The Chinese are masters of the rational, and also of the absurd.

So no bird sings in Chungshan Park as the light begins to shift and grow stronger in the east and the authoritative delicacy of the Imperial Palace roofs asserts itself in silhouette behind the trees.

Grass does not grow easily in Peking. The winter brings intense cold (a distinguished Russian on an embassy to Peking in the eighteenth century swore that it was colder than Moscow), while summer, between the downpours of rain, burns out the surface moisture. Under the trees in the park lies that velvet coating of dust that silences the feet. Because of this and the stillness of the city just before dawn, to walk there is a through-the-looking-glass sensation that makes of every object a sort of dream. It is the quality of some Chinese landscape painting whose realism is thinned out and distributed evenly over the scroll without focus, and in which the insignificance of man is noted as an aside, as a tiny counterpoint down near the bottom of the scene. Moment by moment the sky grows lighter, glows, and then glints as if it had achieved something, on the yellow roof tiles of the palaces, while the guardian figures (one of whom is generally a mythological fire insurance) stand in little fretted rows down the corner ridges, poised for launching into the Chinese heaven.

In a thin haze of dust some old men are standing with equal assurance on one leg, arms raised and heads thrown back. For a second or two in the silence they stay quite motionless. Slowly their arms move, the position of their bodies changes, their heads follow a prescribed arc. Like flowers in a slow-motion film, the blue-clad men in their black-canvas shoes merge one position into another, hands folding over in the manner of petals, heads inclining like withering stamens. Nearer, you can see the individual hairs slightly trembling in the beard of one of the men. Graceful in spite of their shapelessness, the old men take no notice of you and continue slowly forming new Chinese characters with the co-ordinated movements of their bodies and arms and heads and legs.

Obviously it takes long practice to reach the stage of smoothness and sureness in this "shadowboxing." And it is also evident that a long tradition has been required to perfect the exercises. The practice, in fact, is a lifelong recreation, with a history going back at least two thousand years. It is not some mystical activity like Yoga, but a very ordinary one in China, aimed at co-ordination of muscular action and breathing.

Some of the dancers (it is hard not to use this word to describe them) have brought

YIN-YANG SYMBOL. *Here, like two fish head to tail, the symbol is enclosed by the Eight Diagrams. Said to be derived from a continuous straight line denoting the male principle and a broken line denoting the female, these diagrams symbolize the evolution of nature and its cyclic changes.*

their cronies with them, and four or five old gentlemen are sitting on a park bench not far away, resting their hands on their walking sticks, their faces ineffably bland in the soft morning light. We talk a little about *t'ai chi ch'uan,* as the exercises are called, and what it does for them. "It keeps the *yin-yang* balance right," one says, the other nodding approval of the explanation.

To the uninitiated the answer is as odd as the performance. But in those two laconic-sounding words lies one of the fundamental concepts of Chinese thought—the harmonious balance of complements. To call it that is to oversimplify. *Yin* originally meant the shady side and *yang* the sunny side. The characters for the words begin to appear somewhere around the fourth century B.C., *yin* conveying the ideas of dark, weak, female, night, moon, shade; *yang* denoting bright, strong, male, day, sun. With their human passion for order, the Chinese gradually formulated a theory of nature and the natural order of things. And underneath all later philosophies and religions which have ebbed and flowed over China and left their essences and their dregs on life and thought there, this theory of the ideal balance of complements has persisted. It would not be too sweeping to assert that because of it, and because of the codification of custom derived from the ideas of Confucius, the one being in many ways dependent on the other, Chinese civilization developed on the lines which are peculiar to it. After all the arguments that fill so many learned volumes on the subject of Chinese culture, underneath the whole structure there is left this pervading sensation of the necessity of *yin-yang* balance. So the old man has orthodoxy on his side, and an intense Chinese-ness which, in Peking perhaps more than in many other places, is very obtrusive.*

The Chinese-ness of Peking may seem a rather obvious fact to stress; but, much more than in the great cities of the West, the people of China's capital give the impression of a limitless particular strength and a complete confidence that things Chinese are not just the best, but the only ones worth considering. Nowadays when, under the new regime, the old life has radically altered, much that is new and foreign is already visibly in the process of being sinified. It is not that Peking people make the foreigner feel an outsider. On the contrary, they are very friendly. But he feels an outsider none the less. At first

* René Grousset (see Bibliography for full information on works mentioned in the text or footnotes) suggests a lyrical and rustic origin for the *yin-yang* idea. He recalls the spring-to-autumn period of labor in the fields, followed by cold winter when outdoor work was largely impossible and most people kept inside their houses. With the coming of spring the ceremony of first ploughing took place (performed in Peking by the emperor; see back endpapers) and thereby not only the soil was fertilized but human beings also. Then summer and outdoor work ensued, and the harvest with its festivals, followed once more by the closed winter season. It was not unnatural that within this all-important agricultural pattern everything became classified. The *yin* or closed season when indoor women's work predominated, and perhaps women's authority too; the *yang* or outdoor season of heat and the expansion of growth. The two principles, in opposition and in balance, were capable of being modified by each other, and coexisted in everything. The order which decided their alternation, year to year, was the order of the universe and of society. The Chinese called this order *tao,* and it is a concept central to all their philosophies.

this can be a slightly alarming thought. The millions, the six hundred and fifty millions, of the Chinese, so much at one with each other in outlook, constitute in themselves a group of alarming proportions; and the knowledge that, by their numbers and their confidence in themselves and their way of life, they have quickly absorbed everything and everyone who ever impinged on their lives disturbs one's tranquillity: perhaps because it makes one feel utterly unimportant in their scheme of things. The emotion soon disappears in contact with the individual friendliness one meets everywhere, only to return at other times. The spectacle of Chinese workers on a building site taking a half-hour nap in every conceivable uncomfortable position while a nearby pile driver makes the air and the ground shudder fills the foreigner with a mixture of surprise and envy.

Spring, the Chinese say, is as changeable as a stepmother's face. In Peking this is very true. The gentle light of sunrise quickly strengthens as the sun surmounts the morning mist of the horizon. The old men finish their dance, faces now emblazoned by luminous sunlight, and sit awhile with their friends on the benches before wandering off home. The water of the palace moat—dug many hundreds of years ago and beautifully confined—begins to sparkle, to mirror the bird-bone fineness of the corner tower high on the palace wall, and to throw little spotlight reflections up to the branches and trunks of weeping trees. Voices of children from a kindergarten situated not far away in a Ming pavilion carry on the air toward the light. An area of those contorted rocks and miniature shrubs and trees much prized by generations of Chinese gardeners begins to emerge as an entity from the more commonplace park. The wonder of its suggestion of wild scenery and of its cosmological overtones—an aesthetic cultivated since early times and resulting in a definitive catalogue of such stones written in the twelfth century by a relative of the famous T'ang poet Tu Fu—is a department of Chinese culture hard for the foreigner to understand. The diminutive perspectives of such gardens remind one of an artfully made doll's house, the stones resembling craggy peaks as much or as little as model Louis Quartorze chairs resemble the originals. "The Chinese mind is curiously haunted . . . by this admiration of resemblances," says Osbert Sitwell. "Thus, for example, in Peihai, on the Island of the White Dagoba, an inscription written by the Emperor Ch'ien Lung specially praises a predecessor of the Sung dynasty for having brought to this hill 'many rocks from the South and placed them here in fanciful positions to make them look like dragons' scales.' It is a love which . . . we shall never share for long, only during a passing surrealist phase. . . ."

Now the morning sharpens in the sun. The sky assumes its typical daytime character. The light is strong but blunted by fine dust hanging thousands of feet above the ground. From the blanket of yellow loess soil radiating fanwise from Lanchow in the far west, toward the China Sea, the slightest breeze lifts a layer of particles and raises it far above, forming a translucent canopy over the whole North China Plain. This plain, on whose northern border Peking stands, was formed by loess blown from the Central Asian deserts

DRAGON AND PEARL PAPERCUT. *Papercuts, used in this book as chapter-head decorations, are an old and popular form of Chinese folk art. Here is one of the many variants of the dragon and pearl motif—the dragon symbolizing the emperor, and the flaming pearl, an old Buddhist device, standing for divine truth or the wisdom of heaven. A sculptured version of the dragon and pearl appears in Photo 55.*

and by the eroding effects of rain and river which transported the yellow mud eastwards through long stretches of time. It is worth remembering this genesis of the plain, and of the dust in the Peking sky, because the two are the same substance, and because the beginnings of Chinese history take place within the yellow-earth area, on the banks of the Yellow River. There, not far from the modern Sian, have been found the first vestiges of a culture whose artifacts, more than three thousand years old, are recognizably Chinese, and from which the great tradition of later Chinese motif and cosmology in large part derives. Indeed, Sian, now an industrial town amid the minutely terraced loess mountains, is built on the site of Ch'ang-an, the capital of T'ang China. To the color of this soil we perhaps owe the connection between yellow and the imperial appurtenances— robes, roofs, etc.—and the title of Huang-ti, the Yellow Emperor, mythical founder of the Chinese empire and developer of agriculture.

Almost the whole of this plain is treeless. The forests which must once have softened its contours were buried hundreds of feet under this yellow skin. (From one such ancient forest comes Peking's coal.) And the trees which grew later have long ago been felled for fuel, for housebuilding, and for the construction of temples and palaces. The dust storms afflicting Peking are proverbial, though now, with the recent planting of belts of millions of saplings to the west of the capital, they are less choking and less frequent. The massive afforestation program of the present government, which is gradually covering the friable surface of the plain with groves, seems likely in time to improve things even further. The familiar muted sun of Peking, a light which makes colors glow and prevents even the gaudy reds from jangling with the greens and yellows and purples of painted eaves, seems doomed to lose its kindness. But the inhabitants of Peking are not likely to complain. Their noodles will not be intermittently mixed with grit any more.

It is this gentle light which takes the sadness from the look of the *hutung,* the narrow lanes whose houses unanimously turn their backs on the pedestrian and look instead inwards to their courtyards, just as the thoughts of China have until recently been turned inwards. Peking is a city of walls. The organic connection between walls and city is demonstrated by the ideograph *ch'eng,* which means either. The walls are of every age since the founding of the city. Most of them look old: the dust and the violent extremes of winter cold and summer heat and humidity are responsible for that. The city itself is limited by its Ming walls, within which, until some decades ago, were the walls of the Imperial City; within which, in turn, are the walls of the Forbidden or Palace City. These concentric squares of massive walls are duplicated in diminishing scale in the walls of temples, shrines, and the ordinary *hutung* house.

Traditionally no wall whatever had a window looking outwards. The absence of break in the brick or stucco surfaces gives a vital clue to Chinese ideas about architecture, just as the almost universal presence of rows of windows reflects Western cultural ideas as they materialize in its buildings. In these days when the transition can be made abruptly

Moods and People of the City ▶

The ancient, mellow, expected scenes of Peking are 1 ▶
the ones that first insinuate themselves into the thoughts,
loaded with the nostalgia peculiar to China. Here, by
the Ming wall and watchtower at the southeast corner
of the Imperial Palace, the sweet glow of medieval
China is partly sun, partly color, and partly the settled
peace of things made long ago for purposes now super-
seded.

In China it is still the grandparents who look after the smaller children. As spring colors the winter branches of Peking the old and the very young take the air in the parks. And in the early morning, before the sun has had time to warm up, men practice the slow, balletic movements of shadowboxing. Figures move through the trees and past the chilly faces of palace walls, often in traditional costume as if they had strayed across the boundaries of dynastic time into a present which is now not quite their place.

2 ▲

3 ▲

In the great walled courtyard before Wumen, the front gate 4 ▶
of the Forbidden City, color blends with morning haze and
the impression of former times intensifies. From the parapet
of this gate emperors sometimes received the groveling
tributaries of far countries.

5 ▲

6 ▲

The outer walls and the imperial-yellow roofs were formerly all the average Chinese saw of the Forbidden City. From a high vantage point the palace roofs hover serenely above trees and the grey sea of hutung *houses. The tiled wall, center, with its ceramic insert, forms part of the Imperial City's east boundary. On the skyline, left, is the roof of Wumen, the gateway to the palace.*

Vast cobbled courtyards, vistas of noble but never oppressive proportion, follow one another from south to north through the imperial buildings of Peking. At the Temple of Heaven, where emperors came each year to supplicate the heavens, by whose mandate they ruled, a long avenue reaches northward between dark trees. The low gate at its northern end leads to the circular Temple of the Happy Year, whose conical roof crowned with a gold bud rises above. In its court, children find a spacious playground.

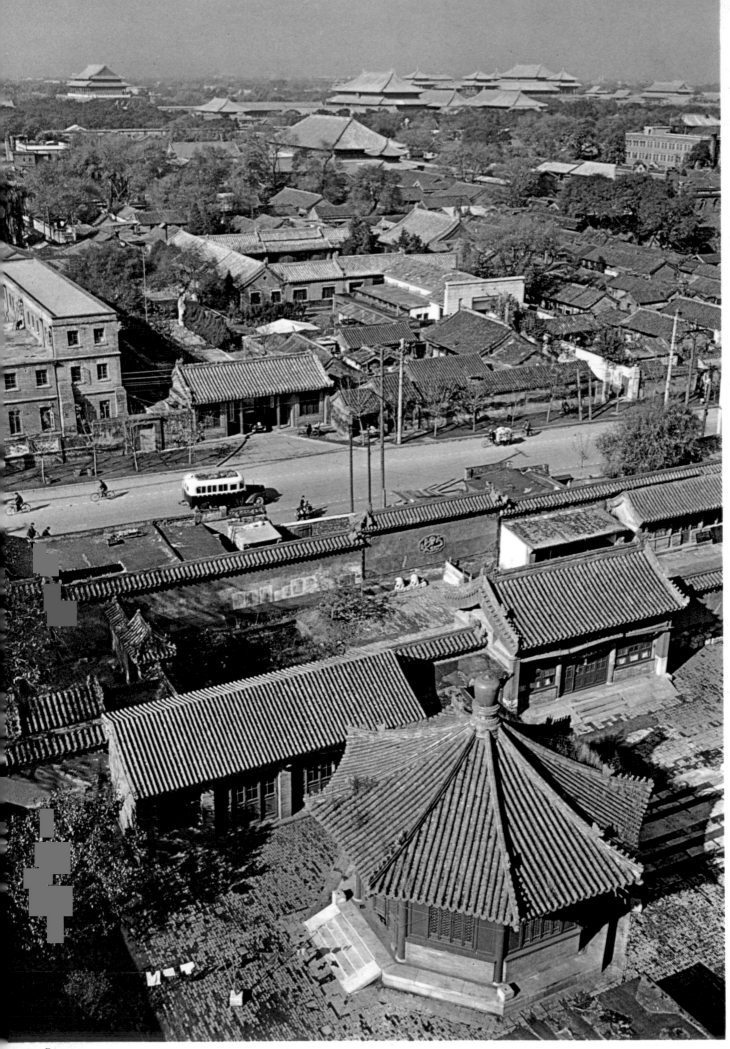

◀ 8 *Peihai, northernmost of the three artificial lakes within the Imperial City, was formerly the pleasure ground of emperors and their birdlike flocks of concubines. Since the fall of the last dynasty it has been open to the public. The White Dagoba on Emerald Isle dominates a sight, familiar now in Peking as in other cities—young men taking their girl friends for a row. The first impression of a timeless Peking begins to dissolve into the facts of contemporary life.*

Photo by Brian Brake, © National Geographic Society

10 ▲

9 ▲

The family climbing Coal Hill is definitely of today's Peking. The boy's cap and the badge with a red star are both postrevolutionary objects. Down the hill is one of the five pavilions. In the haze to the right lie the northern roofs of the Forbidden City.

The delight of the Chinese in their children is often explained as mere insurance against the hard times of old age. But an hour in the Peking hutung *makes it obvious how mistaken such a notion is.*

In one of the city's many Chinese medicine shops—this one is more than three hundred years old—the attendant wears contemporary clothes, but the old customer could have come in unremarked on the first day the shop opened its doors. The abacus has been in use in China from the much more distant past.

13 ▲

There are times in Peking when the past begins to take its place in the background, as it does in old Western cities. The eighteen-year-old concentrating on his book as he sits having tea on the shores of Peihai, the student (from a college in a distant province, his badge proclaims) gazing at the rather sugary beauty of the Summer Palace, and the youths with bicycles pausing a moment or two on Marco Polo Bridge—these are as much Peking at its fabric of old walls.

15 ▲

16 ▲

Until two or three years ago there were itinerant markets in Peking, moving from the yard of one temple to that of another. Some boasted a Peking opera in miniature (18) in which the grand figures of Chinese history and romance strutted on a tiny stage under an awning. Backstage (15) is one of the musicians with his two-string fiddle, and hanging ready for the next act is the false beard indispensable to any wise or powerful character. In another market, near the Temple of Heaven, a formal portrait against a painting of the Gate of Heavenly Peace is still in demand. And a teahouse storyteller recounts traditional tales of mighty men and mighty deeds to an attentive audience (17, 19).

18 ▲

17 ▲

19 ▶

21 ▶

One of the many beasts of Chinese fancy (21) that stand guard in the courtyards of the Forbidden City. In a courtyard in the northern precincts of the palaces two snarling Ming lions of gilt bronze flank the steps to a gateway. Their curly eyebrows, stiff whiskers, and nostrils flared with wrath (23) give them a daunting look belied by the fact that each rolls a cub playfully under one forepaw.

22 ▲

◀ 20 A modern reproduction of a T'ang pottery camel looks out on Liulichang, the street of curio shops in the Outer City, recalling the days when real treasures were on sale there.

23 ▶

24 ▲

25 ▲

The adjustable jets of a fountain outside the exhibition hall given by Russia to China are seldom properly aligned due to the efforts of schoolboys who try to train them on their friends.

From the steps of the Monument to the People's Heroes the Gate of Heavenly Peace is dwarfed by the immense size of a newly created square. May Day and other national celebrations find the square tightly packed with half a million people. Here, young men from the new University of Peking, many of whose students come from distant parts of China, take a look at the sights of the capital. Photo by Brian Brake, © National Geographic Society

27 ▲

In the Western Hills, where Ming temples slumber on the wooded slopes, a former China reigns unchallenged. A gingko tree shades a courtyard and only a garden seat recalls the present. On the door of another temple, the red lacquer peels a little more each year from the carved character shou, whose meaning, fittingly, is "longevity."

28 ▲

29 ▲

In the streets of the city old and new intermingle. A barrow of ancient design has a pneumatic tire, and in the background reams of paper are transported by pedicab; the flag of the People's Republic is probably homemade. On Ch'angan Boulevard traffic is light. The new lamp posts have built-in loudspeakers. Wumen, just visible above a bus, faces big new buildings across the great width of the street.

by plane, the difference between a Chinese and a Western city is dramatic indeed. At first sight, traditional Peking has the look of a prison or a fortress, an impression which is utterly incorrect.

A comment of the emperor K'ang-hsi in the eighteenth century when he was shown sketches and plans of European houses underlines the Chinese attitude: "Undoubtedly this Europe must be a very small and pitiful country; since the Inhabitants cannot find Ground enough to spread out their Towns, but are obliged to live up thus in the Air." Attiret, the Jesuit priest in Peking who reported this, goes on to give a graphic account of Chinese opinion on the same subject: "The Height and Thickness of our Palaces amaze them. They look upon our Streets as so many Ways hollowed into terrible Mountains; and upon our Houses, as Rocks pointing up in the Air, and full of Holes like the Dens of Bears and other Wild Beasts. . . ."

In the *hutung,* which generally follow the grid pattern on which Peking was designed, only doorways break the flat wall surfaces. Topped with a trim of tiles, more or less ornamental according to the size of the house inside, the doors themselves are often of a plain wooden beauty, opening to reveal a screen of wood or ceramic which conceals the courtyard beyond, preserving the privacy of the house. Through these long zigzag corridor-streets, narrow and mazelike, you can only find your way by asking. The answer from any Chinese is couched in terms of the points of the compass (a device which they invented some time before the rest of the world). "It's second turning to the north and first east," they will say, their feeling for position as unerring as is ours for left and right. Conversely, the Chinese distinction between left and right is often faulty and uncertain.

And when the door of the house is reached there is little indication whether it is a mansion with a proliferation of interior courts, or a simple one-courtyard home. Until little more than fifty years ago when the first republic was set up after the collapse of the last Chinese dynasty, Peking was a one-storey city. Only temples vied with the stately roofs of the imperial palaces, only pagodas rose above them, and then at some distance. The palaces too have only a single storey, but it is a massive storey three times the height of the average house and raised on triple terraces of white carved marble. Yet even they are almost invisible from outside their red walls, only the roofs curving serenely against the sky. It would have been unthinkable, probably punishable, for a Chinese under the imperial system to add a second storey to his house. By tradition, and because of that humility which dissembles pride, the greatest mansions of the rich and noble remained no higher than the humble norm. Only through the doorway and past the screen did the succession of courtyards reveal the extent of the house. Even in establishments sheltering several hundred persons—four generations of the family together with the wives of sons, concubines, and a legion of servants and grooms—there was no such thing as the baronial hall of great European houses. Only the emperor was provided with rooms of height and breadth symbolical of his sway over the vast regions of the world.

And even he actually lived in smallish rooms laid out on precisely the same plan as the houses of the *hutung*. (See the floor plans on page 116.)

Hundreds of *hutung* still exist in Peking today—as if London still contained whole quarters of Tudor housing. They are still unpaved, though now cleared of the ordure which used to make the air thick as soup and arouse travelers to vivid condemnations. In spring their shut and almost forbidding aspect is suddenly enlivened by sprays of blossoms that peer over the dark walls with fragile pink and yellow smiles. For every courtyard has its tree, preferably a blossoming variety, and spring comes suddenly—a drama, a revelation—like first love. With the delicate air of a Chinese court beauty on a T'ang scroll it appears in the grey door of Peking with a whiff of perfume and wearing a new embroidered gown. Blossoms cluster exuberantly on every dark branch, whose skin is still so cold from winter that the flowers are all the more miraculous. In courtyards the bamboos begin to spear the air with their tiny pins of green. Potted plants much loved by the family, Chinese date trees, make a new start in life. Children come out in cotton prints whose outrageous flower patterns far outdo the tentative efforts of nature; and men and boys climb homemade bamboo ladders to the roofs to inspect the damage to tiles from winter frosts and snow, and to make it good before the violent summer showers begin.

The places of Peking are swaddled in history. Much of it is history that has not yet been fossilized in books and thus forgotten by the inhabitants. In this, and in other senses, Peking exists still in the credulity of medieval life. Every structure and every street is known to people not only in the common context of their lives, but also as the site of some historical, mythical, fabulous, or supernatural event. The names of great emperors and great rogues, the eras of turbulence and of the horror and sweetness of Chinese life, have left their tales glowing like the Peking light. There is hardly a corner lacking its story, and many carry the written characters dictated by some emperor and cut in stone in an effort to underline the past to which he was proud to conform. For there exists perhaps no people in the world with such a passionate interest in their own history, such a deep desire to make it fit the tenets of their orthodoxy, and such a genius for falsifying facts in favor of this desired perfection.

It is hard indeed to disentangle even the simplest and most basic truths from the filigree of delightful myth with which this inventive race has protected the events and objects of their past. The precedents for this baffling activity are hoary and unimpeachably valid. In the first century B.C. Ssu-ma Ch'ien, the first and perhaps the greatest Chinese historian, wrote an account of history from its beginnings which is just such a mixture of fact and of fact made to fit the pattern of events as he and his age conceived history ought to have followed. And the energies of generations of Chinese and Western scholars have been applied to unraveling the truth from his work (and in many cases to making it fit some other equally conceptual form). Granted that no historian can claim complete objectivity, yet the Chinese must still be allowed to win all prizes for squeezing the round pegs of their past into the square holes of contemporary opinion. And the tendency is far from dead today. Coming to an actual example—the two artificial hills in the otherwise level area of the capital, one of which we want to climb in order to see the expanse and pattern of the city—this maddening process can be appreciated more readily. The two hills are called Coal Hill (also Prospect Hill or the Protecting Hill of the Great Within) and the Emerald Isle (also Hortensia Isle or the Island of the White Dagoba). In some ways it is the second hill that better illustrates the point, but let us deal with them in geographical order as approached from the palaces.

Coal Hill is directly north of the north gate of the imperial palaces, while the latter lies a little farther on, in the artificial lake called Peihai (North Sea), somewhat to the west of Coal Hill. They are the highest points in Peking and the area is charmingly described by Marco Polo as it was in the very early days of the city in the Mongol dynasty: "Not far from the palace, on the northern side, and about a bow-shot distance from the surrounding wall, is an artificial mount of earth, the height of which is a full hundred paces, and the circuit at the base about a mile. It is clothed with the most beautiful evergreen trees; for whenever his majesty [Kublai Khan] receives information of a handsome tree growing in any place, he causes it to be dug up [a very ancient and highly skilled procedure which is still common in China] with all its roots and the earth about them, and however large and heavy it may be, he has it transported by means of elephants to this mount, and adds it to the verdant collection. From this perpetual verdure it has acquired the appellation of the Green Mount. On its summit is erected an ornamental pavilion, which is likewise entirely green. . . ."

Except for the presence of four other pavilions disposed in line, two at either side of the central and highest pavilion, which must have been added later, this is a good enough description of Coal Hill today. Marco Polo continues: "In the northern quarter also, and equally within the precincts of the city, there is a large and deep excavation . . . the earth from which supplied the material for raising the mount. It is furnished with water by a small rivulet and has the appearance of a fishpond, but its use is for watering the cattle. [Fishponds, then as now, were common in China, but apparently the Mongols, not long ago nomads from the steppes, kept herds near the palace. The pond has disappeared since then.] The stream passing from thence along an aqueduct, at the foot of Green Mount, proceeds to fill another great and very deep excavation formed between the private palace of the emperor and that of his son [Chen-chin]; and the earth from thence equally served to increase the elevation of the mount. In this latter basin there is a great store and variety of fish, from which the table of his majesty is supplied [served, as we have seen, by attendants wearing face masks]. . . . The stream discharges itself at the opposite extremity of the piece of water, and precautions are taken to prevent the escape of fish by placing gratings of copper or iron . . . at its entrance and exit."

PEIHAI AND EMERALD ISLE. *A view of Peihai or North Lake showing Emerald Isle, its summit crowned by the White Dagoba. (From an 18th-century engraving.)*

Historically it is certain that both hills are artificial, but why Coal Hill is so called is less certain. There is good reason for thinking that its position due north of the palace was dictated by the desire to guard the imperial household from the evil influences believed to emanate from the north. Perhaps at some point the household had its stock of coal, which until a few years ago used to be brought to Peking on camels, piled at this place (a custom attested to by similar coal heaps in the T'ang capital many centuries before). The hill was built by one of the early Mongol emperors, almost certainly by Kublai Khan himself, since the earlier capital city had been utterly destroyed by his grandfather Genghis Khan, and the Mongols had had their capital elsewhere until Peking was rebuilt. Marco Polo arrived at Peking in 1275, fifteen years after the enthronement of Kublai Khan, and the new city was by that time largely finished.

Uncertainty about the reasons for Coal Hill's name is matched by a whimsical fog of stories about the building of the five delightful pavilions along its crest, stories which have formed the subject of interesting and often amusing articles written by sinologists in their lighter moments. But there is one story which is both dramatic and true—the suicide of the last Ming emperor by hanging from a tree at its base (see p. 112).

Around Peking's other hill, Emerald Isle in Peihai Park, many fascinating tales have been woven by generations of Chinese, all of them examples of manufactured history. One is worth retelling because it is typical of the way in which the Chinese have collected ideas from many places and fused them into accounts supposed to explain the origins of things.

In T'ang times (seventh and eighth centuries A.D.) an emperor is said to have offered one of his daughters as a bride to a Uigur prince in exchange for the miraculous Mongolian mountain called the Hill of Bliss (in this case a euphemism for the Mongol's domain). Now, many Chinese emperors found it convenient to offer their womenfolk in this way to tribal leaders on the fringes of the empire ; it was cheaper and easier than waging long wars of conquest to subdue unruly chieftains, and it also served to secure the line of communication with India and the West. The Hill of Bliss is a projection of Mount Meru or Kailasa, abode of both Hindu and Buddhist gods—the latter religion having reached a flourishing state in China in the T'ang dynasty. The barbarian prince accepted the offer of a bride, but the mountain proved very large and hard to transport. The Chinese, however, were undismayed (they had, after all, built the Great Wall a thousand years before). They prayed to the God of Hindrances and Obstacles (a typically Chinese god), and then, practical and superstitious as they are today, they built a fire round it and poured vinegar on top. Whereupon the mountain disintegrated and they easily moved the pieces to Peking.

Unfortunately for the credibility of the story Peking was at that time a small provincial town, the seat of a mere military governor, and was located southwest of the present capital—far from Peihai. The story, like so many others, was invented later than T'ang times, probably to explain the construction of the White Dagoba on top of Emerald Isle by the Ch'ing emperor Hsun-chih in the late seventeenth century. The dagoba, called by Juliet Bredon "a mighty monument glowing like a phantom lotus bud in the sunshine," is shaped like a Tibetan *chorten* and was put up for political, not religious, reasons to celebrate the visit of the Dalai Lama to Peking at that time.

The story illustrates in the eclectic Chinese way one of the imperial problems of many ages—how to keep fringe territories of a sprawling empire tied to the central control. Like an old ramshackle vehicle, the body of China has moved through the centuries alternately shedding parts and having them welded back on again. The dagoba and the Dalai Lama's visit were part of a welding operation. As recently as 1959, when the priest-rulers of Tibet showed signs of defecting from the Chinese orbit, they were once again gathered into the Chinese fold. No student of history should have been surprised at the Chinese reaction.

The climb to the top of Emerald Isle is steep, and every footfall is a step on the artifacts of Peking history (real or invented). Since Mongol times Peihai and its shores have seen a succession of palaces, pavilions, temples, and monuments put up by rulers for their pleasure, aesthetic satisfaction, and personal aggrandizement. The court dramas and intrigues centered on the imperial pleasances of the area are numberless. But now, in the reality of this spring day when the sun has climbed well up in the Peking sky, the shadow of the White Dagoba falls sharply down the slope to the northwest (where, according to tradition, it is supposed never to cast a shadow at all). From the terrace round its base the whole city spreads out—in nearby detail, in general lines of middle distance, beyond the walls to the misty hills of the northern horizon which are as much a part of history as of contemporary Peking life.

Not far from the foot of the hill, to the southeast, lies the Center of the World—the

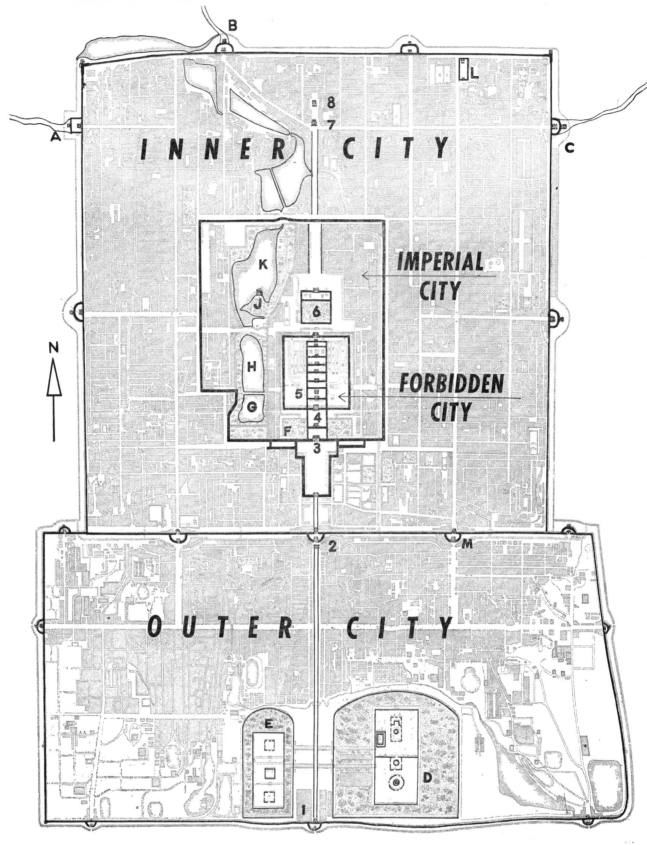

PLAN OF PEKING IN MING-CH'ING TIMES *(based on the plan in
Father Hyacinth Bitchurin's* Description of Peking, *1829).*

NORTH-SOUTH AXIS	OTHER PLACES MENTIONED	
1. *Yungtingmen, south gate of Outer City*	A. *Road to Summer Palace*	H. *Chunghai, Middle Lake*
2. *Ch'ienmen, front gate of Peking*	B. *Road to Ming Tombs*	J. *Emerald Isle and the*
3. *Gate of Heavenly Peace*	*and Nan-k'ou Pass*	*White Dagoba*
4. *Wumen, the Meridian Gate*	C. *Road to Jehol*	K. *Peihai, North Lake*
5. *Hall of Supreme Harmony*	D. *Temple of Heaven*	L. *Lama Temple*
6. *Coal Hill*	E. *Temple of Agriculture*	M. *Hatamen (gate)*
7. *Bell Tower*	F. *Chungshan Park*	
8. *Drum Tower*	G. *Nanhai, South Lake*	

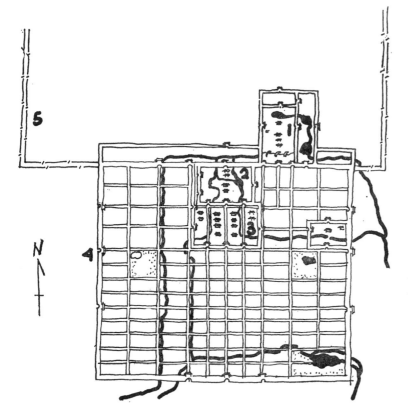

PLAN OF THE T'ANG CAPITAL, CH'ANG-AN. *Though slightly smaller in size, the Inner City of Peking, together with its Forbidden City, was modeled on Ch'ang-an, following the pattern closely both in its south-north alignment and in the arrangement of its streets, palaces, and pleasure gardens. (Based on a contemporary stone bas-relief.)*

1. *Imperial pleasure palaces and gardens*
2. *Imperial Palace*
3. *Administrative city*
4. *Perimeter wall of city, 22 miles around*
5. *Portion of wall of Imperial Park*

palaces which were the nucleus of the known molecule called Chung Kuo or Middle Country; which in its turn was considered by the Chinese to be the only civilized terrain in the world. From there the geomancers, astrologers, and even court astronomers plotted the immutable lines of force that passed unerringly south to north, threading the line of needles' eyes of the great gates and halls of the palaces. Here in Peking they chronicled the movements of the Chinese heavens, whose sailing stars, planets, and moon foretold the fortunes of the only race on earth, and signified nothing else at all.

We of the twentieth century may afford a smile and be excused a gasp of incredulity at the apparent self-importance of those long visions of power as we stand under the bulge of the White Dagoba. But it was largely this absolute conviction, with others such as the belief in the *yin-yang* balance, the Confucian system of morality and polity, together with the legacies of philosophies such as Buddhism, which animated and made truly great the long civilization of China.

Here in Peking under the roofs of golden tiles, within the smallish square of the fat city walls, and in the small rooms of houses along the *hutung,* all visible from the hill, this strange, rational but in some ways blind society took up the legacy of T'ang days after the fall of the capital on the Yellow River, and made of it an astonishing entity, alternately overrated and undervalued by the rest of the world.

From the vantage point of the hill one recalls again how remote Peking still is. A tall middle-aged lady in crow-black trousers and jacket, her hair pulled back into a scanty bun held with a small jade clasp, arrives on the terrace. She is with a young man who must be her son. Her face, in common with many ageing Chinese faces, has a soft, lined look. It is stripped to the essentials of a face. She totters and rolls a little, a long walking stick held in both brown-spotted hands. Her bound feet—three-inch golden lilies, the Chinese call them, which are an increasing rarity as the older generation dies out—are gorgeously encased in embroidered shoes. Her son wears army uniform of mustard khaki and a winter hat with earflaps lined with brown fur. He supports his mother by the elbow, and they begin pointing out to each other the landmarks of the city which is perhaps as

DRAGON AND PHOENIX. *Another papercut, the dragon symbolizing the emperor and the phoenix the empress.*

unfamiliar to them as it is to us. The traditional old lady and the modern young man remind one in human terms of the meeting of medieval and contemporary which is part of the essence of China today, and of its capital spread out below the hill.

By now it is midday, the sun due south, exactly opposite Ch'ienmen, the front gate of Peking, which stands against the ground mist and the fog of cooking smoke over the Outer City beyond. It is a five-mile walk from the south gate of the Outer City directly northward to the northern wall of the Inner City, a route which none but imperial processions could follow until the opening of the palaces some time after the Republic of 1912. From the South Gate to the absolute center of the dynastic world, the Hall of Supreme Harmony, where the emperors gave audience, is a distance of three and one-eighth miles. The area of the Palace City within its red walls (the Great Within and the Forbidden City were two of its names) is something over 250 acres; and the area of the Imperial City enclosing it, most of whose wall has gone now, is nearly 1,500 acres.

A glance at the map on page 40 shows Peking bounded by its walls in the shape of the Chinese character *tieh* 凸 and split down the middle by the backbone of the long processional way, on or around which lie all the buildings connected with the functions of imperial power. The grand design of the capital is an ancient one, and with small variations a similar design has served the Chinese for most of their history since the unification of the country under one central authority.

At this point we need not go further into the meaning and functions of this deliberate creation of a city, except to recall that its persistence as a model town plan gives one more clue to the unique quality of Chinese life. A civilization which could successfully preserve such a rigid form in its capital might be expected to have preserved a similar rigidity in its institutions. And this indeed was the case. Even the manner of writing, the ideographic character, has persisted, so that it is quite possible to recognize the scripts of the earliest Chinese written material. This too is unique. No other language has managed to achieve this continuity over three thousand years, remaining the spoken and living means of communication today.

As we stand on the hill, the palaces lie to the southeast, a sea of wavelike yellow roofs. Much farther away in the same direction, the blue-tiled roof of the Temple of Heaven can be seen—one of the most perfect creations of Ming architecture. Directly south the two lakes called Chunghai and Nanhai (Middle Lake and South Lake) shimmer between trees, surrounded by their pavilion-encrusted banks. And turning due north there are, beyond the shores of Peihai, three more lakes, all artificial. In Peihai Park itself virtually every corner is studded with buildings and such strange fancies as the Nine Dragon Screen—a ceramic-tile barrier, standing before a now-vanished temple, on which some of the most ferocious and arresting dragons in China cavort in high relief and lively color. To the north also stand twin structures—the Bell Tower and the Drum Tower—forming the last architectural eyes through which the south-north axis passes. The Drum Tower is probably that described by Marco Polo but later moved from its old position to the east so as to fit the new alignment of Peking when it was rebuilt in Ming times.

Almost in the northeast corner of the city walls the roofs of the Lama Temple break through the level of the surrounding structures, as do the many gates in the walls themselves. To the east also it is sometimes possible to see a thread of water approaching the city. Like the lakes, this too is artificial. It connects with the end of the seven-hundred-mile Grand Canal, one of the most remarkable of Chinese engineering feats, linking the capital with the distant grain-bearing lands of the south since A.D. 608.

So much, then, for the general look of the Peking within the walls which has remained unaltered for centuries. But there is another Peking, of vast concrete buildings far larger and higher than anything from the past, which has sprung up in the last decade amid the buildings of the old. At first glance this seems almost an upstart city.

Opposite the Gate of Heavenly Peace, the front door of the Imperial City, one of the world's biggest city squares has spread out west and south and east, and is now flanked by a huge hall on one side and an equally huge museum on the other. Each of these is a quarter of a mile long. Between them at the southern end of the square a tall monument in the form of a memorial stele stands alone, inscribed in the excellent calligraphy of Mao Tse-tung with the words: "The People's Heroes Are Immortal." Ch'angan Boulevard, running straight as an arrow east and west across the city as it always did, has been cleared of those decorative triple arches called *p'ai-lou* and broadened until it is as wide the Champs Élysées in Paris; and on its northern side there is a whole row of multistorey buildings raising their raw-concrete, many-windowed bulk into the shocked air of medieval Peking. Away to the southeast the vast new railway station breaks through the level of the old city. And there are many more new buildings—hospitals, a sports stadium, hotels, blocks of apartments.

There is still little vehicular traffic on Peking streets, at least in comparison with the congested gushers of Western capitals. Even the dash of Moscow's not too numerous vehicles finds no parallel in Peking. Along Ch'angan Boulevard an odd mixture of old and new conveyances proceeds at moderate pace—Czech buses, Chinese-made trucks, large red taxis from West Germany, bicycles of Chinese manufacture, handcarts of all descriptions (but all with pneumatic tires, however old they may be in structure), and a steady procession of pedicabs which have now completely replaced the former rickshaws. The impression this traffic gives is that of an emphatic trickle on an outsize street.

Outside the walls to the east and northwest the formerly irregular clutter of suburban construction which clung to the safety of the walled city as far back as it existed has mushroomed into industrial complexes, an enormous new university which resembles a series of factories, and a morass of blocks to accommodate the several new millions of Peking's population.

All this is now an integral part of Peking. Fundamentally there is nothing surprising about it, except the rapidity with which it has appeared. We may regret the formerly inviolate, imperial, yet unpretentious face of Peking which is changing so rapidly, just as we could regret the obliteration of medieval London or Paris which the industrial revolution achieved by gradual stages. The word "gradual" is the key. Peking—like many another Oriental city—is having its industrial revolution in instant form. And Peking, more perfect, more purely medieval than most other Oriental places, appears to suffer more from the sudden change. Yet broadly speaking the change is a waking up, the pains of a difficult birth. In the middle of the twentieth century it is not possible for any city to remain at the same time a museum piece and the capital of the most populous country in the world. And what we are regretting is really the fact that we can see the perfection (and also, if we look more closely, the filth and human misery) of an old city actually changing before our eyes into a shape more familiar if less aesthetically pleasing. If we had been doomed to exist for several centuries in any Western city, some similar tears would have rolled down our romantic cheeks, not without cause, but without real reason.

But farther away, still only an hour's bus ride from Peking, the country takes up again. Indeed on a clear day in autumn when the air is sharp as a prism the Western Hills rise out of the dusty land, dotted with temples and pagodas, with "lofty trees surrounding summer-houses and cabinets contrived for retreat and pleasure" having "the appearance of enchantment."* Here are the tombs of the Ming emperors and the Summer Palace; and a building where, until quite recently, the last survivors among the eunuchs of the last emperor lived on in perplexed seclusion in a world which had no further use for them.† In this countryside, for centuries the delight of courts and of individuals sensitive to its special beauties, so much loved by them that they adorned it with structures that make the pleasure even more acute, the people of Peking nowadays take their own form of pleasure at weekends. Spring draws hundreds of thousands of them to sit under the blossoming trees—students with their books and their friends, boys with their girls, families with children and a hundred small packages of the odd ingredients of a Chinese picnic.

And farther still the brick-scaled serpent of the Great Wall rampages along the crests of mountains whose summits, well into early summer, are still drifted with snow, and whose bulk delineates Peking's northern limits. Here too Peking people come in fat bus-loads to scramble along the top of the wall and enjoy the freedom of a fortification that for centuries excluded the barbarous tribes from the terrible north, but through which trains and trucks now go roaring to the industrial northwest.

On such a day in spring the capital shows its modern energies and its old lethargies, its soft beauty of palace and temple, and the spiky towers of modern communication—

* This description by Staunton actually applies to the area of the palace lakes in Peking.
† In *Escape with Me* Osbert Sitwell gives a gently satirical description of them.

all jumbled together. The pandas in the zoo begin to pant a little, regretting the passing of winter, which they enjoy, perhaps already looking forward to the blocks of ice on which their keepers will set them as relief from the summer heat. The Soviet Exhibition Center, a gift from Russia and a confection of positively eye-searing ugliness, houses a show of China's new industrial products and is crammed with people all and every day. All those lathes and surgical operating lights, those cheap cameras, those plastic objects ranging from busts of Chairman Mao to combs of virulent green, still fascinate people simply because they are made in China, whereas formerly they would have been imported. Round one exhibit there is a wedged crowd of adults and children, some smaller ones sitting on their fathers' shoulders. Now and then they give out a concerted cry of delight and awe. In the center of the crowd is a young Chinese manipulating a pair of remote-control mechanical hands used in dealing with dangerous or radioactive substances. The attention of the children is hardly more rapt than that of their fathers and mothers, for there is something in this slightly uncanny sight of a pair of metal hands performing delicate operations with tiny objects that appeals to the innate inventiveness of the Chinese mind. One remembers that centuries ago the ancestors of this same people invented such astonishing devices as a carriage with a mechanism that always indicated the south, no matter what direction it might be going or how twisted the route; who anticipated the Western invention of the crossbow by thirteen centuries, printing with movable type by four centuries, and the rotary winnowing machine by fourteen centuries.

On this and later days in Peking, when the changeable spring has let fall a crisp layer of startling white snow on the blossoms and the pedicab drivers are beating their arms to keep warm, you may speculate on what happened that Peking and all China sat tight in medievalism and never burst out with its own industrial revolution. In Peking, if we follow its history and the story of its birth and growth, the epic of its great men and their ideas, we may find some clues. For the story of Peking is the story of adult China: of a long dream and sudden waking.

EARLY CHINESE INVENTIONS. *These two postage stamps are from a series recently issued in Peking depicting early Chinese inventions. The seismograph (upper) was the first in the world, invented by one Chang Heng in the early 2nd century. It consists of a bronze jar inside which is balanced a vertical rod connected loosely to the four dragons curling down the outside from the lid. Each dragon holds in its jointed mouth a ball. When an earthquake took place, the internal rod was displaced and caused a movement in the jaws of the dragon facing in the direction of the tremor, whereupon the ball in that dragon's mouth fell with a crash into the open mouth of the frog placed directly below. Thus both the time and the direction of the quake were known, though not its strength. Turning to another Chinese invention, one of the earliest compasses (lower) consisted of a magnetized iron spoon floating in a pool of water. The spoon's handle pointed north and the directions were marked on a surrounding plate. Compasses were undoubtedly in use in China by the year 800, while the first description of a workable compass in the West does not arrive until 1269.*

The First Peking

THE PERIODS OF CHINESE HISTORY

(Adapted from Joseph Needham's *Science and Civilization in China*)

Hsia kingdom (legendary?)		*ca.* 2000 to 1520 B.C.
Shang (Yin) kingdom		*ca.* 1520 to 1030
Chou dynasty (Feudal Age)	Early Chou period	*ca.* 1030 to 722
	Spring and Autumn period	722 to 480
	Warring States period	480 to 221

First Unification

Ch'in dynasty		221 to 207
Han dynasty	Earlier Han	202 B.C. to A.D. 9
	Hsin interregnum	9 to 23
	Later Han	25 to 220

First Partition

Three Kingdoms period	Shu kingdom	221 to 264
	Wei kingdom	220 to 264
	Wu kingdom	222 to 280

Second Unification

Chin dynasty	265 to 420
Liu (Sung) dynasty	420 to 479

Second Partition

Northern and Southern dynasties	479 to 581

Third Unification

Sui dynasty	581 to 618
T'ang dynasty	618 to 906

Third Partition

Five Dynasties period	907 to 960
Liao dynasty	937 to 1125
Hsi Hsia state	990 to 1227

Fourth Unification

Northern Sung dynasty	960 to 1126
Southern Sung dynasty	1127 to 1279
Chin dynasty	1115 to 1234
Yuan (Mongol) dynasty	1260 to 1368
Ming dynasty	1368 to 1644
Ch'ing (Manchu) dynasty	1644 to 1911
Republic	Established 1912
People's Republic	Established 1949

2. The Long Beginnings

Chinese civilization, and with it Chinese architecture, are less remarkable for their antiquity than for their continuity. The early advances in agriculture and metallurgy and the first great civilizations based upon them were all further west in Asia. When the ziggurats were being built in Mesopotamia and the drainage systems laid out at Mohenjodaro, China like Europe was deep in the stone age. Bronze, which was in use [in West Asia] before 3000 B.C. appears in China about 1600 B.C. . . . later than it appears in Britain. . . . There are not even many old buildings remaining in China as in Europe. . . . What there has been, however, is, straight from the brilliant flowering of the bronze age in about 1500 B.C. right up to the present, a completely continuous, individual and self-conscious civilization of an extremely high level: one might say, one nation with (basically) one language, one script, one literature, one system of ethical concepts, one tradition in the arts, including one architecture.

—Andrew Boyd, *Chinese Architecture*

It is simple coincidence that one of the most important Stone Age sites in the world was found at Chou-k'ou-tien near Peking. The bones of Peking Man dug up in a cave there belong to a time half a million years ago, before the west winds from Asia had transported the loess soil in that colossal airlift and dropped it on North China. After Peking Man there is a gap in Chinese prehistory until the neolithic peoples of four to five thousand years ago.

Ancient Chinese history, which starts with legends of wise kings who invented everything from agriculture to silk and writing, is lumped together in the semimythical Hsia dynasty, and is the product of Chinese imagination of a much later date. Archaeological findings have begun to substantiate parts of it in excavations around the middle Yellow River. For it was there, and not in the Peking area, that the first flickers of Chinese light in the dark Eastern world began.

As a capital and as a great city Peking's story is comparatively brief—not nearly as protracted as that of London, which was important even in Roman times, two thousand and more years ago. Contrary to the ideas of both Chinese and Western scholars of the nineteenth century, Chinese history itself is fairly short; the civilizations of the "fertile crescent" in the Middle East evolved their written scripts long before the first Chinese began to scratch picture-words on tortoise shells and on the shoulder bones of oxen. But after a late start, civilization in China was concentrated, more compact. Likewise the story of Peking, the capital city, reflecting the condensed historical span of China just as it reflects many other qualities peculiar to the Chinese, runs on at a good pace once it gets going. It has, almost, the succinct form of a short story as opposed to the more

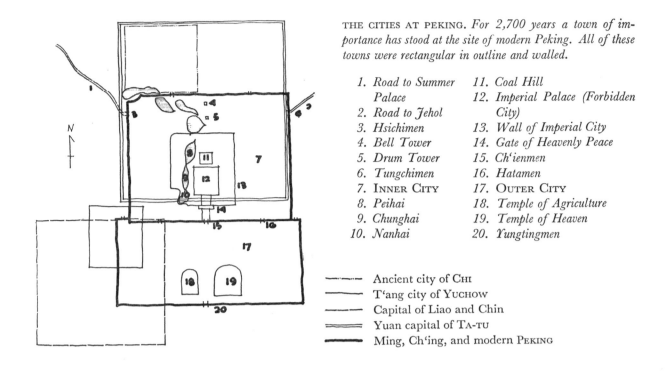

THE CITIES AT PEKING. *For 2,700 years a town of importance has stood at the site of modern Peking. All of these towns were rectangular in outline and walled.*

1. Road to Summer Palace
2. Road to Jehol
3. Hsichimen
4. Bell Tower
5. Drum Tower
6. Tungchimen
7. INNER CITY
8. Peihai
9. Chunghai
10. Nanhai
11. Coal Hill
12. Imperial Palace (Forbidden City)
13. Wall of Imperial City
14. Gate of Heavenly Peace
15. Ch'ienmen
16. Hatamen
17. OUTER CITY
18. Temple of Agriculture
19. Temple of Heaven
20. Yungtingmen

------- Ancient city of CHI
——— T'ang city of YUCHOW
——— Capital of Liao and Chin
═══ Yuan capital of TA-TU
▬▬ Ming, Ch'ing, and modern PEKING

leisurely pace of the novel. But the short story of Peking as a full-fledged great city and capital of China does not start until many of the greatest achievements of the Chinese have already flowered, and until many of the most important men and ideas that moulded its history have left their mark on Chinese life.

In the present book we are mainly concerned with the three great eras of Imperial Peking, capital of all China—the Mongol, the Ming (and its continuation under the Ch'ing), and the far-reaching changes of the present day. But the following brief summary of pre-Mongol events, together with the chart on page 55, will set the stage for our "tale of three cities."

Like most things in China the story of Peking begins in the inspiration of legend. Thirty-one hundred years ago, in the early Chou dynasty, which consisted of a collection of petty states under the suzerainty of kings reigning from a town on the Yellow River, the ruler named Wu is reported to have settled a group of his subjects in the Peking region. No archaeologist has yet discovered a settlement in the area which would substantiate this tale. But, as with Homer's story of the siege of Troy, which was supposed to have taken place on the other side of Asia about this time, and whose legend was dramatically converted into history by the spade, it may be as well to accept this first little scrap of evidence about Peking. Even at this early time the Chinese had evolved a considerable civilization which was distinctively their own. The superb bronze vessels with their masterly use of decoration, which can be seen in many Western museums, coming from tombs of Chou and even earlier kings and princes, show how this extremely difficult technique had reached a perfection never equaled before or after, either in China or elsewhere in the world. At the same time the distinctive Chinese way of writing in ideograms or characters was already well advanced and their written language was capable of expressing ideas as well as facts. The first use of writing was in divination. Astrologers at court scratched questions on the shoulder bones of animals. The bones were then put in a fire and the resulting cracks interpreted. Often the answers to the questions were then written on the bones also. The form of writing that thus developed is the same script, vastly expanded and capable of the utmost subtlety, which is in use to the present day—the sole example in the world of a writing method which has survived intact throughout the history of a country.

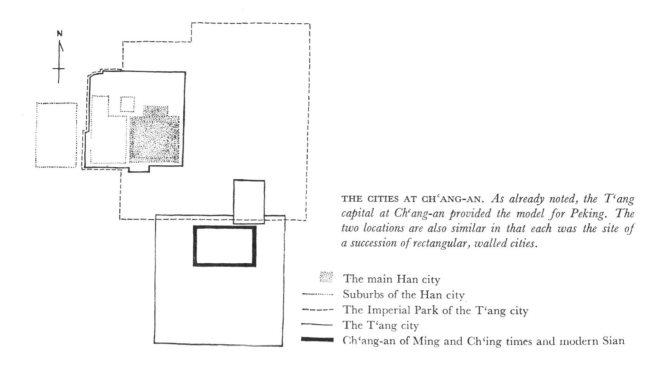

THE CITIES AT CH'ANG-AN. *As already noted, the T'ang capital at Ch'ang-an provided the model for Peking. The two locations are also similar in that each was the site of a succession of rectangular, walled cities.*

▓ The main Han city
············· Suburbs of the Han city
----- The Imperial Park of the T'ang city
——— The T'ang city
▬▬▬ Ch'ang-an of Ming and Ch'ing times and modern Sian

Written Peking history, as distinct from the writing on "oracle bones," begins a little later when the powerful state of Yen, a Chou tributary, made its capital there and called it Chi. The significance of this event lies in the choice of the Peking region for a town. The same reasons have motivated the choice throughout its history. Peking stands sentinel on the north edge of a great plain, conveniently located about twenty-five miles from the easier of two passes through the mountains that form the northern boundary of the plain and constituted its protection from the barbarian tribes who lived beyond. From the very beginning of Peking history these aggressive and hungry tribes were ready, at the slightest sign of Chinese inattention, to descend like the Assyrians wolflike on the rich fields of the North China Plain. The only other pass through the folds of the mountains lies to Peking's northeast and leads to Jehol, of which we shall hear more in later years. This pass is also defensible from the city. Eastward, a long strip of low land follows the coastline of the Gulf of Chihli, giving access to Manchuria, but it narrows almost to vanishing point and invasions from this direction could easily be choked off. From Peking, therefore, the tribal danger could be controlled.

The state of Yen was only one of many states loosely ruled by the Chou dynasty from its successive capitals on the Yellow River. In later Chou times, around 330 B.C. and after (approximately during the lifetime of Alexander the Great in the West) there were eleven such states. Almost every one of them had been formed by a coalition of several earlier petty states in each area, or by the conquest of several by one of their neighbors. These times are rightly called the Warring States period. The ferocity of the conflicts which raged throughout the epoch was matched only by their inconclusiveness. The total area of China within which these fierce little states contended was very restricted in Chou times, stretching from approximately the Great Wall (not yet properly built) southward to the Yangtse River.

In one of those warring states, whose territory consisted of the Shantung Peninsula to the south of Yen, there lived one of the very few Chinese whose name is a household word in the West—the philosopher Confucius. At this time ancient Greek civilization in the Mediterranean was at its height, and in India Buddha had lived and died a couple of hundred years before. Though he never journeyed to the Peking area, Confucius is nonetheless important in our story of the future capital because his teachings formed

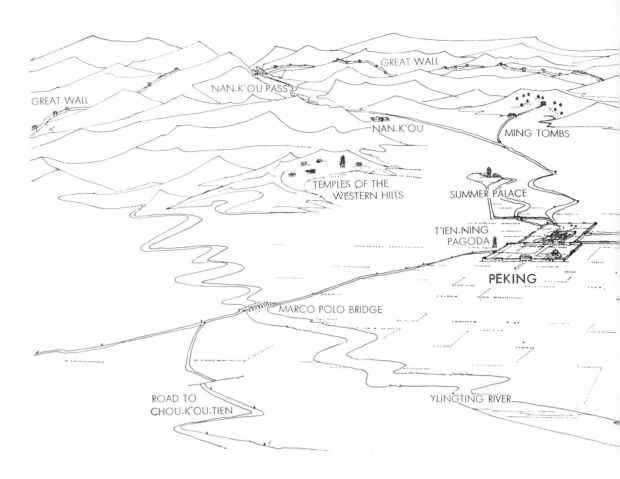

AERIAL VIEW OF PEKING AND ENVIRONS. *In this simplified view of Peking at the edge of the North China Plain the strategic value of the site becomes clear. Hemmed in by the mountain barrier to the north and northeast and by the Yellow Sea to the east (off the map), and almost equidistant from the only two near passes, it was ideally situated to ward off attacks from barbarous regions beyond the mountains on the far side of the Great Wall. Among the site's amenities was easy escape, for those*

one of the chief foundations of life and conduct in the China which was to develop later. His conservative doctrines of obedience to rulers and to parents and elders, and his implied idea that all things were perfect when the legendary emperors ruled and everyone knew and agreed to his status in life, were to have results which set much of the pattern of Chinese civilization for the 2,500 years until the coming of the twentieth century.

During the later centuries of Chou times, when Peking was a small provincial garrison town called Chi, the power of the Chou rulers became less and less, until one of the petty states called Ch'in emerged as undoubted leader of China. The Ch'in dynasty overthrew the Chou and reunited the several states whose adherence to Chou had diminished to vanishing point. The little frontier town of Chi, a rough-and-ready place where men were always on the alert, sleeping with their weapons in the midst of foes, was situated a little to the north of the present city of Peking. The fact is attested by the eighteenth-century emperor Ch'ien-lung, who put up a small pavilion on the spot to house a marble tablet on which he wrote: "Here stood one of the gates of the ancient city of Chi." At this point in history the area falls into limbo with the destruction of Peking by Ch'in Shih-huang-ti.

Here we come to a man, his name practically unknown in the West, whose succession of bloody victories over his rivals made him the first effective emperor of the country. His name, Ch'in Shih-huang-ti, means First Emperor of the Ch'in dynasty. In 221 B.C. his state, called Ch'in (from which comes our word China), having conquered the other states of which China was then composed, was strong enough to create a centralization

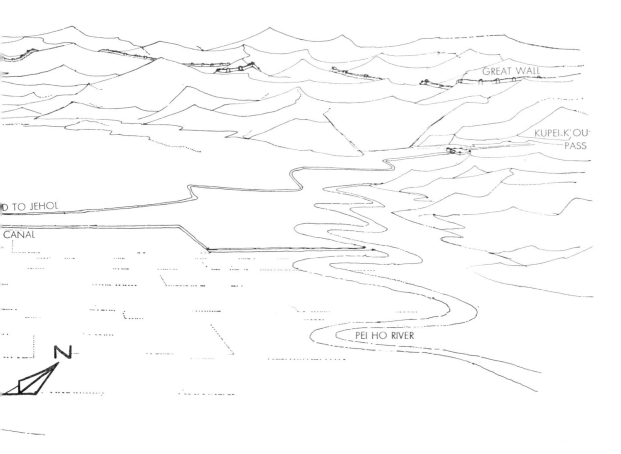

GREAT WALL

KUPEI-K'OU-PASS

D TO JEHOL

CANAL

N

PEI HO RIVER

who could afford it, from the hot summers—in the Western Hills, in the court's Summer Palace, and elsewhere on convenient wooded slopes where a semblance of rustic retreats could be contrived. The Grand Canal, main artery of commerce between North and South China and the route by which the provinces remitted their huge taxes in grain, connected with the capital via the Pei Ho and a smaller canal linking this river with the eastern part of Peking.

of government. This was the first united Chinese state, established two hundred years before the birth of Christ, and its concept was to endure for twenty-one centuries. The pattern of this first Ch'in emperor's rule is the basic pattern of the imperial system in China which, with modifications, was to last so long, and which eventually gave birth to Peking as its most splendid capital.

At this time, when northern Europe was a rabble of tribal hunters, Ch'in Shih-huang-ti was standardizing the written language of China and its weights and measures, and even decreeing the exact gauge of all wheeled vehicles throughout the land.* He was assuring his lines of communication by a network of main highways shaded by trees, and he was joining up the existing walls built in the north to form the Great Wall, so as to secure the frontier against invaders. He was decreeing mass movements of population and organizing Chinese settlements in areas south of the Yangtse River. In broad outline his system of rule through provincial governors responsible to the emperor formed the enduring basis of all future governments of China. In this manner, ruling through agents appointed from the center, Ch'in Shih-huang-ti unified the agglomeration of states whose allegiance to the Chou dynasty had ceased to exist. The area of China still did not effectively extend south of the Yangtse River, but for the first time it had come under really central control.

* This standardization of the axle lengths meant that all over China the ruts made by wheels in the unpaved roads were the same distance apart. Carts could then go from place to place without the former trouble of their wheels' not coinciding with the ruts.

In the succeeding centuries, as dynasties rose and fell, Peking's fortunes, and its names, varied. Its strategic position meant that it was always important, while its remoteness from the centers of imperial control, which were generally located around the Yellow River far to the south, made for chronic instability. The era between the dissolution of the Ch'in dynasty and the establishment of the T'ang about eight hundred years later was a time of flux in the North China Plain. Under the Han the town was the capital of a virtually independent state called Yen, while later, in the succeeding Chin times, the area fell under the control of tribes from north of the Great Wall. In the Sui dynasty Peking was reabsorbed and became the administrative center of a district. But, apart from the years when it was controlled by barbarian tribes, its role did not greatly vary. Peking, then and for most of its later history, was controller of the vital passes beyond which waited hungry tribes ready to swoop down on the fertile expanse of the plain. Information about the area during these times is scanty, but without doubt Peking was mostly a garrison town. Viewed from the dynastic capitals around the Yellow River, its function was a protective one—to exclude those barbarians who lived outside the limits of Chinese control. For several centuries, at this point in history, the Chinese had felt the superiority of their civilization to be so great that they classed all those outside their borders as barbarians. It is worthwhile noting this early habit of disbelief in the possibility of other nations' being civilized, for it is one more aspect of Chinese thought that persisted and eventually led to strange unrealities in the Chinese concept of the outer world.

Ch'in Shih-huang-ti was succeeded by his son who, like many a son of a forceful and successful father, proved an ineffective ruler. Almost at once revolts broke out here and there in the country, and after eight years of plot and assassination involving rival claimants to the throne an army officer named Liu Pang emerged victorious and founded the Han dynasty. With a brief interregnum between A.D. 9 and 23, when a dynasty called Hsin divided the existing empire, the Han dynasty continued until the year 220, its capital at Ch'ang-an near the Yellow River and then at nearby Loyang. The decline of this dynasty came about through the usual economic troubles culminating in palace revolutions and peasant revolts in whose suppression various generals managed to gain great power.

The Han dynasty crumbled away and for the next half-century China was divided into the Three Kingdoms (San Kuo) of Shu, Wei, and Wu. This division is significant since the areas conform to the basic economic divisions of the country, a factor which is later reflected in the division of China into three comparable areas just before the Mongol conquest. The three hostile states of this period—Wu in the south and southeast, including the Yangtse valley; Wei in the north and northwest, with its capital on the Yellow River; and Shu in what is now the provice of Szechuan and controlling the southwest—form one of the sources of high romance in Chinese literature and folk tale. From their wars and from the exploits of a wide selection of typically Chinese individuals come the materials of such classic novels as the *Romance of the Three Kingdoms,* which was written much later.

The end of this deeply troubled era came in A.D. 265 when the northern area achieved domination over the other two, and for a second time all China was unified under a dynasty which took the name Chin. But this dynasty proved short-lived, losing its capital Loyang and later Ch'ang-an, retreating south to Nanking while a rabble of seventeen "dynasties" fought it out among themselves in the north. Of these seventeen only three were Chinese peoples. The remainder were of Turkic, Hunnish, and Mongol stock emanating from various parts of Central and Northeast Asia. These "barbarians," as the Chinese always called them, were, however, to some extent sinified during this period, accepting the obviously superior life of Chinese agriculture, even acquiring Chinese names and intermarrying with the Chinese. In the latter part of this period of a hundred years a dynasty called Sui was formed by conquest (581–618). Thus yet another reunification of the country occurred. Brief though it was—a mere thirty-seven years—the Sui dynasty served as a preparation for the coming of the great T'ang age (618–906). The fall of the Sui dynasty was brought about by simple bankruptcy, the coffers of the

PEKING BEFORE THE MONGOL CONQUEST

DYNASTY	DATE	NAME & STATUS OF THE CITY
Chou	1030–221 B.C.	Chi, capital of the kingdom of Yen, 723–221
Ch'in	221–207	Chi, destroyed by Ch'in Shih-huang-ti
Han	202 B.C.–A.D. 220	Yenching ("Capital of Yen"); then Yuchow, capital of an independent kingdom
Chin	265–420	Yuchow, generally under the control of the Hu tribes
Northern & Southern	479–581	Uncertain
Sui	581–618	Chochun, administrative center of a district
T'ang	618–906	Yuchow, residence of military governors
Period of Five Dynasties and Northern & Southern Sung (907–1279)		
Liao	937–1125	Nanking, then Yenching; southern capital of Liao after 937
Chin	1115–1234	Chung-tu ("Central Capital"), capital of Chin

HSUAN-TSANG, BUDDHIST TRAVELER OF THE T'ANG DY-NASTY. *In a cosmopolitan era Hsuan-tsang was one of many Chinese monks who went to India to obtain authentic copies of the Buddhist scriptures. In this rubbing from a carved stone in a Ch'ang-an temple, he is shown returning laden with scrolls of sutras he had collected abroad during a stay of many years. In T'ang times not only were scriptures brought from India, but many Indian monks as well were encouraged to come and live in China.*

state emptied by huge expenditures on public works and by the cost of expeditions in Central Asia. The family which eventually overthrew the Sui emperors was in fact related to them. Ch'ang-an, the Sui capital, fell in 617, and the first T'ang emperor ascended the throne of China in the following year, ruling over an area which included all geographical China together with large tracts in the northwest (Sinkiang).

Under the T'ang dynasty China seems for a time to have discarded her traditional illusions of exclusiveness. Within the capital at Ch'ang-an—a city fortified with great walls forming a square—a cosmopolitan society flourished. Though the pattern of the city's walls and streets might be a traditional one, long established and lasting right up to modern times, the pattern of its thinking was refreshingly new.

To many historians, Chinese and Western alike, the T'ang dynasty is the peak of Chinese civilization. It is certainly true that China at that time knew an era of great peace and material progress, and that the xenophobia which led at other times to its cultural isolation from the rest of the world did not operate in the centuries of T'ang rule.

Ch'ang-an must have been an astonishing city. Built on a plan that, much later and far to the northeast, would be followed almost exactly at Peking (see maps on pp. 40–41). it housed merchants, scholars, envoys, and every manner of wanderer from the ends of the known world. Buddhism, which had come from India to China in the first century A.D., had reached a point at which its influence was supreme in China. Its adherents had built glorious temples and pagodas, had commissioned some of the most profound works of sculpture and painting in China to serve their religious purposes. Monks from India had long lived in Ch'ang-an teaching the Buddhist sutras and techniques of meditation, while a Chinese monk, starting out from the capital of the T'ang made one of the greatest journeys recorded in any literature up to that time. His name was Hsuan-tsang. His purpose was to find the true Buddhist scriptures, and his nearly always solitary travels on foot took him in a great curve right across the Central Asian deserts and down over the formidable Pamir Mountains, through Afghanistan and northern India to the birthplace of Buddha. More than twenty years later, after learning the language of his hosts, collecting what he could of the scriptures, and living in Indian monasteries, he returned by a similar route to Ch'ang-an and spent the rest of his life translating the books into Chinese. The pagoda built for Hsuan-tsang by the T'ang emperor of the time to house his library still stands.

Aside from religious and philosophical developments of great sophistication (and here we can only mention the development of the great Chinese system of thought called Taoism), the arts of poetry and painting, sculpture and architecture contributed to a brilliant efflorescence of Chinese culture in almost all its departments. More great poets lived in T'ang times than ever before, or ever after. Painting, although its absolute heights came somewhat later, showed astonishing brilliance and variety, while the architecture of the T'ang palaces and temples reflects vividly the intensity of a conscious revival of the arts, without sign of decadence.

Meanwhile, the materials, the manufactured goods, the wonders, and the languages of the whole of Asia flowed into the capital with nationals of distant countries. In Chinese painting and sculpture of those times we see Persians and Indians, Arabs and Armenians —perhaps even Greeks. With them came ideas to which China was not at all hostile; and with those travelers, on their return trips, went Chinese silks, Chinese pottery, Chinese medical techniques, and much else whose influence can be traced in the cultures of western Asia.

T'ang Peking was a small town called Yuchow, the seat of military governors-general, one of whom, An Lu-shan, has come down in history because of his amorous escapades. The rebellion which he led against the ruling T'ang dynasty was raised, it is said, partly to acquire for himself the seductive, petted, witty, and tragic empress Yang Kuei-fei. Originally the mistress of one of the emperor Hsuan Tsung's sons, Yang Kuei-fei had accepted the advances of the emperor when he fell in love with her. She became the imperial favorite and, as these things generally turned out in Chinese courts, gathered around her considerable influence, which she used to advance her family and friends. An Lu-shan owed his position as a trusted general to her favor, with the emperor's con-currence. But in 755 General An seems to have awakened to his opportunity and, taking advantage of the peripheral revolts against T'ang rule in a country by that time worn out with wars of conquest, he raised the standard of revolt. Within a few weeks he had

A Heritage of Art ▶

On the eve of the Mongol invasion of China a brilliant and sophisticated culture, peculiar to the country, had already been in existence for hundreds of years. The T'ang dynasty (A.D. 618–906) is often called the Golden Age of Chinese art, and assuredly there were painters, sculptors, poets, and courts of astounding luster, to be followed by those of the Sung dynasty, whose achievements in painting, to mention only the best known facet of that time, were no less great.

But, beginning in the distant past in the Shang dynasty (prior to 1000 B.C.), the art of bronze had already run its surprising course for a thousand years until Han times, its strange vessels never surpassed in technique and feeling for the medium anywhere else in the world. Likewise, painting, pottery, architecture, sculpture, fabric design, the working of jade—all these had flourished in their turn through the long ages before the coming of the Mongols. The arts of jade carving and of bronze casting are unmatched elsewhere, and it could be argued that Sung painting has little to fear from comparison with the painting of the rest of the world.

Into this elegant, impressive, and scintillating culture the barbarian rabble of the Mongols irrupted. Their first instinct, destruction, was akin to childish rage in the face of an adult form of life they could not comprehend. The Mongols spluttered with anger, with the impotence of their cultural inferiority, but it was not long before, in the arts, they knuckled down to the elegant steam roller of the Chinese way of life. At this point the capital was built at Peking.

The objects shown in the following plates, though all too few in number for the diversified grandeur they represent, nevertheless give an idea of the great heritage of pre-Mongol art in China, of the artistic background against which the new city arose.

The Guardian of the World (31), made in the unusual sculptural material of cast iron, was supposed to protect the Buddhist faithful by the ferocity of his appearance. The immense and solid power of this T'ang figure is probably unique in iron. Also unique is the jade disc or pi (32). When it is realized that jade is more brittle than glass and that the disc is extremely thin, some idea of the skill required to carve it is apparent. The artist has connected the outer rings with a finely drawn dragon, and has utilized the original shape of his piece of jade to carve a pair of masterly figures on the outer rim.

The pottery T'ang camel (33) exemplifies the lively art of ceramic tomb figures which flourished at the time, while the stone stele of the earlier Wei dynasty (34) shows another side to the bewildering virtuosity of Chinese art. As with most Chinese Buddhist sculpture, the head is the bearer of significant messages while the body is relegated to a minor role. But the figures are beautifully related, conveying an expression, peculiar to Chinese Buddhist art, of austere sweetness.

In contrast, Liang K'ai's apparently simple brush drawing of Li Po (35), the great T'ang poet, has the immediacy of an actual portrait. More than that, it has the hint of movement, of the poet's animation. Of a later date and entirely different style is the painting of Yang Kuei-fei (39), one of the great beauties of the T'ang court; this was executed in the early years of the Mongol dynasty. Ch'ien Hsuan, the artist, refused Mongol honors.

The landscape of Ma Yuan (36), one of the great Sung painters, shows yet another kind of Chinese painting. It belongs to the so-called one-corner style which conformed to the idea: "In one corner to make the nature of the other three clear . . . that is like daily bread to the disciple. . . ." But, more than its suggestive power, its spacial effect shows something of the consummate mastery of Sung art.

Leaping back in time about two thousand years to the Shang dynasty, the bronze vessel (37) shows another kind of achievement, a very early refinement of form and decoration harmoniously married in metal. Already some of the decorative motifs of later Chinese art were well developed.

The Sung vase of Tz'u Chou ware (38) represents a category of ceramics little praised by the Chinese themselves. Yet its elegance and the assured perfection with which the dragon design fits the shape and space available lend a spontaneity which only the great objects of art achieve. Another artist whose life-span bridged Sung and early Mongol times was Kung K'ai. He too spurned Mongol acclaim. The painting attributed to him (40) achieves with almost incredible simplicity the effect of a moment snatched from time and place—as if the viewer had just parted the last sticks of a bamboo grove and come upon the scene.

All photos in this section have been supplied by the institutions named in the captions and are used with their kind permissions.

*A Guardian of the World. Cast iron. T'ang dynasty. Height
21 in. Rietberg Museum, Zurich. (Photo by Ernst Hahn)*

Jade disc or pi *found near Loyang on the Yellow River. About 250 B.C. Diameter
6 1/4 in. William Rockhill Nelson Gallery of Art, Atkins Museum, Kansas City.*

Camel with Pack. Earthenware with cream glaze.
T'ang dynasty. Height 17 in. Seattle Art Museum.

(34) *Buddhist stone stele from Shansi Province. Wei dynasty, about the beginning of the sixth century A.D. Height 5 ft. Von der Heydt Collection, Rietberg Museum, Zurich. (Photo by Ernst Hahn)*

(35) *Portrait of the T'ang Poet Li Po Reciting His Poems. By Liang K'ai (ca. 1140–1210). Ink on paper. Sung dynasty. Height 3 ft. National Museum, Tokyo.*

Landscape: Mountain Retreat Under Pines by a River. In the manner of Ma Yuan. Ink and color on silk. Sung dynasty. Approx. 48 × 75 in. Smithsonian Institution, Freer Gallery of Art, Washington.

37 ▶

(37) *Bronze* chia. *Shang dynasty* (ca. *1600–1027 B.C.*). *Height 16 1/2 in. Seattle Art Museum.* (38) *Vase with dragon design. Ts'u Chou ware, engraved slip. Northern Sung. Height approx. 22 in. Nelson Gallery of Art, Atkins Museum, Kansas City.* (39) *Yang Kuei-fei Mounting a Horse (detail). By Ch'ien Hsuan (1235–ca. 1300). Ink and colors on paper. Yuan dynasty. Approx. 18 × 12 in. Smithsonian Institution, Freer Gallery of Art, Washington.*

38 ▲

9 ▶

*Man Asleep in a Boat Near the Shore. Attributed to Kung K'ai. Ink on paper. Sung
dynasty. Approx. 22 × 41 in. Smithsonian Institution, Freer Gallery of Art, Washington.*

marched on Ch'ang-an and the emperor was in flight toward Szechuan in the southwest, taking Yang Kuei-fei with him. On the journey the soldiers of the imperial escort ran short of rations and mutinied. They demanded the life of Yang Kuei-fei, who they thought, rightly or wrongly, was the cause of their troubles. Defying the emperor, they led her away and strangled her. Thereupon, their grievances appeased, they rallied round the emperor again and the flight continued. Hsuan Tsung's son, on his father's virtual abdication, became the new emperor Su-tsung. The rebellion was crushed and An Lu-shan killed by his own son.

Although the T'ang dynasty lingered on for another century and a half, its decline had definitely begun with the disorders represented by An Lu-shan's rebellion. In embroidered and heavily romanticized form this episode has become one of the staples of Chinese opera and romance. But like that of many another court intrigue (and such stories embellish Chinese history with somewhat wearisome regularity), its importance has been inflated. The end of the T'ang dynasty, precipitated as it was by An Lu-shan's rebellion and his love for Yang Kuei-fei, came as the result of economic causes. But not before the great poet Li Po had immortalized Yang Kuei-fei in verses of supreme delicacy; nor before such eloquent pictures of the court at her capital, Ch'ang-an—descriptions which it is interesting to compare with those of later courts at Peking—had been written by other poets such as Tu Fu:

> On the third day of the third moon, the weather is fresh and clear,
> Beside the waters of Ch'ang-an are many lovely women;
> With graceful step and distant air, so virtuous and demure,
> Their figures curving evenly, their skin so smooth and fine;
> Their garments of embroidered silk reflect the light of spring;
> The gold-brocaded peacock and the silver unicorn.
>   What are the ladies wearing on their heads?
> Iridescent feather-flowers that hang before their ears.
>   What does one see when looking from behind?
> Sashes sewn with pearls and fitting closely to the waist.
> Beneath their cloud-worked awning are the sisters of the consort
> Ennobled with the titles Lady Kuo and Lady Ch'in. . . .*

On the fall of the T'ang dynasty China, in the apt words of Joseph Needham, "reverted to its original cellular unaggregated state" similar to that which existed before the conquest of Ch'in Shih-huang-ti. A profusion of small states then fell heir to the glittering civilization of T'ang China which had at that time no equal in all the world. "It is interesting to reflect," Needham continues, "that this fragmentation represented a state of affairs which in Europe would have been thought perfectly natural. But the

* Translation from Grousset. "The consort" of the second last line is Yang Kuei-fei.

ACUPUNCTURE. Left, *diagram showing acupuncture points for treatment of kidney diseases, and,* right, *for diseases of the spleen. Long before the Mongols built their capital at Peking, Chinese medical sciences and skills were firmly established. These traditional methods have continued in wide use up to the present, as indicated by these pages from*

Chinese, in spite of the vastness of their country, had a tradition of unity." Among these small states we must single out one in the north of China established by a Mongol people called the Khitan Tartars. After destroying T'ang Peking (Yuchow), they built their capital on approximately the same site, calling it Nanking, Southern Capital, to distinguish it from other capitals in their Manchurian homeland in the north. The Liao, as this people called its dynasty, ruling Mongolia and Manchuria, made its court in the new town, whose walls, again bounding a square, were twelve miles in circumference, thirty feet high, had eight gates, and enclosed a fine imperial palace. The basic Chinese town plan was thus repeated once again.

Chinese history at the ends of great dynasties such as T'ang is always confused, and we need not here follow in detail the shifting powers and alternately rising and falling fortunes of various states within the country. The Liao survived the setting up of the great Sung dynasty in 960 and indeed were paid an annual tribute by the Sung (a unique reversal of the usual procedure whereby a "barbarian" people paid tribute to the central Chinese authority) and grew very fat indeed on the proceeds. Only one more point need be mentioned about the Liao: the Mongol rulers of Liao became so sinified as to be all but indistinguishable from the Chinese themselves. This absorption process is worth noting because it is repeated time after time in later history, with the most profound effects. It proved true that no conqueror of China, or of part of it, could withstand the powerful force of Chinese culture, which soon converted his barbarian ways to those of the Chinese themselves. The Chinese are less a race than a continuous civilization.

In the confusion after the end of the T'ang dynasty the innate desire for unity among the Chinese lacked only a focus. "Only the man was wanting," says Needham, "and he appeared in the person of Chao K'uang-yin, who in A.D. 960 was raised to power by the army after the manner of later Roman emperors. He and his house kept it much longer than most of them." Chao belonged to a Chinese military family from just south of Peking. The Sung dynasty which he founded endured, in the south, until 1279. Its capital was first at Kaifeng on the Yellow River, almost due south of Peking, but in 1135 it fell to the Chin, who were successors to the Liao.

The Chin people were yet another group of nomadic Tartars (a branch of the Mongols)

a Ch'ing manual and by Photos 101–4. Among the physical treatments—as opposed to the medicinal ones—was a method of curing a certain range of ailments by the insertion of needles at points explicitly delineated in manuals of very ancient date. These points lie along lines with no relation to the nerves or arteries of anatomy, and even less relation, very often, to the part under treatment. But recent scientific research both in the West and in China has proved that along these particular lines there is in fact an increased electrical conductivity. The treatment by needles which, being of metal, are of known electrical potential presumably alters or modifies the natural electrical currents along the lines specified. There is no question that in conditions such as arthritic and rheumatic complaints, migraine, and others, all resistant to alleviation by Western methods, acupuncture makes definite improvements in measurable lengths of time. Chinese medicine as a whole has yet to come under the close scrutiny of Western scientific investigation, but in Peking there is now an institute whose function is exactly this.

called Nuchen. They came from the Amur River in the far north and were in fact the forefathers of the Manchus who conquered all China five hundred years later. For their dynasty the Nuchen took the name Chin, meaning "golden"—a pretentious enough title for the house of a semibarbaric people. But their pretensions did not extend to altering the Liao Peking they found, and they contented themselves with renaming it Chung-tu, Central Capital.

Meanwhile, the Sung, having been driven out of their capital at Kaifeng by the Chin armies and having lost to the invaders their emperor and many government officials, fled south and set up the Southern Sung dynasty under one of the princes, establishing their capital at Hangchow south of Nanking. Their northern border from that time onward lay along the Huai River some distance to the south of their former frontier on the Yellow River. They had no success in their expeditions northward against the Chin, just as the earlier, or Northern, Sung under their emperor T'ai Tsung, marching against the Liao and besieging Peking in 979, had also been defeated near that city.

But let us retrace our steps a little and have a look at this Central Capital of the Chin. They built summer palaces in the area now occupied by the Three Seas (Nanhai, Peihai, and Chunghai), a fashion well established in China and continued to the end of the dynastic system. And it is likewise during the Chin dynasty that we have for the first time an account of the city and court of Peking. Fan Cheng-ta, a courtier from the Southern Sung emperor, whose domains lay to the south, writes in tones of amazement at the magnificence of the Chin city. Entering one of the gates of the palace, he was confronted by the spectacle of over two hundred guards dressed in flowered red brocade robes and wearing turbans sprinkled with gold. At the audience hall of the emperor a huge carpet with a design of phoenixes was spread opulently over more than half the courtyard outside. The buildings on either side of the great audience hall, contrary to later custom, were of two storeys. In front of them stood lines of armored guards—those on the west wearing blue cloth and carrying spears decorated with gold, and headed by a white banner emblazoned with a yellow dragon, those on the east side wearing red and bearing a yellow banner with a green dragon.

Conducted inside the audience hall with impressive ceremony, the Sung courtier discovered the emperor of the Chin seated on his jeweled throne, positively embowered in lacquer and painted screens of great beauty, with tapestries, gold lions, and carpets and perfumed mats for worship. Even the rafters of the hall were sheathed in embroidered cloth. Flanked by high officers in magnificent jade and other precious belts signifying their rank, the emperor himself wore a red robe.

Much of this prodigal display of finery doubtless came from Kaifeng, the capital of the Northern Sung emperors, which, as we have seen, the Chin had looted. The palaces themselves, says Fan Cheng-ta, were innumerable and extremely fine. To build them 800,000 laborers and 400,000 soldiers were employed—a number which we may think exaggerated, but which, even halved, is still large and wholly commensurate with the manpower easily impressed by emperors since the industrious Ch'in Shih-huang-ti a thousand years before. The Chin palaces and their ostentation strike a rather *nouveau riche* note, but serve to show how far on the road to technical mastery in the arts and crafts, and how far on the road to absolute imperial power, China had progressed. Nothing in the West at this time even remotely compares in magnificence and authority.

Elsewhere during this era the arts of painting and of pottery attained what are probably their most sublime heights under the Sung dynasty, while the Sung refinement in life and manners among the leisured and ruling classes constituted one of the most sophisticated and controlled human societies that the world has ever seen.

It is hazardous in the extreme to attempt to guess what Peking and China would have become, in what further manner they might have developed from the glories of the Sung, had history decreed a continuous evolution from that time. But it is safe to suggest, perhaps, that a civilization which had bloomed with such genius, far outstripping the achievements of the rest of the world, would have gone on, in at least a few aspects of human endeavor, to even further glories.

The chance of continuing was not, however, allowed. For, into this intricate embroidery of cultured life, through the spreading minutiae of Chinese fields, bursting through the Chinese dream, came the Mongol hordes of Genghis Khan. This cataclysm, one of the most astounding and terrible events in history, burst on China in the years 1211 and 1212 with the force of a typhoon. It is not sensation but literal truth to say that, at this precise moment in history, the fate of the whole Far Eastern world hung on frayed and tenuous threads which the Mongols, with their primitive energies bred of a hard and starved existence on the meager pastures of Asian steppes, all but snapped in their lust for the riches and ease of Chinese soil and Chinese life. The civilization of China was the bait which lured the Mongols on. Its riches caused its own near destruction.

Surprisingly enough, the beginnings of Peking as the most brilliant capital of half the world appear soon after the Mongol conquest, for reasons which are as curious as they are Chinese. No one could have guessed it at the time, but Peking, the first of three great capitals of that name, was soon to rise in all its fabled splendor, phoenix-like from the ashes of the old.

3. A Destroyer and a Builder

The greatest joy is to conquer one's enemies, to pursue them, to seize their property, to see their families in tears, to ride their horses, and to possess their daughters and wives.

—Genghis Khan

Fierce, pitiless, rapacious, gorged with booty and inflated with pride in their conquest of the rest of Asia, the Mongol cavalry of Genghis Khan turned their horses toward China. Fabled over the whole continent and beyond for its riches, its limitless rice plains, its immense superiority in the arts and sciences of life, China was a prize which the Mongols, a primitive nomadic people racially different from the Chinese, had no mind to forego. The conquest, if not easy, was less troublesome than it might have been, because China was weak, divided against itself into three mutually hostile parts (see map on p. 72).

Nearest to the Mongol area in the Central Asian steppes was the Tangut kingdom in the west, called Hsi Hsia, where a people related to the Tibetans lived in what is now Kansu, the Ordos, and Alashan. In 1209 this people was conquered and the Mongols turned their attention, together with Genghis Khan's military genius, to the Chin domain and its capital Chung-tu on the site of modern Peking. To the south lay the Sung country, the third of the Chinese states at the time; but this Genghis left alone for the moment. His cavalry, many thousands strong, swept through the Chin state toward Chung-tu, elated by their easy victories in the west. But face to face with the Great Wall the nomad prowess of Genghis Khan was baffled. He remained for two years in the region of Jehol in the mountains north of the capital before his armies were able to storm the passes and flood down to the walls of Peking.

During these two years, in a period of truce between the Mongol and Chin armies, the emperor of the Chin, Ai Tsung, escaped from the blockaded Chung-tu in June, 1214, and raced south to Kaifeng on the Yellow River—but not before he had paid out to the Mongols a ransom of enormous and humiliating proportions. Jewels and other precious articles, five hundred youths, five hundred girls, and three thousand horses were handed over, together with the adopted daughter of the previous emperor, who was an ugly girl but nonetheless a prize in Mongol eyes.

The ferocity of the battles of the Great Wall and the valiance of the Chin army are saluted by the writer of an old Mongol chronicle, *The Secret History of the Mongols*, in admiring terms. Evidence of the horror of these battles was the sight, described nine years later by travelers on the road from Peking to Kalgan in the northwest, of great heaps of human bones and skeletons of horses piled up at the sites of the encounters. The Chinese, not only in the Chin state but elsewhere during the Mongol conquest, were for

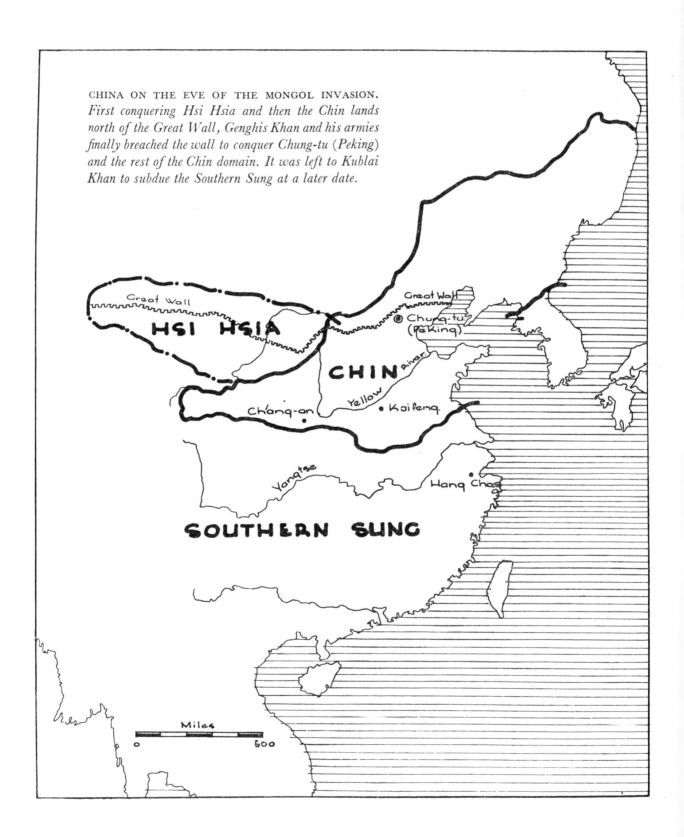

CHINA ON THE EVE OF THE MONGOL INVASION.
*First conquering Hsi Hsia and then the Chin lands
north of the Great Wall, Genghis Khan and his armies
finally breached the wall to conquer Chung-tu (Peking)
and the rest of the Chin domain. It was left to Kublai
Khan to subdue the Southern Sung at a later date.*

Great Wall

HSI HSIA

Great Wall

Chung-tu
(Peking)

CHIN

Yellow River

Ch'ang-an

Kaifeng

Yangtse

Hang Chou

SOUTHERN SUNG

Miles

0   500

their part amazed at the mobility of an enemy whose armies, mounted on steppe-toughened horses, appeared capable of innumerable forced marches, of lightning strikes at this and that widely separated point, where they let loose a rain of accurately placed arrows—and then dispersed like the wind. The melancholy words of an anonymous Chinese poet, writing, it is true, of a preceding era, come to mind, more fitting than other descriptions to point the aftermath of Mongol drives through the countryside: "So men are scattered and smeared over the desert grass."

On hearing that the court had fled, Genghis angrily gathered up his armies and breached the Great Wall by sheer force of the numbers of his horses and men, ruthlessly squandering both in the assault. His armies descended on the Peking plain, rounding up the grazing horses of the Chin and bewildering their men in the same way that the Red Army of Mao Tse-tung and Chu Te was to bewilder the forces of Chiang Kai-shek in the 1930's. The parallel between the mobility of the Mongol forces and that of the Communists is remarkable and interesting, as is the apparent inability of both the Chin and the Kuomintang leaders in widely separated historical times to respond in a militarily effective manner to similar tactics.*

The Mongols laid siege to Peking, probably using the metal-barrel cannon which was comparatively new and not used in Europe until about fifty years later. With "glorious slaughter" (to quote *The Secret History* again) the invaders at last stormed into Peking in May, 1215. The carnage, by all accounts, continued for a month until the whole population was exterminated and the last valuable in the treasure city of the Chin was torn from its place and borne away on horseback to the camps of the victors. It is hard to encompass with the modern imagination the scenes of uncontrolled lust and slaughter which made the cowering city at that time a sudden and final hell. The people were not only defenseless, but had no thought of defense. For, more so in the China of those times than in Western countries, the prevailing attitude and custom made them wholly dependent for safety on authorities whom they had not put in governing positions, and whose intrigues and whims and care for their own safety seldom included the slightest consideration for the populace. Power to rule, to make decisions, was entirely in the hands of emperors and a few court officials. These authorities in Peking now deserted their people.

Then, the rapine and pillage complete, the wrecked buildings of the capital were set alight and the whole broken fabric and the butchered denizens of Chung-tu went up in flames, a crackling bonfire whose pall of smoke rose up and joined the canopy of yellow dust above the plain.

Four months later in the same year, 1215, Kublai Khan, grandson of Genghis Khan, was born. Unlike his half-savage grandfather, whose experience of China was confined

* One of the best descriptions of the Red Army's tactics can be found in Robert Payne's excellent biography of Mao Tse-tung.

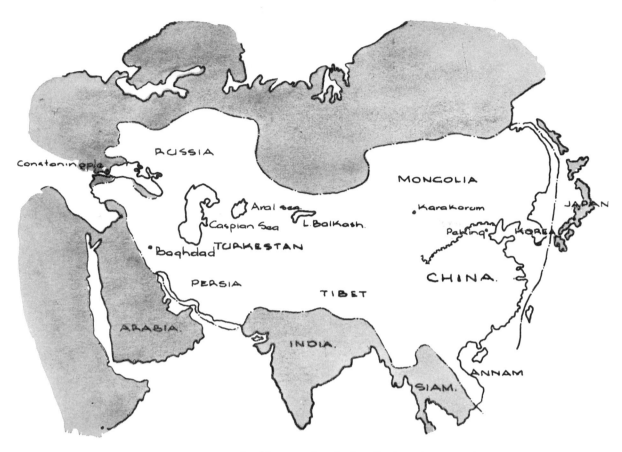

THE MONGOL EMPIRE OF KUBLAI KHAN. *In this great though short-lived empire, stretching from the Mediterranean to the Pacific, the old barriers to movement and trade which had grown up since the T'ang dynasty were dissolved. China was once more open to the West, and the West to China. In terms both of money and of culture it was the West which benefited more from the new freedom of movement.*

to its conquest, Kublai Khan, while completing the Mongol conquest of the country ruled by the Sung in the south, grew up to be almost a Chinese gentleman. Like the Chin before him, he was conquered by the country which he ruled. He was forty-five years old when, in 1260, he was elected successor to his brother Mangu, the Mongol emperor, while still heavily engaged in the south against the Sung in his capacity as governor of the provinces. On receiving the news of Mangu's death, he at once came to terms with the Southern Sung emperor, who was delighted to make concessions in matters of vassalage, tribute, and territories in return for what turned out to be but a brief respite; and then Kublai hastened north to the Mongol country, where in 1264 he defeated a younger brother who was making pretensions to the throne. In 1271 he officially proclaimed a new Chinese dynasty, the Yuan, of which he was emperor.

In the long years of warfare against the remaining parts of China which held out against the Mongols, Kublai completed his conquest of the whole realm. Apart from the wars of foreign conquest in which he engaged, for the most part with little success, it was not until 1279 that all China fell to Mongol hands. Meanwhile Kublai determined to build a new capital, abandoning the old Karakorum in the Mongolian hills.

He was a Mongol, emperor not only of China but of almost the whole of the Asian continent. His grandfather, after breaking the back of Chinese resistance, had returned with an apparently compulsive longing to the steppes and deserts of the Mongol west; hence it seems at first surprising that Kublai should choose to construct his own capital on the site of Peking. For Peking, in Mongol eyes, had stood for all that was essentially Chinese and essentially Chin—and therefore antagonistic to them. For these reasons as well as out of contempt for cities, Genghis had razed it to the dust. But here we come once more to the old story—the uncanny power of Chinese life, and the Chinese environment, to convert even its most alien conquerors into something akin to itself. Genghis Khan—in the words of Grousset, "a nomadic savage dressed in the skins of wild beasts and with no thought but to kill and burn"—had been dead only forty years when his grandson began what marks him as almost completely Chinese in outlook—the building of Peking.

Half a century earlier, Genghis had hardly been able to imagine any meaning to conquest but the subjection of the country by the murderous violence of his armies. Still less, at first, could he imagine what to do with the settled agricultural land and its peoples, nor with its culture and its cities, all utterly foreign to his nomadic way of life. His outlook at that time, when the Mongol armies were searing their way like branding irons through the rural treasury of China, when the whole land lay at his mercy, has been aptly compared to that of a tribe of Sioux Indians rampaging through the farms of North America. With one of the world's richest agricultural countries and the world's most advanced civilization at his feet, he could conceive only of destroying all of it. The impulse sprang not from any innate depravity but quite simply from ignorance and the consequent absence of a more constructive plan. Basically Genghis was a nomad, though a brilliant man within the compass of warfare on nomadic terms, and a shrewd man within the terms of the herdsman's life to which he was born. The abstract values—that of human life, for example—were unknown to the Mongols, and it was by sheer chance that one of the few captives taken during the destruction of Chung-tu happened to be its governor, a man called Yeh-lu Ch'u-ts'ai, a Khitan Tartar, descendant of the royal house of the Liao dynasty which had preceded the Chin as rulers from that city.

Yeh-lu Ch'u-ts'ai was a cultured, Chinese-absorbed product of the process which makes a Chinese out of anyone. Genghis Khan took a liking to him because the governor avowed his loyalty to the Chin rulers despite the fact of his Liao ancestry. It was this dynastic loyalty that appealed to the Mongol chief, who gave Yeh-lu great power. His influence on Genghis was a moderating one, and it is due to Yeh-lu Ch'u-ts'ai himself that the excesses of Mongol marauding did not end in much greater damage to Chinese life and property. To him we owe in large part the setting up of a new administration, which Genghis could not have managed on his own, and also the penetration of that administration, at least at the lower levels, by Chinese officials and Chinese concepts.

So it was that Kublai had grown up, if not exactly Chinese, then in an environment strongly influenced by Chinese ideas, in a government with the bones of a typically Chinese officialdom. The established form of Chinese bureaucracy had survived the Mongol trauma—but only just.

The grandson of the conqueror of China was by now the thrall of his conquest's way of life. He ceased to have any heart for living in Mongolia. He dreamed of the final act,

CONSTRUCTION OF A SMALL BUILDING. *Chinese building methods and architectural idioms had been worked out through preceding centuries and were ready at hand when Kublai Khan started the building of his capital at Peking. This sketch is based on a fresco in one of the Buddhist cave-temples at Tun-huang on the far west borders of China and antedates the Mongol era by several centuries, but much the same methods were used in the building of Kublai's Peking. The typical curved form of the Chinese roof and the long flat shape of Chinese bricks (used for the base on which the wooden structure rests) are already seen. The master builder, distinguished by his lighter skin and beard, sits pondering as workmen go busily about their tasks. Their darker color is perhaps an indication of their lowly status, or perhaps they were not Chinese.*

the final crown of achievement. He dreamed of himself, who was in fact the ruler of the greatest dominions any man has ever ruled, stretching from the Middle East to the China Sea—as the Son of Heaven on the Chinese throne, the next in line of that ancient and heraldic succession of Chinese emperors stretching back into the legendary distances of the Chinese imagination. It was an odd ambition for a Mongol, but one which demonstrates dramatically once more the alchemy of Chinese ideas which converts, then as now, each iota of foreign substance into the yellow gold of its own peculiar entity.

It is there that we find Kublai Khan, on the throne of China. To him it was more valuable than all the rest of his domains throughout the world of that day. It is there that we find him in all Chinese majesty a few years after the new capital, Ta-tu, had been built at his orders to form the proper setting for his dream, the first Imperial Peking. Even through the factual, pedestrian, and utterly unpoetic eye of the Venetian merchant Marco Polo, the contrast between this emperor Kublai and his wild and woolly grandfather is mordant and surprising. For here, in a sparkling new city built on an antique Chinese model, surrounded by traditional phalanxes of Chinese counselors and courtiers, embowered like the Chin emperor whose capital Genghis destroyed and which in its turn was a copy of more ancient Chinese capitals and palaces—here we find the Mongol emperor Kublai issuing his edicts like a T'ang or a Han from the Center of the World in the Middle Kingdom, to which all the peoples of the globe owed tribute. He is without question the Son of a Chinese Heaven.

From Ta-tu, the Great Capital as it was called, now for the first time the capital of all China, Kublai ruled as emperor of the Yuan dynasty with pomp, but also with some humanity: and for the most part in an entirely Chinese manner. And the fame of Ta-tu, together with the fame of its ruler, began to spread—the newest and most surprising of Chinese legends—across the deserts of Asia, which were now once more open to the east-west, west-east caravans of former times. With few and brief interruptions Ta-tu and its successors on the same site have been the capitals of China ever since.

4. City of the Great Khan

The sun is almost down, sitting red and flat in layers of mist and dust on the western horizon. Its light is still strong enough to throw long east-sloping shadows from the small grave mounds in the fields. The road and the shadows point toward the walls of Ta-tu, a mile or two ahead.* To the south, rising as if miraculously from the ground mists, the delicate octagonal height of the T'ien-ning Pagoda, only a little over a hundred years old and one of the few buildings to survive the sack of the former city, is poised almost asleep in the evening air. Two separate columns of dust are approaching Ta-tu along the road. As the first comes near it reveals a train of shaggy Bactrian camels, their heads moving like those of birds in unison with their thin feathery legs. They look very like outlandish four-footed birds, swollen at the flanks with sagging black bags of coal from the Western Hills. Their coats, impregnated with coal dust, are almost black. The camel drivers walk beside them in twos and threes, silent with fatigue, wrapped up already against the cold of November in an assortment of coal-colored garments, their feet, resembling those of the beasts, tied in clods of matted cloth.

Behind the fuel supplies for the capital the other column of dust, much longer, is quickly catching up with the camels. At its head are several riders trotting briskly with banners on tall lances fluttering importantly. Then come two palanquins one after the other, each borne by a dozen men, bouncing in unison with the coolies' trot and with the resilience of the carrying-poles. Their bright curtains conceal the persons of two ambassadors from the other side of Asia, come to bring their country's tribute to the Son of Heaven in the city. And in the rear, strung out over a hundred yards in the swirling dust of the horses' hooves, come the retainers, the servants, the guards, and the baggage train stuffed with the strange, barbaric, costly, and peculiar presents which the sovereign vassal of this petty state has sent to the Great Khan.

The caravan of the ambassadors is not long in overtaking the camel train and with an exchange of oaths and shouting pushes it off the road so that the envoys may pass swiftly to their night's lodging in the suburb without the city wall. For them it is the end of a journey of many months. Ahead, the outriders can see the jumble of one- and two-storey houses of the suburb which spreads from each of the three gates of the west city wall as if the buildings had spilled out for lack of room inside. The smoke of cooking fires drifts on the air as evening meals are prepared. Beyond the unpretentious houses of the suburb the mud wall of Ta-tu rises a strong thirty feet or so, topped with elaborate

* The following reconstruction of the city of Ta-tu is drawn from several sources. The writings of Marco Polo are supplemented by those of the Christian priest Odoric of Pordenone, who came to Peking after Marco Polo left. Use has also been made of Du Halde's *Description* and De Guignes's *Voyages*. In this first description of Peking my intention has been to give the reader an outline picture of the Mongol city which can be compared with descriptions of the city in later eras.

THE WEST GATE OF PEKING. *Depicted toward the end of the 18th century by William Alexander, the artist who accompanied the Macartney embassy from George III of England. A romantic treatment of the subject, typical of European sentiments in those days, the engraving nevertheless preserves the basic features of the scene.*

crenelations, each of its gates crowned with a big fort with tiled roof under which the garrison, having closed the gate in their charge, are preparing to sleep. Closer, a few men on duty through the night watches can be seen on the parapet looking down on the roofs below and watching the approach of the tributary party, whose arrival they will report to the captain as soon as he comes on his rounds.

The sun is now almost over the horizon, half of a dimmed-red circle in the embers on the edge of the world. The land between is bare of trees, a sea of dust and desiccated autumn fields. The corner towers of the west wall—one six-mile-long side of the city wall that is twenty-four miles round, enclosing the almost perfect square of Ta-tu—are beginning to disappear in the evening mists. The cloudless dome of the sky is thickening with the twilight as the cavalcade of the envoys rumbles into the suburb and pulls up at one of the hostelries allotted for the reception of visiting dignitaries. The people who live in that street come out of their houses and crowd around to stare at the foreigners with their beards and long Semitic noses as the two noblemen are ushered into their rooms. The remainder of the party makes for the yard of the inn, where the tired animals are unburdened, the personal baggage of the envoys taken inside, the treasure stacked and a guard set over it for the night. The grooms wolf down their bowls of gruel and curl up in corners in the soft yellow dust to sleep. Dark has fallen by now and the suburb is settling down for the night.

In the hotel the captain in charge of prostitutes comes to offer a choice to the two envoys—a service for which the women are not paid since it is regarded as a tribute to the emperor, who has commanded that travelers of rank be "honorably treated." The ambassadors make their choice and retire.

Outside, the noises of the suburb are quieting. The dry rawness of the air, moving slowly in from the steppe and desert of Mongolia to the west and north, is no ordeal to the city's inhabitants: many of their fathers were cattlemen in the Mongol heartland. The great wooden gates of Ta-tu stand soberly closed under their towers. Even the guards are not visible on the parapet against the sky, whose blue is lightening with the rising crescent of the moon. Only the porcelain monsters at each end of the ridgepole of the roof stand alert like quotation marks enclosing the elegance of their subject exactly stated beneath.

Soon it is the second watch of the night and over the huge bulk of the wall comes the sound of the great bell that is struck with a wooden pole once every two hours from eight in the evening until the light of a new day comes up over the square of Ta-tu, whose form represents the world in miniature. At the third watch three strokes of the bronze bell in the Bell Tower beyond the wall signal midnight. Complete silence falls over this microcosmic world and its drifts of suburbs, in which, aside perhaps from the envoys, the populace are now asleep.

At dawn the deep chill of the night lingers in frosty air, and the camel drivers rise, beating arms to drive the cold out of their fingers. The camels cough and munch straw while they are reloaded with the ungainly sacks of coal. The sun is a frosty red, almost as large as it was last evening, but with a halo of vapor. The men of the garrison stamp up and down on the parapet of the gate, which is now open. The envoys have been advised to wait in the hotel till Kublai, the Great Khan, signifies his pleasure and designates a day for receiving them. For he has not long returned to the capital from his summer palace at Shang-tu in the north—Xanadu, whose fame has already spread across the world in the stories of the caravan men.

Inside the rhomboid of the gate the dust of the city streets is laid by the night's dew. The populace are already busy, bustling along in the cold with steaming breath. A regiment of cavalry trots toward the gate bound for some destination unknown, pennants fluttering, quivers and bows joggling on the riders' backs. Most of the Chinese living in the city come from the settlement which sprang up on the gutted ruins of Chung-tu after Genghis destroyed it; and when the new city of Ta-tu was ready, and by command of Kublai, they moved within its walls. The whole plan of the city is regular, the streets in general dead straight, so that if it were not forbidden to climb up to the gate towers and look straight ahead across the city, the opposite gate on the other side of the city would be exactly at the end of the street starting at the viewer's feet.

All the main thoroughfares in Ta-tu are lined with shops and stalls and booths catering for the needs of the population. And behind the main avenues the houses are set on square sections of ground, "each allotment being sufficiently spacious for handsome buildings, with corresponding courts and gardens. One of these was assigned to each head of a family: that is to say such a person of such a tribe had one square allotted to him, and so of the rest. . . . In this manner the whole interior of the city is disposed in squares, so as to resemble a chessboard, and planned out with a degree of precision and beauty impossible to describe." This regularity of plan is reflected in the laws governing the people, for "it is not to be understood that" the garrison of a thousand men to each of the walls of the city "is stationed there in consequence of the apprehension of danger from any hostile power whatever, but as a guard suitable to the honor and dignity of the sovereign. Yet it must be allowed that the declaration of the astrologers has excited in [Kublai Khan's] mind a degree of suspicion with regard to the Cathaians [the Chinese]

A TRAVELER ARRIVING AT A PEKING INN. *Another 18th-century engraving which, though several centuries later than the Mongol times of which we are speaking, nevertheless suggests the mood of the ancient city.*

. . . and after the third stroke of the great bell no person dares to be found in the streets, unless upon some urgent occasion such as to call assistance to a woman in labor, or a man attacked with sickness; and even in such necessary cases the person is required to carry a light.

"The small roads [the *hutung*] which run into the avenues have doors made of wooden trellis-work which, however, do not prevent one from seeing who walks inside . . . and these doors are closed at night by the city guards, and they can only rarely be prevailed upon to open them except to people who are known to them, who carry a hand lantern and who are about for some good reason such as to call a doctor. . . ."

Crossing the city to the east by one of those straight streets, threading a way among the throng of merchants and travelers from every part of Asia, another great wall bars the way—the wall of the Imperial City, within which is a third walled enclosure, the Palace City of the Great Khan. The wall of the Imperial City encloses a vast area surrounding the palace, an area which contains buildings, parkland for the emperor's pleasure, two artificial hills, the lakes, and quarters for the Mongol army. Of the big buildings there are eight for military stores, disposed at intervals round the inside of the wall. "Thus, for instance, the bridles, saddles, stirrups, and other furniture serving for the equipment of cavalry, occupy one storehouse; the bows, strings, quivers, arrows, and other articles belonging to archery, occupy another; . . . cuirasses, corselets, and other armour formed of leather, a third storehouse. . . ."

Between the outer wall and that of the Palace City itself—"the distance of perhaps a bow-shot" and on the western side—lies the focus of imperial pleasure, the lakes with their flying bridges connecting one to another, the boats lazing on the waters, shaped like dragons and so built that they pass easily under any of the arches of the bridges. Emerald Isle rises out of the North Lake more than a hundred feet, garnished with strange and suggestive rocks, and still bearing on one side, halfway up, the remains of a temple where the Chin rulers used to play chess. On the western shores of the lakes lie specially built baths and ladies' rooms, enclosed parks for animals, and a library. And, on the lakes, "there be such multitudes of wild-geese and ducks and swans . . . that there is no need for that Lord to go from home when he wisheth for sport." A whole wilderness, tamed in the Chinese manner, has been concentrated within the walls of western Ta-tu for the emperor's amusement.

"The spaces between one wall and the other are ornamented with many handsome trees, and contain meadows in which are kept various kinds of beasts . . . stags, the animals that yield the musk, roe-bucks, fallow-deer. . . . Every interval between the walls not occupied by buildings, is stocked in this manner. The pastures have abundant herbage. The roads across them being raised three feet above their level, and paved; no mud collects upon them, nor rainwater settles, but on the contrary runs off, and contributes to improve the vegetation."

Inside the inner wall, four miles round, "stands the palace of the grand khan, the most extensive that has ever yet been known. It reaches from the northern to the southern wall, leaving only a vacant space (or court) where persons of rank and the military guards pass and repass." The palace "is of vast size and splendor. The basement there is raised about two paces above the ground. . . . It has no upper floor but the roof is very lofty. The paved foundation or platform" has "a wall of marble, two paces wide. . . . The wall, extending beyond the ground plan of the building, and encompassing the whole, serves as a terrace, where those who walk on it are visible from without. Along the exterior edge of the wall is a handsome balustrade with pillars. . . . The sides of the great halls and the apartments are ornamented with dragons in carved work and gilt, figures of warriors, of birds and of beasts, with representations of battles. The inside of the roof is contrived in such a manner that nothing besides gilding and painting presents itself to the eye. The hall is about one hundred and thirty paces long . . . and the columns supporting the roof are about six or seven feet in circumference at the base, encrusted with a kind of paste covered with red varnish. . . . The roof is covered with glazed tiles of such a lovely yellow that even from a distance they appear hardly less striking than had they been made of gold." It is a palace fitting for the majesty of the most powerful ruler in the world, its beauty and refinements contrasting with the dirt, the absence of sanitation, the unpaved streets, and the brutality of life in surrounding Ta-tu.

"In the rear of the body of the palace there are large buildings containing several apartments, where is deposited the private property of the monarch, his treasure in gold and silver bullion, precious stones and pearls, and also his vessels of gold and silver plate. Here likewise are the apartments of his wives and concubines; and in this retired situation he despatches business with convenience, being free from every kind of interruption.

"When the Lord Khan is seated on his Imperial throne, the queen is placed on his left hand; and a step lower are two others of his women, whilst at the bottom of the steps stand all the other ladies of his family." In the vast audience hall are forty columns of gold, and "all the walls are hung with skins of red leather." The headdresses of the women are curious, of a Mongol type foreign to Chinese beauties, formed from some substance like bark and about a "cubit and a half in length"; draped and set with cranes' feathers on top and adorned with pearls. Some are in the form of a man's riding boot to show the women's subjection to their jealous Mongol husbands and perhaps to remind them of their masters who, in nomad life, are often absent from home. The great opulent Chinese audience hall is still somehow, by token of those headdresses and the skins hung on its walls, near to the yurts or black camel-hair tents of the steppe.

Thus Kublai holds court. On his right hand, but lower, is his son Chen-chin (who did not live to succeed him), and below, their heads at the level of Kublai's feet, all others of the royal blood are at tables with their women and accompanied by the wives of the nobility and military officers. Overlooking them is Kublai, his back to the inauspicious north, face to the south. At the New Year festival in February he "appears in a superb dress of cloth of gold, and on the same occasion full twenty thousand nobles and military officers are clad by him in dresses similar to his own . . . but the materials are not equally rich. . . . At each door of the grand hall . . . stand two officers of gigantic figure . . . with staves in their hands, for the purpose of preventing persons from touching the threshold with their feet," an act regarded as a bad omen and punished with the bastinado. But, heavy drinkers as the Mongols are, there is often trouble over this point of ceremony when the company finally breaks up for the night. "In departing from the hall, as some of the company may be affected by the liquor, it is impossible to guard against the accident, and the order is not then strictly enforced."

But while the feasting lasts the drinks are called by Kublai. The page who brings him the cup then retires among the body of the guests while everyone kneels down and prostrates himself. "At the same moment all the musical instruments, of which there is a numerous band, begin to play, and continue to do so until he has ceased drinking, when all the company recover their posture; and this reverential salutation is made so often as his majesty drinks."

From the ritual distance the ambassadors, when they are eventually permitted to have their audience with the Great Khan and when they have made their prostrations before him (probably the nine kowtows with the forehead touching the floor), see another spectacle of equal grandeur. Kublai, seated on his throne, is of middle height, with well-formed limbs. His complexion is fair, occasionally suffused with red in the manner of Mongols, whose cheeks, in the steppes, are often as rosy as those of Tibetans. His eyes are black and handsome and his nose well-shaped and prominent, quite unlike the noses of his Chinese subjects. Around him are disposed the courtiers and high officers in their heraldic robes of rank and distinction; outside in the courtyard three thousand of the Khan's personal guard of twelve thousand horsemen stand in rows. A dead silence, only broken by the clicking of the accouterments and an occasional staccato order, reigns over the whole palace. The focus, the crux of all men's eyes and all men's thoughts and fears is Kublai, seated on the throne under the gold-shining roof of the exact Center of the World, in tremendous and terrible majesty: impassive, absolute in the knowledge that he may if he chooses lift one finger and destroy a hundred thousand men, or send an army a thousand miles and more to the conquest of some far country. Both of those things he has done and will do again.

No wonder then that the ambassadors tremble and offer their presents with abject humility. Kublai is graciously pleased to accept these strange and barbarous objects "of which we have no need in the Middle Kingdom, since our domain contains everything of every kind whatsoever that man can desire"; and in return he makes them each, and their petty king as well, some presents of great value within the range prescribed in the rules as fitting to such vassals who show their allegiance. The ambassadors retire, like well-trained dogs given a bone, ordered to repair on such and such a date decreed by the court to their own country and to convey the imperial pleasure of Kublai that their kinglet will remain within the global protection of the Son of Heaven.

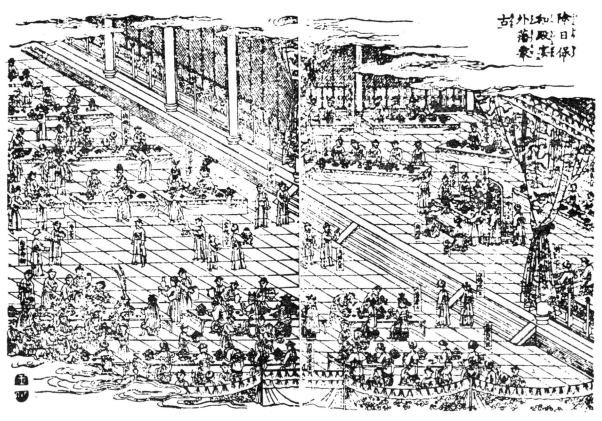

A BANQUET IN KUBLAI KHAN'S PALACE. *The "Grand Khan" sits at table in the center of the upper level of the court-yard (right). The guests, on the lower level, are various Mongol chieftains and courtiers. Principal personages and functionaries are identified by the Chinese ideographs in cartouches. (From a Chinese woodblock print.)*

Kublai is borne away to his private apartments, where his four wives of the first rank reside, each of them attended by no fewer than three hundred girls, besides pages, eunuchs, and ladies of the bedchamber. "When his majesty is desirous of the company of one of his empresses he sends for her or goes himself to her palace." Or, since he has several hundred concubines—mostly of the Uigur race, whose women are distinguished for their fair skins, selected not only for their beauty but for the tranquillity with which they sleep and do not snore, have sweet breath and no unpleasant odor or imperfection—he selects from the party of five such maidens which is on duty in his inner apartments for three days and nights in rotation.

Outside the absolute sanctuary of the palace is the densely peopled city of Ta-tu, where no corpse is suffered to be buried, but where the stench of overcrowded living ascends among the eaves of the delicate temples. The vast concourse of merchants and officials gathered in the center of the largest and most populous country of the world arrive and depart, plot and negotiate, discuss and extort. They come and go on foot, holding their long robes out of the dust and the garbage, or in palanquins springing from the shoulders of stumbling men, and with long rowdy escorts of horse and camel, and a thousand slave retainers, tons of baggage—from and for the ends of the earth. Here in Ta-tu once more, as was the case in T'ang days at Ch'ang-an, the capital near the Yellow River, all the tongues of Asia, and several from Europe, are heard, and the techniques and ideas of all three great civilizations of the age—of India and the Mediterranean as well as those of China herself—mingle. In former times it used to be said that all roads led to Ch'ang-an. But now with the Mongol rule established at Ta-tu and the whole of China compelled to pour out its tribute and taxes in coin and in kind, with the whole of Asia sending its ambassadors to the marble steps of the Great Khan's palace, all roads are *being made* to converge on the new capital, on the palace of that unseen and terrible emperor whose tribes have mastered the world.

Kublai Khan, emperor of a China much greater in extent than that ruled by any former dynasty, first alien master of all the Chinese, is at last the Son of Heaven. He is the cynosure of that universal eye which—the Chinese believe—observes his deeds, and gives him the Mandate of Heaven. This mandate will not finally be withdrawn from the Mongols until eight of his descendants have followed him on the throne of the Middle Kingdom.

5. The Mongol Century in Peking

By 1267–70 the Grand Khan, as Marco Polo reverently calls him, had well begun the building of Ta-tu as the capital of China. Doubtless he thought as did the early rulers of every dynasty that his royal house would rule forever. But, although this did not happen, Kublai had unwittingly established the site of the Chinese capital once and for all. Ta-tu and its successors remained, with few and brief interruptions, the focus of the bureaucratic centralization which the Mongol dynasty consolidated.

The city which he built to be worthy of his enormous empire was constructed by Chinese forced labor—a means employed by previous rulers, and to be used many times in the future also, so that one may see in almost every large project, whether tomb or canal or wall, an example of the unrewarded effort of thousands and often millions of Chinese pressed men. Booty accumulated in the Mongols' Chinese and other campaigns provided money for materials on a lavish scale. The work was done at no cost at all by peasants press-ganged from all parts of China: doomed men whose farms failed in their absence and were taken over by others, and whose families often perished of starvation, while those with sufficient influence and money easily bribed their way out of the obligation.

It was one thing to build a new city—however faithful you might be to ancient Chinese models in so doing—and quite another to make it the effective capital of the vast country of China. In the preceding dynasties of Liao and Chin, though the capital was on the same site, it controlled an area which never embraced the whole of geographical China. Ta-tu, completed in a few years, did. No capital in the world until that time had been deliberately planned in this way, destined and designed to rule a great terrain. From the Tibetan mountains to the China Sea, from Manchuria to Canton and the Burma borders, the land to be administered from Ta-tu stretched into the extreme distances. For the first time a Chinese capital controlled the actions and conditions of people in the remotest southern and western places formerly considered either beyond, or only just within, the natural influence of the central government.

The immediate result of the greatness thrust on the new city was to show its inadequacy for the role. First, there had to be a rapid expansion in the numbers of officials administering the affairs of the scattered and teeming provinces. Second, Ta-tu had to be made into the *physical* focus of the country. To multiply the numbers of officials was as easy in Mongol times as it is now when government departments seem ever larger and ever more expensive to run; but in the circumstances of early Mongol China it meant employing a majority of Chinese in most positions—for there were not enough Mongols competent to do the jobs. This was the first and probably most significant event in the process by which Mongols absorbed Chinese ways and forgot their own traditions. But it also meant

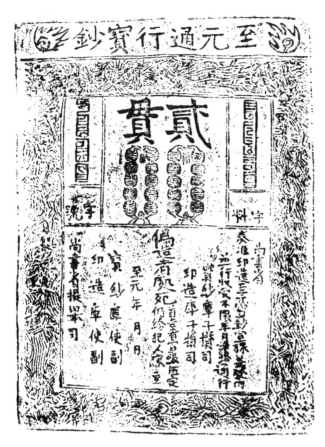

PAPER MONEY ISSUED BY KUBLAI KHAN. *Such paper money was copied from Sung models. Note the sketches of strings of "cash," the basic metal coinage that persisted in China until recently.*

that many decisions below the top level were made by Chinese, who once more began to control their own countrymen.

The Mongols, in fact, contributed nothing new to the method of governing the Chinese. And that they failed to do so is not only a measure of their total lack of administrative flair, but more importantly an indication of the basic strength of institutions which the Chinese, from Ch'in Shih-huang-ti onward, had formulated and refined in practice, in order to govern themselves.

For a little over one hundred years the Mongols were the real owners of China, the rulers and the lords of Ta-tu. Yet for only twenty to thirty of those years were they in effective control of all China. This was not entirely due to resurgence of the Chinese, but also to the miserable inadequacy of the Mongol administration. After the death of Kublai Khan in 1294, the government grew more and more oppressive because it was so inefficient. But the energetic Kublai himself was without any doubt the greatest emperor of Yuan times, and his reign stands comparison with those of the illustrious Chinese emperors who came before him—as with those who came afterward, such as Yung-lo of the Ming dynasty and K'ang-hsi of the Ch'ing.

Like all emperors of China, Kublai Khan was by designation an absolute monarch, and his personal character, like that of other emperors good and bad, had a direct influence over the government of Ta-tu and China. His motive force seems to have been pride—pride in his achievement of the throne of the Son of Heaven, and of ruling such an enormous prize as China, at that time the richest land in the world. But with pride was coupled an understanding in theoretical if not in practical terms that the wealth of China came from the peasants and from the international trade in which merchants engaged. His legislation to facilitate trade was considerable, his attempts to expand agriculture lamentably ill-directed. His care for the position of Ta-tu as the physical center of the country caused a network of roads shaded by trees to converge on the capital from all parts. He introduced the Mongol postal system, consisting of relays of post horses galloping along those roads between post stations at twenty-five mile intervals. This was to stand later dynasties in very good stead: six hundred years later an emperor in Peking received word of the landing of an English embassy at Canton only five days after the event—and Canton is over a thousand miles from Peking.

There was, however, yet another aspect of Kublai Khan's character—his firm faith in the Shamanistic beliefs of his Mongol ancestors, which led, while he ruled from Peking, to the adoption of Lamaism from Tibet (one of the most debased and deplorable offshoots of Buddhism), and to the power of the astrologers which was exercised on him with adverse effects. Partly from this superstitious side of his nature came his deep suspicion of the Chinese, which led him in turn to make sure that all offices of any major importance were in Mongol hands, and to prohibit the Chinese (at first) from learning the Mongol language.

Because he was familiar with their ways, and for no other reason, Kublai encouraged Central and West Asian elements among his adherents to monopolize foreign trade. And this led to progressive impoverishment of the country, since these traders sent their profits to their Asian homelands. The Grand Canal might now have been made to approach Peking, but the silver from Peking and country treasuries drained westward out of China. Gradual increases in taxation, coupled with steady inflation (the complete failure of the paper-note system which Kublai copied from the Sung dynasty), added to a picture of progressive economic weakness which, because of the busy construction of roads and buildings and the luxury of the court, seems to have remained unnoticed by travelers in the China of the Grand Khan.

In Ta-tu another facet of the unworkable Mongol system was only too evident. The city swelled daily with myriad clusters of Mongol officials appointed to administer imperial business and state finance (to name only two of a battery of state departments). Their upkeep made a deep hole in actual food and monetary supply. In the countryside the same cancer of bureaucratic officialdom was added to the old leisured gentry, and both classes financed their high standards of living from the product of the overburdened peasantry. The number of peasants cultivating the fields decreased as the number of Mongols who were virtually state pensioners rose, month by month. Meanwhile the wealth of the foreign merchants filtered off the silver backing for the paper currency and, as the modern historian Wolfram Eberhard puts it: "The imposing picture of a commerce made possible with every country from Europe to the Pacific . . . led to the impoverishment of China . . . simultaneously with a great display of magnificence."

Marco Polo was one of many privileged persons who traveled at state expense through-

MARCO POLO. *It is surprising that no contemporary portrait of the famous Italian traveler exists—but then, at a later date, the face of Columbus also went unrecorded by his generation. All we have of both are imaginary portraits such as this 17th-century one of Marco Polo.*

out the Mongol empire. All his contacts were with men in high office. While easily taking his attitudes from theirs he apparently remained almost blind to the evidence of his own eyes, and his much-praised picture of Mongol China and its capital is, to say the least, one sided, and in many ways utterly false. The banknotes for whose invention he incorrectly credits Kublai, and which he calls the "philosopher's stone," a gift from the Grand Khan who was the "perfect alchemist," were—as we have seen—rather less than that, and soon worth little more than the bark of the mulberry tree from which their paper was probably made. Marco Polo's touching and doubtless true reports of the Khan's tender feeling for his subjects have, however, some foundation in the edicts on "regulative and charity granaries." Again copied from the Sung, these were supposed to relieve want in China's proverbially faminous summers by dipping into the imperial storehouse and distributing grain free of charge as required. But unfortunately Kublai did not ensure that the uncontrolled peculation by provincial officials was curbed, and the granaries can hardly be said to have done much except provide yet another treasure-trove source of wealth for those who did not labor.

Marco Polo's naïveté (to call it by no worse a word) is immense. His excellent narration of the events leading up to the assassination of Kublai's finance minister, Ahmed—an *éminence grise* whose like we will meet several times in later dynasties—and his accurate statement that Kublai was surprised to find the extent of Ahmed's embezzlements, are nullified by his conclusion that Kublai was "infatuated" by this man. He exonerates the emperor from all blame for his total blindness to what was going on under his imperial nose and attributes the infatuation to spells.

A strange man, Marco Polo. Very close to Kublai Khan over many years in Ta-tu, he had every chance to assess his qualities both as man and as emperor. Yet, writing long after, when Kublai was dead and the Polos were safely back in Italy, he never attempted such a thing. "The most puissant of men, in subjects, lands, and treasure, that there is on the earth or ever was, from the time of our first father Adam to this day," is his over-all report. Far from squaring with the facts (many of which must have been known to him), Marco Polo's portrait of Kublai and Ta-tu and China is often more revealing of himself and his own background. His amazement at Chinese achievements highlights the inferiority of pre-Renaissance Europe.

In other matters too, Marco Polo is strange. To have understood the real meaning of the Yuan dynasty in China was beyond him because he was too close to it. But it is odd that, even the rather dull merchant that he was, he never mentions the many inter-

MARCO POLO AS A BUDDHA. *In China, Marco Polo not only gained high favor with Kublai Khàn but also so impressed himself on the Chinese that he was remembered both in fact and in fancy throughout later eras. Generations of tourist guides have even awarded him Buddhahood, saying he is immortalized in the European-featured statue sketched here, one of five-hundred life-size wooden images in the Temple of Five Hundred Buddhas in the Western Hills outside Peking.*

esting things he must have seen every day. Was he so unimpressed by the Great Wall that he thought it not worth a sentence? Why does he never talk of the tea which he must have drunk in gallons every week of his time in China, and which was unknown in Europe? Why was he so impressed by the use of coal and asbestos and by certain sheep in Asia, while he fails to tell us the stories he must have heard of the sack of Peking by the Mongols? Did none of the bevy of sycophants (of whom he himself was one) who surrounded Kublai ever tell him of the glories of the Mongol army and its cavalry that conquered China? Chinese painting, which he must have beheld so often, arouses not one word from Marco Polo—but neither do the Yuan china cups of marvelous colors from which his unmentioned tea must have been drunk several times a day.

Under the Mongols Ta-tu grew fat on the shrinking fields of China. Its population increased, while that of the country (already halved to a mere fifty-nine million in Kublai's time according to Grousset's estimates) remained static. The palaces were more and more stuffed with treasure, while the court, the military, the provincial officers and the civil service in general, together with those who traded with them, prospered greatly. The opera, which began in Yuan times, was much patronized, and as will be pointed out in a later section, this new form of art was to enrich Chinese culture in an important aspect.

Meanwhile Kublai was attempting to cement the fragments of a dissident empire in the west, waging wars of conquest in Tibet, Burma, Indochina, and the petty kingdoms of Java and Borneo. His invasion of Japan was foiled by the courage of its defenders and by what the Japanese call the *Kamikaze* or Divine Wind—the typhoon that destroyed the Chinese armada. Except in Burma, Kublai failed in all these territorial ambitions because of his Mongol lack of understanding in the realms of sea power and jungle fighting. His relatives out on the steppes of Central Asia, still hard-riding, tent-living peoples, considered Kublai had gone soft in the Chinese cultured way by relinquishing his ancestral mode of life. His peace feelers made them curl their lips in disgust. But in Ta-tu until his death after a reign of thirty-four years (1260-94) he was unquestionably the great and omnipotent emperor of all China.

After the death of Kublai the façade of his administration, which so thoroughly hoodwinked Marco Polo, began to crumble, and the train of incompetent figureheads who replaced him one after the other on the throne did nothing to arrest the decay of real Mongol power. While great temples and magnificent mansions sprouted thick as weeds in Peking, the first serious uprisings against the Yuan dynasty were beginning in 1325. More than ten percent of the population of China was starving in 1329. At first the rebels, who came initially from the most depressed classes, aimed solely at the removal of the rich, but it was not long before their target became the Yuan regime itself.

Their leader was Chu Yuan-chang, son of a poor peasant from Anhui province, which lies between the Huai and Yangtse rivers. At the age of seventeen Chu found himself the sole survivor of an epidemic which had carried off all the members of his family. With no means of support he had no choice but to enter a Buddhist monastery, where he was at least assured of food. There he lived until a popular revolt against the Mongols broke out in the area, an event which appears to have inspired his future actions. It is not long before we find him at the head of a similar revolt, the chief of the rebel band. His innate political good sense, together with an unusual humanity toward the villagers whose land his little army crossed, gained him a popularity uncommon among such leaders. He forbade his men to loot and pillage, and soon achieved the status of a liberator in peasant eyes—a liberator not only from Mongol tyranny but from the depredations of the many bandits who, at this time, roamed the country. Acting on sound advice, he soon ceased to pit his forces against the gentry and officials and won them to his side. In 1356 he captured Nanking and established his capital there, quelling the anarchic conditions which had prevailed in the town. His principal rival in revolt and in the battle for power at the time was another peasant—the son of a fisherman—who had made himself master of the provinces of Hupei, Hunan, and Kiangsi. This area, standing to the north of Chu Yuan-chang's small empire, lay in his path to the Mongol capital at Peking. But not for long. In 1363 the armies of Chu defeated and killed this rival, clearing their way north to the Yellow River. After subduing the Canton region to the south in a prudently directed campaign, Chu marched on Peking. The Mongol armies, who had caroused away the years of power in complete and delightful idleness, by now hardly knew how to use their arms. Garrisons offered little resistance and most fled northward. Ta-tu, the Mongol Peking, fell to the rebels almost without violence on the night of September 14, 1368, as the last of the degenerate Yuan emperors raced ignominiously on horseback from his treasure-laden capital toward the ancestral wastes of Mongolia.

The century of the Yuan dynasty, now ended, left a curiously mixed legacy to China. Ta-tu, the first of the great cities at Peking, was no mean achievement and one, more-over, in what was basically a Chinese idiom. After centuries of isolation since the T'ang dynasty, the capital, and China as a whole, had been opened up for the first time to world influences. But the disastrous effects of foreign trade which we have seen, and the revulsion that Chinese increasingly felt for foreigners such as their late masters, now succeeded in closing China's doors more firmly than ever, as soon as the Mongols left.

It was this reaction, natural enough in itself, that had such baneful effects in later times. The quality of Chinese civilization which the Mongols inherited, they could not at first understand; and after a little, when they began to be sinified and to comprehend their new cultural surroundings, they proved to have very little to contribute to that

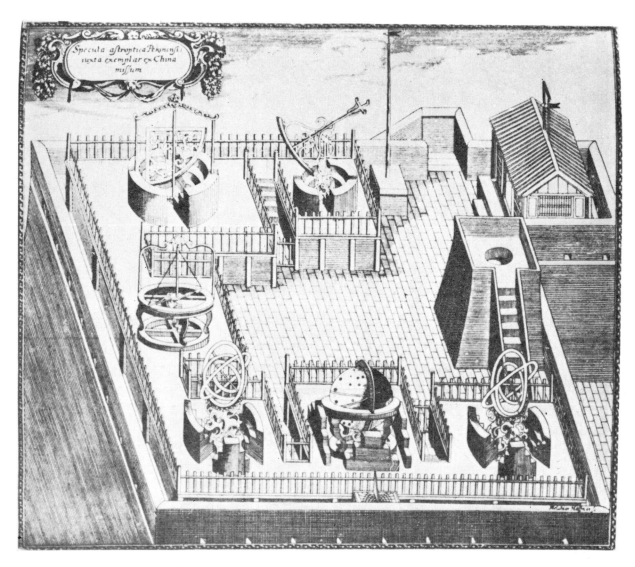

THE PEKING OBSERVATORY. *An engraving of 1687 showing the Peking Observatory as refitted by the Jesuit priest Ferdinand Verbiest in the reign of K'ang-hsi. A Ming observatory occupied the same site and was itself successor to a Mongol one set up in the latter part of the 13th century. This view is from the south. The east wall of Peking, not shown, should run on the right of the picture, the observatory being situated on a battlement of the wall. Reading counter-clockwise from top center, the instruments are: sextant, quadrant, horizontal circle, ecliptic armillary sphere, celestial globe, and equatorial armillary sphere. The Jesuit Matteo Ricci records that while the Chinese astronomers were perfectly adept at calculating when an eclipse of moon or sun would take place, they nonetheless vigorously beat gongs to scare away this evil occurrence when it approached.*

culture. The Chinese, on the other hand, seem to have been stopped almost dead in their tracks by the Mongol invasion; and it is during this century of Yuan rule that Chinese civilization begins to copy its former masterpieces without achieving many new works that vitally reflected the spirit of the age.

In Peking while the Mongols were there, the only significant development in the arts was Chinese opera. Cloisonné and carpet-making were imported from the west, and Peking cloisonné has been famous ever since, as indeed have North Chinese carpets. Painting and sculpture for the most part stood still, architecture absorbed some Indian influences, and literature achieved little of importance. The sciences fared a little better and Ta-tu's imperial observatory was re-equipped in the latter part of the thirteenth century with instruments which were remarkably advanced in construction. Chinese astronomy was in fact well ahead of its European counterpart at the time, and the Jesuit scientist Matteo Ricci, arriving in Peking in the Ming dynasty, was very surprised indeed at the perfection of the observatory's equipment. In Yuan times, too, thanks largely to the restless campaigns of Kublai Khan, the source of the Yellow River was at last discovered—a piece of information whose absence had bothered Chinese mapmakers for ages. And publications such as the remarkable Great Atlas of 1311–20 attest the continuing Chinese interest in geography.

Ta-tu saw a new university rise within its walls before the Mongols departed—not that it taught scientific subjects. Teaching in China remained concentrated on the ancient classics with a doggedness and a complete disregard for the observable fact that this training fitted no one for public life; it was not until the turn of the twentieth century that scientific subjects began to be given space in institutions of learning.

Such, very briefly, was the enigmatic legacy of the Yuan. When the scholars and literati had come out of retreat in the early years of the indigenous Ming dynasty that followed it, not even they seem to have realized that a century of foreign rule had broken the spirit of Chinese civilization, which had suffered such a deep trauma that it was never wholly to recover its former brilliant creativeness. Their reaction, and that of so many later Chinese, including even the most enlightened of the emperors, was in general to try to return to the glories of the past, which they now proceeded to emulate with incredible—but dead—perfection. Apart from architecture and ceramics, which went forward, the most vital of Chinese arts were the popular ones—the opera, and the novel which was soon to be born.

But if this seems to paint a gloomy picture, we should remember that it is not the whole canvas. The abundant vitality of the Chinese under the coming Ming dynasty breaks out with flashes of brilliance and a pervading magnificence. The Chinese were about to come into their own again. If their civilization did not become more profound, it certainly became more rootedly and more splendidly Chinese.

The Second Peking

6. The Brilliance of Ming

Moreover, the work of the greatest Ming and his architects doubly compels our admiration when we remember that in their time Versailles was an insignificant shooting lodge, the Kremlin still surrounded by a wooden palisade and Hampton Court not yet built.

—Juliet Bredon, *Peking*

Ta-tu, the Mongol capital, fell to the peasant emperor and founder of the Ming dynasty Chu Yuan-chang in 1368, just over a hundred years after it had been built by Kublai Khan. Once more China began the classic cycle of change: the fall of a dynasty at the hands of popular rebellion, the establishment of a new dynasty, a period of fresh approach and vigorous government sweeping away the laxity and incompetence of the old; then gradual enfeeblement of rule, progressively more incompetent and hedonistic emperors under the thumb of their *éminences grises* and of the eunuchs, rising popular revolt against injustice and starvation in the countryside; and finally rebellion and the fall of the dynasty. . . .

With the arrival of the Ming, China's capital was set up far to the south at Nanking in the heart of the agricultural lands which were, and still are, the chief wealth of the country. Not until fifty years had passed was Peking reinstated as the center of imperial government. Now for the first time the city was actually named Peking; for the first time in over a century the actors in the urban drama were Chinese of the Chinese. This time— as every new dynasty must have assured—itself, things would be different.

In many respects, things *were* different in the Ming epoch, which was to last almost three centuries, from 1368 to 1644. But the basis of Chinese rule did not change between the setting up of the first unified state of China by Ch'in Shih-huang-ti in 221 B.C. and the coming of the Republic in 1912. Only the dramatis personae, the state of Chinese civilization, and the intentions of the outside world toward China were different. There were a thousand rebellions in China in those two thousand years, hundreds of emperors, and thousands of millions of individuals—but there was no *revolution* till 1911. On no occasion in that tremendous stretch of time, and within the long trajectory of human progress in almost every department of living, did any faction in China succeed in establishing any way of ruling the country except through another dynastic system modeled very closely and consciously on one or another of its predecessors.

In this one important way China is unique among all countries whose civilized way of life reached the twentieth century intact. In the struggle between rulers and the ruled, which in most other countries resulted in curbing the power of the rulers, the Chinese did not succeed in elaborating a single democratic idea—far less in putting any such change into effect. By the very end of the last dynasty, the effective ruler—the Empress

SELECTING A CITY SITE. *A Ch'ing drawing depicting the method of selection supposed to have been used in Chou times when, according to legend, the first settlement was built at Peking. The geomancer, skilled in calculating favorable auspices in accordance with topography and directions, is shown using a magnetic compass, which is, of course, an anachronism, although at a later date it was the Chinese who invented the instrument. Until recent years such geomancy preceded each major architectural plan for Peking throughout its long history.*

Dowager, who died in 1908—was still as absolute a monarch under the yellow roofs of the Forbidden City in Peking as was Ch'in Shih-huang-ti on the Yellow River more than a couple of millennia before her. And the powers of landowners, gentry, and officials all over China became, if anything, more complete as years passed. Democracy, to the Chinese until the twentieth century, was as foreign and incomprehensible an idea as cannibalism.

If the story of Peking through the Ming dynasty adds nothing to the story of democracy, it is certainly not negative in other ways. History, whose initially fervent gaze gradually cools to an icy and crystalline stare, will doubtless remember the Emperor Yung-lo, the son of Chu Yuan-chang, largely for the gift of Peking. It is substantially his Peking that survives to the present day. Little of the former Mongol city escaped his rebuilding, and now almost nothing but the Drum Tower north of the palace, the low hump of the old city's north wall, and the pagoda of T'ien-ning remain as faint reminders of those times. Vistas of shining yellow tiles laced with the abundant green of spring trees, with jet tracery of winter branches—these are Ming and also contemporary Peking. But so is the grey drab of wall in street after street, with the feeling that the houses prefer to look inward on themselves, while only the blossoming trees in the courtyards dare cast a flirtatious glance at the outside world. There is palace enchantment, architectural nobility, classicism of concept, and at the same time a warm homeliness about Peking. It is a city in which fact and fancy, geomantic abracadabra and extraordinary human skills, and a highly civilized but unsophisticated people are all mixed together. Hints of the turbulent, the vile, the miserable as well as the transcendental are there; and here the poetic, rustic, sexy, and the infinitely delicate and plainly idiotic particulars of Chinese life and its history come to a sort of grand total. In the man-made landscape round the lakes you can see the poetic and passionate side of the Chinese character. In princely and religious buildings is couched that resilience and conservatism which is the unromantic aspect of the Chinese being.

It was Yung-lo, when he rebuilt Peking, who focused all those fragments of a blurred image. From them he made a city fit for the greatness of China and the Chinese. Perhaps in no country in the world is the character of a people and their aspirations so well matched by its capital. While the character of T'ang and Sung life in China was undoubtedly its brilliance, that of the Ming is richness.

Peking had always been a square city—most Chinese towns are, if the land is flat enough to allow it—and Yung-lo's new city was no exception. What has surprised historians is that the great Ming ruler should have chosen to move his capital, first established at Nanking, northward to Peking. For the first fifty years of the purely Chinese Ming dynasty, Peking had been named Peip'ing ("Northern Peace," a title it was to have again later on). Now it became Peking or Northern Capital in contradistinction to Nanking or Southern Capital. Modeling the new dynasty on T'ang principles as Yung-lo consciously did, it is all the more interesting to find him breaking with the hitherto uninterrupted tradition of Chinese dynasties in making their capitals on the Yellow River or at least centrally, as a nucleus in the great cell of China. His reasons—they turned out to be bad ones—were probably connected with the fact that Yung-lo had ruled the Peking region in the time of his father, the first Ming emperor.

As Prince of Yen, Yung-lo,* the fourth son of the peasant founder of the Ming, had usurped the throne by force, driving out the sixteen-year-old boy emperor (his nephew) from the capital at Nanking. In the civil war which followed, the country's allegiance was divided between the north and the south. The north, under Yung-lo, won. The dethroned emperor, Hui Ti, disappeared in circumstances of mystery and high romance. He managed to escape detection and death by becoming a wandering monk, and it was not until over forty years later that he was recognized and captured. He was sent to Peking.

Fortunately for him Yung-lo, who had long searched for Hui Ti in vain, was dead by that time, and Yung-lo's grandson Cheng-t'ung was reigning. The former boy emperor, now an old monk, was identified by an even older eunuch, Wu Liang, who had known him in his boyhood. When the old monk was confronted with Wu he asked the old man: "Are you not Wu Liang?" The eunuch, perhaps fearing his former association with the hunted emperor would do him no good, replied: "I am not." Then Hui Ti, former emperor and now aged monk, recounted a story of his boyhood days known only to Wu and

* One of the problems confronting anyone in writing about China in a Western language is how to render the names of emperors. To be strictly correct, the emperor Yung-lo ought to be referred to as the Yung-lo emperor, since the words Yung-lo refer to his reign period. It was the first Ming emperor who established the precedent of retaining a single reign title throughout the rule of any one emperor. In Chinese, Yung-lo may also be called Ch'eng-tsu or T'ai Tsung, which are his posthumous and temple titles; or he may also be designated by his memorial title. Before the Ming dynasty the emperor is sometimes called by the family name of his dynasty plus his personal name, and in fact the first Ming emperor, Chu Yuan-chang, was so called. In the case of earlier dynasties the emperor was sometimes called by the dynastic name (e.g., Ch'in) with his memorial titles (Shih-huang-ti, in the case of the famous founder of the first unified Chinese realm). In general the normal Western usage, however inaccurate it may be, has been followed in this book, utilizing the most familiar name. It would be both nonsensical and pedantic, for example, to call the well-known Kublai Khan by his unknown but correct title, the Chung-t'ung emperor, especially so since at a later date this title was changed to yet another.

himself. Wu turned away weeping. The former emperor was recognized and identified. But the embarrassed government, with a one-time Ming emperor on its hands, decided to keep the matter quiet and allowed Hui Ti to spend the remaining years of his life peacefully in Peking, incognito.

As we have said, this was years after Yung-lo's death. To take up the story of Peking again we must return to a time when Yung-lo was still very much living. With China subdued, the warrior emperor turned his hand to the arts of peace, but not exclusively. Such was the energy and verve of the new dynasty that he could afford not to forego the delights and rewards of war. Following closely (and as we have seen, significantly) the T'ang outlook on life and imperial functions, he fostered peace at home and expansionist wars around the borders of China. But in a final assessment of Yung-lo's reign, it is undoubtedly the city of Peking and its palaces that still stand "as the most eloquent testimony of his power and the civilization of his period."

The plans were started in 1406, four years after Yung-lo was enthroned. They involved such extensive rebuilding that almost nothing remained of the first Peking, the Mongol capital which Yung-lo had known as a prince for years before acquiring the Mandate of Heaven. Outside the north wall of today's city there is a long shapeless hump of earth which was once the rampart of Kublai Khan's capital; here and there stands a *chorten* whose story goes back to the Yuan dynasty, and the Drum Tower north of the palaces is probably Kublai's also, although moved east from its original site. And that is about all there is of the Mongol dream and its Chinese setting.

Yung-lo's Peking was enclosed in brick-faced walls, but it occupied a smaller area than its predecessor, the north wall being built some distance south of the former one. Between 1417 and 1420 the main structures of ramparts and palaces were raised. The walls, bulkier than those described in Mongol times, were matched in grandeur by the palaces, whose size and beauty were thought by contemporary authorities far to outstrip those of Nanking. Since the city of Nanking was of almost legendary perfection, this was praise indeed. On January 1, 1421, Peking was declared complete.

The reign of Yung-lo, and after him the first half of the Ming dynasty, was a time when the Chinese came as near as at any other to total harmony with that scheme of things which they had evolved slowly and with so much thought over the centuries. The old place of China as the cynosure of heaven's universal eye, as the center of the physical world, and Peking's place as the capital of the Chung Kuo or Central Country of that world—all these concepts matched the temper of the Ming Chinese. One cannot help being reminded of Victorian England with its blind belief in inevitable progress and its self-assurance in the position of the most powerful and the wealthiest nation of the world. In fact it would be hard to say which people—nineteenth-century English or Ming Chinese —was the richer, both in heritage of civilized achievement and in enjoyment of its unique and peculiar qualities.

But before leaving Yung-lo and his times there is an incident which, trivial in itself, is worth recounting since it reveals something of the isolation of Chinese emperors and at the same time reminds us of the important maritime excursions of the Ming. In China, where the dragon had long been recognized as an everyday feature of life, it was perfectly natural that by the time of the Ming the mythical unicorn should also be held in high esteem. It was, to be frank, a rarer species, a special Chinese variety, but if anything more auspicious. Imagine, then, the excitement at the Nanking court of Yung-lo (before the capital moved to Peking) when a living unicorn appeared, treading fastidiously on the cobbles of the palace yards, where lived and reigned the Son of Heaven.

It happened in this way. The Ming was the great age of Chinese voyagers. In the Yung-lo reign it would seem that the vast land of China became too small for its inhabitants—for their imaginations at least—and that they burst out of its confines. Expansion by land westward, to the north, and toward the steamy, lazy countries of Indochina was no new thing and had become the accepted pattern of foreign adventure. But this was the age of the admiral Cheng Ho, the Chinese Captain Cook, who started out with a fleet of sixty-three ocean-going junks and visited many ports in Southeast Asia, returning with travelers' tales and exotic goods, including the kings of Palembang and Ceylon, whom he had abducted.

In the following thirty years seven other expeditions were sent off, each one returning with more tales, more goods and strange peoples. Among their cargoes were ostriches, zebras, lions, tigers—and a giraffe, which arrived in 1414 from Bengal as a gift to the emperor. The giraffe, it is well known, was never at any time an inhabitant of India and must have come from Africa. The riddle of its origin is probably solved by the visit to Nanking in the following year of an embassy from the African country of Melinda, which had previously had relations with the king of Bengal. The Melinda embassy came in fact in a Chinese vessel, proving that the Chinese junks had reached the shores of Africa.

By chance the Somali word for giraffe is *girin*, which sounds to the Chinese ear (for they have no pure *r* sound) like *ki-lin*, their word for unicorn (pronounced *ch'i-lin* in modern Chinese), and they immediately took the new arrival to be this fabled beast, regarding it as "a happy portent . . . of Heaven's favor and proof of the virtue of the emperor." The *ki-lin* was supposed to have the body of a deer and the tail of an ox, to eat only herbs, and to harm no living being. For the eunuchs, the obvious resemblances between the unicorn and the giraffe were enough to start them off on one more round of currying favor with the emperor. In previous years several other strange appearances had already been reported—vegetarian tigers, outsize ears of grain, sweet dew, and suchlike. The arrival of a unicorn, they argued, was therefore expectable. And here it was.

Some excerpts from the nauseatingly flattering and lengthy Memorial of Congratulations to the Emperor presented by the eunuch court officials on the occasion of the giraffe's arrival give a sample of the nonsense which surrounded the occupant of the Dragon Throne. But also they present a charming appreciation of the graceful beast:

"We have heard that the *ki-lin* is the greatest auspicious sign in All-under-heaven. . . .

"UNICORNS." Left: *detail from a contemporary Chinese painting, by Shen Tu, of the giraffe that arrived at court in 1414.* Right: *this papercut showing a more conventional Chinese unicorn carrying a mother and her boy child is a charm to ensure male offspring. Little wonder that such a strange and unknown animal as a giraffe was mistaken by the Chinese for this stranger creature of the imagination.*

When the virtue of the ruler penetrates into the dark waters of chaos and his transforming influence reaches out to all living beings, then a *ki-lin* appears. . . . Of the myriad countries at the four points of the compass, there is not one but submits and honours him. Hereupon Heaven, reflecting the Sacred Virtue, repeatedly causes brilliant favors to descend . . . in the greatest profusion, and the clerks have no respite in recording them. . . . Your servant, joining the throng in the Forbidden Forest [Imperial Park] has daily beheld this auspicious omen the giraffe and he could not master his feelings of admiration and happiness, and has therefore written a song of praise in order to transmit it forever. . . . Amazing is this gentle animal, of strange shape and wonderful form. . . . Its dragon head is carried high, its fleshy horn grows erect; it has purple hair with white lines crisscross in a pattern of tortoise-shell. Its body is glossy and its conduct measured. It has hoofs but does not kick . . . it has horns yet does not butt . . . it walks with balanced tread and its voice resembles classical music. . . . Its brilliant lustre shines in the ether, and felicitous clouds hang down. Its two eyes rove incessantly; all are delighted with it. Wide open is the Reception Hall where the emperor sits to receive it."*

The emperor declined this memorial, but when—in the following year—a second giraffe arrived, even he could not resist. By this time it seems likely he felt the giraffe was really a *ki-lin*. The chronicles relate that Yung-lo went out to the gate of his palace in great state to receive the beast. All the officials made their prostrations and offered their congratulations to the emperor, who replied with what would be becoming modesty if it were not in fact the form prescribed by imperial orthodoxy: "This event is due to the abundant virtue of the late emperor, my father, and also to the assistance rendered me by my ministers. That is why distant people arrive in uninterrupted succession. From now on it behoves Us even more than in the past to cling to virtue and it behoves you to remonstrate with Us about Our shortcomings."

In the meantime the court painters had not been slow in seizing the opportunity of depicting the fabulous animal, another example of which reached Peking after the court moved there. At least one of their efforts survives, its hide looking like the scales of the more familiar dragon or tortoise.

To return to the story of Peking itself, later Ming emperors continued the sturdy and

* This and the following quotation are from the full translation by J. J. L. Duyvendak given in *T'oung Pao*, Vol. 34, pp. 399–410.

intelligent work of the great Yung-lo, each adding some excellent buildings, strengthening or modifying this or that existing one. Emperor Cheng-t'ung, who has two reign periods (1435–49 and 1457–64) because he was deposed and then restored, added to and embellished the walls and gate towers. He built stone bridges in place of the old wooden ones and lined the city's surrounding moats with stone, instituting a system of water-control locks so as to regulate the flow from that famous spring on Jade Fountain Hill to the west of Peking. The water in the moats thus flowed from the northwest corner round the outside of the square of the city walls, the two streams joining again at the southeast corner, as they do today.

An amusing sidelight on Peking conservatism is the fact that, despite Yung-lo's changes in the names of certain city gates, the average Chinese in the city—even to this day—persists in calling them by the names they had in Mongol times. Only a scholar would be able to direct you if you asked for Tsungwenmen, one of the gates on the south wall of the Inner City—because everyone knows it as Hatamen, the old Mongol name.

The Outer City of Peking, appended as it is to the south of the square Inner City, did not exist in Yung-lo's scheme of things. It was an afterthought, its walls raised as protection to the considerable suburb which had grown up there, even in Yuan times, by the emperor Chia-ch'ing, who began the fortifications about 1553. The story of this part of Peking is something of an unfinished symphony. The original plan was to enclose the whole of existing Peking together with all its suburbs in an outer wall so designed that it would form a second barrier against the outside world. The square Inner City would then have occupied the northern part of a much bigger square.

The very fact that the Chinese contemplated strengthening the entire fortification of Peking is indication enough of the decrease in military supremacy at this period of the Ming dynasty. A survey of the ground revealed the prohibitive cost of such a project, which was then tailored to fit the available money. It was decided that the southern suburb should be enclosed first, while the grand design would await some financially healthier moment for its completion. Even the length of each wall originally suggested was drastically cut from a grandiose twenty li (about seven miles) to the present length of the Outer City's south wall, which is about five miles. So the Outer City—which neither the Ming nor anyone else ever completed—remains a not very elegant blob whose walls turn in at each side to join the old walls of the narrower Inner City. The suburb thus protected was a bit of a poor relation, and a rowdy one at that. In the Ch'ing dynasty and right through to the arrival of the Communists in 1949, its reputation was that of a city of pleasure—more especially in the area directly south of Ch'ienmen, where many theaters, restaurants, and brothels (not to use a Chinese euphemism for such establishments) were located.

But there was probably another reason for the decision to build at least the walls round the southern suburb. In the southeast corner of the area lies the Temple of Heaven, built by Yung-lo in 1420, together with the less important Temple of Agriculture, which rose nearby two years later. The Temple of Heaven, where the emperor went to worship twice yearly, was an essential element in Chinese cosmological ideas. It was therefore important to have it protected within the city wall.

The lessening powers of the Ming dynasty which gradually became apparent after the death of Yung-lo were matched by the rising influence of the eunuchs who surrounded successive emperors. The employment of eunuchs by Chinese imperial families goes back to very ancient times, the first records of their dominating influence in politics and government dating to the Han dynasty (202 B.C.–A.D. 220) when the emperor Han Huang-ti gave his eunuchs official rank and titles. But long before that eunuchs had been established as personal servants to the women of the imperial family. They owed this favored position, doubtless, to the fact that they could not father children on the royal women and thus cast doubts upon the legitimacy of the imperial line of male succession. The position of the eunuchs as the only men permitted to enter the royal apartments naturally led in the course of time to their obtaining considerable power. For this reason middle- and lower-class families in China found it advantageous to have a male child castrated and then sell the child through some powerful official to the imperial court. Once established there, in the center of the governmental machine, the son could exert control over much of its activity. The eunuchs rewarded their families with civil-service positions. They sold promotions and appointments for huge sums, while any nonconformist officials who attempted to inform the emperor of unpleasant facts were impeached and tortured or assassinated by eunuch command. Even dangerous popular risings were put down without the emperor's ever learning of their severity or gravity.

In later dynasties, and especially in the Ming times of which we are now speaking, eunuch power often altered the entire course of Chinese history. By this time almost every emperor came to the throne after a childhood and young manhood almost exclusively influenced by eunuchs. His tutors, his playmates, his confidants, his conspirators in every escapade had almost all been palace eunuchs. In many cases, such was the strictness with which the heir apparent was sheltered from contact with the world outside the palace, all he knew of life and of Chinese civilization had come through eunuch intelligence. It was hardly surprising, then, that on attaining power the emperor relied heavily in all important matters on the advice and service of the eunuch mentors of his younger days. And it is even less surprising to find that those same eunuchs quickly amassed huge

BLIND MUSICIANS. *From ancient times it was common practice for talented blind people, like those seen in the two groups here, to become musicians. The old man is accompanied by an assistant carrying a horizontal harp, while the younger musicians play woodwinds made of varying lengths of bamboo. Both types of instruments are common, in slightly different forms, throughout the Far East. (From a Ming treatise on music, dancing, and astronomy.)*

fortunes, and that they became the leaders of palace cliques whose purely selfish influence often guided the destinies of China. While there are touching instances of eunuch devotion to emperors and empresses (see, for example, the end of Chapter 6), the effects of this persistent dependence on eunuchs were overwhelmingly bad. The history of China is often written as a record of imperial power and economic fluctuation, but it would be almost equally valid, at least in later dynasties, to write it as a story of eunuch intrigue and eunuch autocracy.

Thus it is, to return to our story, that the Ming decline was directly related to the power of the palace eunuchs. Yung-lo's great-grandson Cheng-t'ung, whom we have already met embellishing the capital, was only eight when he came to the throne in 1435. He was brought up in such palace seclusion that he may well be forgiven for knowing nothing of life outside the walls of the Forbidden City. At his majority he virtually gave power to a eunuch named Wang Ching who, in 1449, persuaded the emperor to lead an expedition against a Mongol chief on the borders of Mongolia. Not only was the Chinese army annihilated in the mountains fifty miles northwest of Peking, but the emperor was captured by the Mongols. It is related that the twenty-one-year-old emperor was found by the Mongol chief seated on a carpet in his tent, showing not the slightest trace of emotion although surrounded by his slaughtered bodyguard. Whether his composure stemmed from courage or from a belief in his imperial immunity, it is not possible to say. The Mongols then swept right down to the walls of Peking, but retreated from the siege when reinforcements arrived to relieve the city.

The eunuch Wang Ching was killed in this debacle, but there were plenty of other factions at court. The captured emperor's brother was thrust on the thone by one such faction, and on the release of Cheng-t'ung by the Mongols, who made their peace with Peking, was then deposed in the most ignominious manner by a rival palace clique. The released emperor Cheng-t'ung spent a couple of years virtually imprisoned in his own palace on his return to Peking before he was restored.

With the decline in Ming military strength the government, under the usual succession of nincompoop emperors, fell increasingly into the hands of rival groups of eunuchs and generals. Peking, and the China ruled by this "camarilla of eunuchs" from within its walls, stumbled on into the sixteenth century, when new alarms from Mongols and from Japanese pirates came near to ending the dynasty. The Mongols in this case were descendants of Genghis Khan, and in 1550 under Altan laid siege to Peking, the fires of their camps flickering under its ramparts. But the besiegers were finally persuaded to accept Ming sovereignty. Their camp was named by the Ming "Turning Toward Civilization." The combination of irony and Chinese effrontery in the phrase is typical of the arrogance of the authorities at the time.

A vivid picture of the state of the court during this time, and therefore of the quality of Ming government, comes to light in the reign of Cheng-te (1505–21), a little before the siege of Peking by Altan. This emperor, a descendant of Cheng-t'ung, was a youthful eccentric whose main pleasure was to escape from the palace and carouse in the more disreputable areas of Peking (among them the brothel quarter now enclosed with the southern suburb in the new wall). His disguise on these debauches was frequently insufficient, and his adventures caused embarrassment even to the tattered dignity of the court of the day. The emperor's favorite was a eunuch called Liu Chin whose corrupt regime was the scandal of the age. Eventually, when the emperor had been persuaded of the evils of Liu Chin's ways, he had the eunuch assassinated, and his property accrued to the imperial treasury. For this reason we have an official list which casts a very penetrating light on the corruption of officials in general. Apart from a mansion in Peking, said to be as sumptuous as the palaces themselves, the eunuch possessed: gold and silver (expressed in taels worth one ounce of silver each) 251,583,600, twenty-four pounds of precious stones, two suits of solid-gold armor, five hundred gold plates, three thousand gold rings and brooches, over four thousand belts adorned with gems. And the eunuch, who came of a poor family, had been in power only a few years! "An honest magistrate," runs the Chinese proverb, "has lean clerks; a powerful god has fat priests."

The power of eunuchs, as had been proved long before in the Han dynasty, always resulted in diminished efficiency of provincial as well as urban administration. Early Ming emperors specifically condemned their employment, but with weaker monarchs the eunuchs crept back. In the Ming the eunuchs were mostly northerners, and this stimulated already acute southern grievances against Peking. The provinces found it almost impossible to get their point of view through to the emperor. In almost unchallenged control of administration, the eunuchs used their influence in the pursuit of personal wealth and power and the aggrandizement of their families, selling positions for huge sums and extorting further dividends for the retention of those same offices. One direct result of this insidious blackmail was that the provincial officials themselves were forced (not unwillingly, it must be said) to collect higher taxes than was legal; and the whole peasant economy staggered along under a burden that grew increasingly intolerable. While both private and imperial storehouses in Peking bulged with treasure, the rice fields, on whose produce the whole of Chinese civilization has always been based, were tilled by increasingly reluctant peasants, whose share in the proceeds got progressively less, year by year. Hardly surprising, then, that unrest simmered and spluttered angrily in the provinces.

FATHER MATTEO RICCI (1552–1610). *Dressed in what appears to be a combination of European and Buddhist vestments, Father Ricci stands holding a Chinese fan. To the right is the Chinese convert Father Paul Siu Kuang-k'i (1562–1633), in Chinese robes.*

But emperors in the latter part of the Ming era were for the most part so hedged about with eunuchs, through whom every scrap of information passed and who filtered off every fact they did not consider suitable for the imperial ears, that either they did not really know the plight of China or, being so divorced from the ordinary life of the people, didn't care. Shuttered in the gilded courts of the Forbidden City in Peking, swaddled in wealth, choked by petty power, dedicated by upbringing to the empty forms of court procedure—the emperors were only symbols raised like so many jade scarecrows above the spreading weeds of eunuch infamy.

Meanwhile, as things went from bad to worse with Ming government, the first Portuguese traders arrived in South China in 1514, forerunners of many others from European countries whose activities in China were eventually to contribute in large part to the fall of the Ch'ing, last of all the Chinese dynasties, and to the tardy conversion of Chinese life to a modern, in place of a medieval, outlook. The behavior of the Portuguese, who were at first well received by the Chinese, was so reprehensible that it set the pattern of later Chinese antagonism toward foreigners in general.

But, balancing the piratical acts of traders, there were in Peking in Ming times earnest, accommodating, and cultured Christian priests, the successors of a long line of monks and bishops and laymen who had begun to reach the capital as far back as the Mongol dynasty. Christianity, at least as an idea, was well established in the court of Peking and various emperors had accepted priests into their households as painters, tutors to their children, and scientists capable of demonstrating the wonders of European technology. Many of these men have left their comments on life in Mongol Peking—among them the merchant Marco Polo, who, as we have already seen, brought a letter from Pope Gregory X to Kublai Khan; and the Franciscan friar John of Montecorvino, who built two churches in Peking in the early fourteenth century and was appointed Archbishop of Peking by the Pope.

In the Ming dynasty, after initial proscription because of Christianity's connection, slight though it was, with the vanquished Mongol regime, Christians once more began to arrive in Peking. The Jesuit Matteo Ricci in 1601 made himself more acceptable by wearing the robes of a Buddhist priest and taking a Chinese name. Presenting the emperor with a harpsichord, a map of the world, and two chiming clocks, he recited his skills in astronomy, geography, and mathematics, the first of which was to prove the most suitable

A Gallery of Rulers ▶

Studying the portraits and the lives, official and unofficial, of the rulers of China during the centuries when Peking was its capital, it is possible to conclude that the occupants of the Dragon Throne varied from initial barbarity to final depravity. There are elements of truth in this. In the following pages a few of those mysterious figures look out from their common sanctuary of the Great Within, as the Imperial Palace was called. In many cases we have little to tell us how faithful the portraits are. Only now and then, especially after the imperial court began to employ European painters, is it possible to say this or that portrait is probably a fair likeness.

Genghis Khan, even in his official portrait (41), shows traces of the brutish cunning to which his whole life of pillage and conquest attest. And, to turn to someone who could easily have been in his court, the Mongol princess wearing a boot-shaped headdress (42) is obviously straight from the steppes and deserts of Central Asia—as un-Chinese in dress and feature as are true Mongols even today. But Kublai Khan in an unofficial painting (44) looks less of a Mongol. The dynasty was obviously well established by the time his official portrait (45) was painted, for in it he closely resembles many an indigenous Chinese emperor.

The succeeding dynasty, the Ming, set up by the peasant rebel Chu Yuan-chang, was bitterly resented at first by many sections of the populace. The divergence between the two portraits of the founder (46, 47) is the difference between caricature and flattery. In the former he has a spotty face and wears (delight-

ful satire) a hat such as was worn by emperors of ancient times and had gone out of use in the T'ang. Even the carved animal on the corner of the seat of the throne seems to scowl. The great Yung-lo (48), builder of the Peking we know today, despite the formal and by now traditional pose he assumes, is a believable character. The somewhat dashing look of his face, with its mustaches and the alert expression about the eyes, is probably faithful painting.

The Ch'ing dynasty, taking over at the degenerate end of the Ming almost by accident, has left us a drawing of its first emperor, T'ai Tsu (49), probably by a Chinese hand. T'ai Tsu was a Manchu—first cousin of the Mongols—and looks it with his hooked nose. Ch'ien-lung (51, 52), however, at the zenith of the Ch'ing when the dynasty had become sinified, is a cultured Chinese gentleman, as the two portraits show. Their veracity is certain. The younger man has all the features of the older ruler drawn by the Englishman William Alexander in 1793. Ho-shen, Ch'ien-lung's notorious "prime minister" (50), was much craftier and more rapacious than his flattering portrait suggests.

The Empress Dowager, seated in a preposterous nineteenth-century photographer's garden (53), seems fittingly posed, for her taste was on about this level and she was, besides, an extremely ugly old woman. Two young princesses and the empress's favorite eunuch accompany her. Already, Western armies had marched into her capital (54), and the realm of China was in its final, convulsive dynastic years.

Photos 43, 49, 54, courtesy Toyo Bunko, Tokyo; 50, Hope Danby, England; 53, the Mansell Collection, London.
The dragon design is redrawn from the Sung vase of Photo 38.

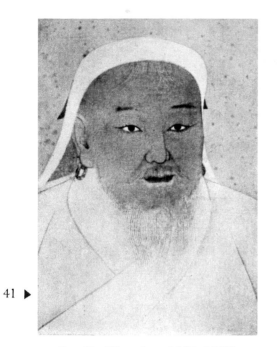

41 ▶

Genghis Khan (ca. 1162–1227)

42 ▶

A Mongol princess, Yuan dynasty

3 ▲

Persian miniature depicting Mongol cavalry

◀ 44

ublai Khan (1215–59), an unofficial portrait

45 ▶

Kublai Khan, an official portrait

46 ▶ ◀ 47

Chu Yuan-chang (1328–98), the first Ming emperor, in a caricature and an official portrait

48 ▶

Yung-lo (1360–1424)

T'ai Tsu (1559–1626),
the first Ch'ing emperor

Ho-shen (1750–99),
Ch'ien-lung's "prime minister"

◀ 50

49 ▲

Ch'ien-lung (1711–99), in a Chinese portrait and a drawing by William Alexander

◀ 52

53 ▶

The Empress Dowager (1834–1908)

Allied forces entering Peking in 1860 during the T'ai-p'ing Rebellion

54 ▼

in gaining imperial favor. With its dependence on the lunar calendar for reckoning time, the Ming court (Wan-li, whom we will meet again later in his tomb, was on the throne) was at first receptive to Ricci's special knowledge of the movements of the heavens. The Jesuit received great honors in Peking, being one of the very few foreigners ever to have his biography printed in official Chinese histories. But while his influence was great, it was to prove temporary; for the Chinese were unwilling to accept, far less to implement, those advances in science which had already begun to revolutionize Western life. This resolute backward and inward gaze of the Chinese in Ming times was neither the first nor the last example of an attitude which in the end proved fatal to the further progress of their civilization

The results of this blindness to the outside world were beginning to show at this point in time. China was beginning to lag behind the West in nearly all departments of human achievement, and in all essentials Peking remained—at least until 1911—a thoroughly medieval city, the capital of a medieval country. It is remarkable that China managed to withstand so successfully the heavy pressure of Western ideas for about four centuries before its traditional system and values finally disintegrated. If nothing else, the fact proves the deep-rooted acceptance of the old values.

By the end of the Ming, Western influence was still negligible, and the fall of the dynasty was entirely due to the corruption and incompetence of the later emperors, the depravity of their courts, and the increasing power of unprincipled eunuchs. By 1640 the end could have been foretold. The peasant brigand Li Tzu-ch'eng was already in control of large areas of western China. Once more a brilliant soldier was to succeed where brilliant thinkers, oligarchies of eunuchs, and ruthless emperors had failed. His final march on Peking was almost unopposed.

While traitorous eunuchs were opening the gates of the capital to the rebel armies, the last of the sixteen Ming emperors, Ch'ung-cheng (1627–44), was searching his heart and finding it barren of hope. In the evening, as the rebels reached the west gate of Peking and lit their fires, the emperor summoned his council. As the bombardment began, say the chronicles, "all were silent and some wept." The imperial regiments fled in panic. Their eunuch commanders surrendered to the besiegers. In the palace, where three or four thousand eunuchs were supposed to defend its walls and the person of the emperor, only one, Wang Ch'eng-en, remained faithful. In impotent rage the emperor seized hold of his Dragon Throne and hurled it to the floor amid his counselors. Leaving them, he climbed to the summit of Coal Hill. Seeing the fires of the rebel army beyond the city wall, he wept. And, back in the palace, he ordered the heir apparent and his other, younger, son to be taken to a place of safety. When they came to say farewell to him, wearing as usual their brilliant court robes, he helped them to change into more humble attire before sending them away.

Then, the chronicle continues, the unhappy emperor drank deeply of wine. The empress consort was brought to him, and some of his concubines. "All is over," he said. "It is time for you to die." Hearing his words, the senior concubine, Lady Yuan, was terrified and started to run away. But the emperor overtook her and struck her with his huge sword. She attempted still to escape, and with another blow he felled her. In the melee the empress consort fled to her Pavilion of Feminine Tranquillity and hanged herself there.

Then, sending for the princess imperial, who was a child of only fifteen, he cried out: "By what evil fortune were you born into our ill-starred house?" For a moment he glared wildly at her and with an ill-directed blow he hacked off her right arm, and the child collapsed at his feet in a spreading pool of her young blood. Then the emperor rushed out through the silent courts of the palace to the Pavilion of Charity Made Manifest, where he cut down his second daughter. And, reaching the Pavilion of Feminine Tranquillity, he suddenly saw his empress hanging dead from the gaily painted beams of the roof. "Death is best," he was heard to mutter, "the only possible way out for us."

In this night of maddened despair when, for the first time in his life, the emperor found himself powerless to influence its most fateful events, he slew the remainder of his closest family. By five in the morning dawn was breaking. The rebels were flooding through the west gate of Peking. The usual bell which summoned the officials to imperial audience in the palace rang in the deserted courtyards. Not a single soul attended its summons.

The emperor changed his dragon robe of state for another of purple and yellow. It is recorded that he wore only one shoe, his left foot being bare. With the sole faithful eunuch, Wang Ch'eng-en, he quitted the palace for the last time—by a gate whose proud name he may have recalled as he passed through: the Gate of Divine Military Prowess. It is easy to imagine the intolerable weight of his ancestors' condemnation which his orthodox Chinese mind must have felt like a swelling tumor as he left the scenes and the seat of his former lifelong power. The Mandate of Heaven which his house had held for centuries, and of which he was the final recipient, was, manifestly, withdrawn.

Once more he entered the grounds of Coal Hill, which had been built to protect the palace and its occupant from the evil coming from the north. In a final moment of lucid reflection he wrote on the cloth of his robe a formal valedictory decree: "I, feeble and of small virtue, have offended against Heaven; the rebels have seized my capital because my ministers deceived me. Ashamed to face my ancestors, I die. Removing my imperial cap and with my hair dishevelled about my face, I leave to the rebels the dismemberment of my body. Let them not harm my people!"

With that, the last, half-crazed emperor of the glorious Ming hanged himself from a locust tree at the foot of the hill. And his faithful eunuch followed his example.

The cycle of Chinese imperial history was about to begin once again with the first of a new dynasty on the throne in the great hall of the palace whose roofs were glinting in the morning sun as the last scion of the Ming twisted in death this way and that from the tree on Coal Hill.

7. The Grand Design

To the glory and richness of the Ming dynasty there is no more eloquent memorial than the fabric of Peking. The main parts of that second Peking are still, luckily, in existence. Many palaces, temples, and mansions of the great have survived the turbulent centuries since 1421. But what is unique in Peking is that they survived until a matter of fifty years ago in full daily use, and that the over-all plan of Peking changed not at all. Until well after the turn of this present century Peking was, structurally, a city embalmed, resisting the effects of time. Here and there, of course, a building decayed and no one thought to make it good again. Here and there some small modification, some improvement, was made. But the grand design of the medieval capital with its walls did not fundamentally alter.

It is partly this persistence of the old plan in the city which makes Peking so unusual. Approaching by air, you cannot possibly mistake the great walled square of the Inner City, and the wider rectangle of the Outer City attached to it, for anywhere else. The almost perfectly regular pattern spread on the plain is split up the center from south to north by the processional way, on which most of the imperial buildings lie like the bones of a spine. There is only this one important road from the Ming era, leading straight to the center of power in the palace where emperors held audience and, by virtue of their Mandate of Heaven, directed the affairs of the world at large and of China, its most important realm. As if to emphasize the extreme solemnity of the approach to the imperial center of the world, the spacing of the arches and walls and pavilions straddling this sacred way becomes closer, the tempo quickens, as you near the Hall of Supreme Harmony.

This impression is quite as striking at ground level, but in Ming times it was not possible to walk the length of the processional way. Only the emperor himself traversed it, carried in state through the central arches of all the gates. Those whose business took them within the palace courts entered by side doors, fell on their knees, and made the rest of their way to the imperial presence on all fours. Until the close of the last dynasty, a mere fifty years ago, even the highest officers of state spent their time at imperial audiences groveling on their knees before the throne, not raising their heads until spoken to.

Fortunately, although this is strictly a Ming walk, we are all emperors now and can start at the central gate in the south wall of the Outer City and stroll in leisurely fashion directly north to Ch'ienmen, Peking's traditional front gate in the wall of the Inner City. The dark elegant roofs of this front gate are already visible as you start down the long street. And by the time you reach the gate its roofs tower high above every other building of the Outer City around. Through its arch lies the next incident in the chain, the Gate of Heavenly Peace, front door of the Imperial City, red-walled and yellow-roofed, a quarter of a mile away.

This Gate of Heavenly Peace has become the symbol of modern China, a fact which would confuse, if it did not amuse, its Ming builder Yung-lo, who placed it there simply as a suitable gate to his palace. The importance of the palace precincts is made clear by the two tall marble columns, a moat crossed by five marble bridges in front of the gate, and, in Ming times, a small square which was popularly called the Pig Sty because of a willful confusion of the Ming family name with the word for pig. The bridges lead directly through five arches in the great gate to a courtyard, at whose further end is another large gate. Beyond it stretches the longest courtyard of the Imperial City, stone-paved, walled, planted with rows of venerable trees, and ending at a colossal U-shaped structure called Wumen, the Meridian Gate.

Once past the Meridian Gate, the noble, almost daunting proportions of the gates and courtyards then give way to luxurious tranquillity in the buildings of the palace itself. From the steps, at the far end of the tunnel piercing that gate, a much wider courtyard expands on either hand. It is crossed by the Golden Stream running in a marble channel shaped like a bow with its arc facing toward you. Five parallel white marble bridges leap over the stream. A Peking rhyme says:

> One piece bow
> Five piece arrow
> Ten lengths beam
> Can't be seen.

And indeed the water is invisible in its deep channel until you cross one of the "five piece arrow" bridges whose "ten lengths beam" railings are so elaborately carved. Ahead is another gate, but this time in the form of a pavilion with a double roof of imperial-yellow tiles. Other subsidiary buildings, much lower, flank the courtyard across the flagstones.

The great moment comes when you pass through this pavilion and stand, feeling more insignificant than is comfortable, at the edge of the vast square ocean of stone-paved court at whose further end rises the Hall of Supreme Harmony, the crux of the state buildings in the palace. The genius of Ming architecture is first of all in its use of the right space to complement the right mass of building. Here, in this breath-taking courtyard, is contained one of the two supreme examples of the Ming genius in the capital. Over the grey sea of cobbles, triple terraces of that radiant white marble of China, carved and delicate in appearance for all their mass, support the most impressive architectural event in the palaces. The Hall of Supreme Harmony, rising serenely from its brilliant pedestal, embodies the other aspects of Ming constructional genius. Its simplicity and restraint of line is matched and enhanced, but never threatened, by a polychrome decorative abandon in the bracketing of the eaves and the complex carving of its doors and

CH'IENMEN. *The front gate of Peking in the south wall of the Inner City was originally protected by a semicircular bastion as seen in this early drawing. The arch under the pavilion on top of the main wall, which is the actual Ch'ienmen, is here labeled "Main Gate," while that in the center of the crescent wall is labeled "Outer Gate." For a view of Ch'ienmen as it is today see Photo 65.*

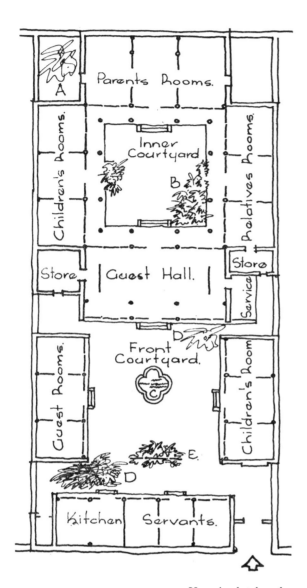

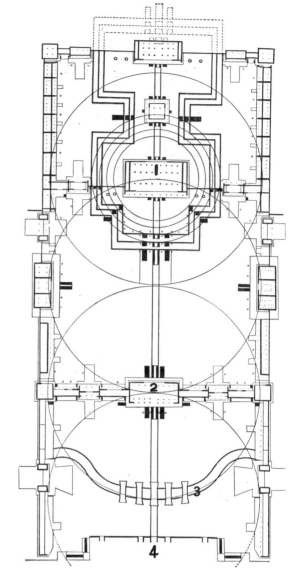

THE BASIC PEKING FLOOR PLAN. *Here, in sketches showing,* left, *a typical* hutung *house and,* right, *the great
ceremonial halls and courtyards of the Forbidden City, is
graphic demonstration of a comment already made in
Chapter 1: that the basic plan for all the buildings of old
Peking was essentially the same.*

The hutung *house shares its side walls with similar
neighboring houses. Its outer walls are of brick while inner
partitions are of wood with paper windows. A, D, D are
date, peach, crab-apple, or other varieties of trees. B is a
miniature stone garden; C, a small pool, generally containing goldfish and surrounded by many potted plants; E,
a screen, sometimes of durable material but often of bamboo
over which vines are trained. (In this house, unlike that of
Photo 30, the entrance is placed to one side so that the wall
of one of the rooms acts as a screen, while the screen at the
entry to the front courtyard conceals the kitchen and servant
quarters from view.) The two courtyards are stone-flagged
or cobbled. The small courtyard at the extreme upper right
is empty and could be used for complete solitude if desired.*

*The absence of bathroom and sanitary facilities is ex-
plained by the large number of servants formerly employed.*

*The plan of the sanctum sanctorum of the Imperial
Palace (after Albin J. Stark, with circles added to indicate
its system of proportions) shows a striking similarity to
that of the* hutung *house, a similarity that is by no means
accidental. On an immensely grander and more imposing
scale, the front courtyard of the palace likewise has its
front gate and screen in the form of Wumen (4), water in
the form of the Golden Stream (3), and flanking buildings
used for a variety of purposes. Beyond this courtyard at the
pavilion (2), equivalent in position and function to the
hutung guest hall where entertainment was done, it was
customary for visitors to the palace to be received. Beyond
lies the inner courtyard facing the master hall or central
being of the structure—the parents' chambers of the hutung
house and the Hall of Supreme Harmony (1) of the Forbidden City. None but the most important or the most intimate ever penetrated to this point, neither in hutung nor
palace.*

the adornment of its walls. Its two roofs are yellow tile. Its walls add up to a dull red with areas of gold. Its pedestal of marble seems almost to levitate the building above the oceanic spread of the cobblestones. Impossible not to realize you are confronted with one of the world's architectural miracles.

There, in the Hall of Supreme Harmony, was the hub of the world. The material form in which Ming architects chose to embody it is such that even today, when all the panoply of dynastic power is a thing of the past, this courtyard and this building still have the capacity to evoke a feeling of ultimate majesty and limitless imperial power.

And so the backbone of Peking passes on north with the flow of benign influences emanating from the south. Beyond the Hall of Supreme Harmony lie other but lesser halls, and also the living quarters of the emperors and their thousands of retainers, a series of courts similar in all except size to those of any small private house of Peking. Past the north palace gate and over the moat, Coal Hill rises, green and fancifully pavilioned. Farther still the sturdy Drum Tower and then the Bell Tower form the last vertebrae in the backbone of the city before it reaches the north wall.

If the plan and design of the palaces have any rival in Peking, it is the Temple of Heaven in the Outer City. After the palaces and their courtyards, it is an experience of an entirely different kind to wander about in the great walled enclosure of the Temple of Heaven. In this park full of dark trees lies the second of Peking's major architectural wonders, the place where the emperor in his role of intermediary between heaven and the world at large, as holder of the Mandate of Heaven, sacrificed at summer and winter solstices every year.

Leaving the palace the day before the ceremonies, the emperor was carried in solemn state down the processional way through the central arch of every gate, southward to the Outer City, where he reached the Hall of Abstinence in the enclosure of the Temple of Heaven. The ruts in the roads had been smoothed, the untidy clutter of booths along the way cleared out, the foreigners in the city warned not to approach anywhere near. And in late Ch'ing times even the railway trains were stopped lest a whistling locomotive disturb the sanctity of the occasion. The Peking people remained indoors, while the ends of streets on the imperial way were curtained off with blue cloth. In his yellow sedan chair borne on the shoulders of sixteen men, with eunuchs mounted on horses and carrying the instruments of the sacrifice, with standard-bearers and guards, the occupant of the Dragon Throne made his way to the place. The following day he went to the Altar of Heaven at the south end of the enclosure, carrying the round jade disc and the macelike jade symbols of his sovereignty, and ascended to the sacrifice.

The altar is the loneliest place in China. In the exact center of a square walled enclosure almost two hundred yards across, sentineled at the cardinal points by tall, delicate white-marble portals, a triple terrace of carved white marble is placed liked a low wedding cake. The square is the world, the circle of the marble altar is the universe. On top,

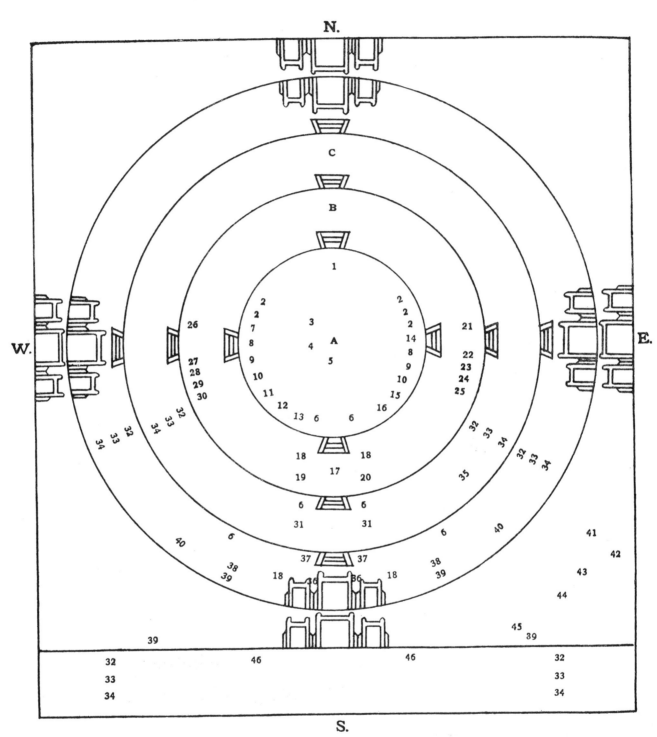

N.

W.

E.

S.

PLAN OF SACRIFICES AT THE ALTAR OF HEAVEN. *This plan gives an idea of the importance attached to the ceremonies performed at the Altar of Heaven as well as of the intricacies of the rituals. (See also Photo 72.) The three circular platforms are labeled, from highest to lowest, A, B, and C, while the outer circle is at ground level. A key to the reference figures is given below. (Compiled from the Ch'ing-dynasty book called "Directory of Worship" and first published in* The Original Religion of China *by John Ross.)*

1. Shrine of Shang Ti, Ruler of the Universe, north
2. Shrines of the Five Emperors (legendary monarchs of ancient times), east and west
3. Place for praying, with a table for prescribed prayers
4. *Tsun* or vessel for sacrificial wine

5. Reciter of the prescribed prayers
6. *Lu* or large censers for incense at ground level, Platform C, and Platform A, south
7. Imperial Guards

(continued at bottom of next page)

standing on the perfect disc of marble perhaps twenty yards in diameter, there is nothing between you and the limitless skies. Everything else recedes into oblivion. A sudden disquieting feeling of isolation surrounds you without apparent reason. There is only one sensation similar to it in the West: the feeling as you stand in the echoing nave of some Gothic cathedral where the walls soar toward dim otherworldly regions. Neither there, nor standing on the Altar of Heaven in Peking, is it necessary to subscribe to the beliefs these structures serve in order to be deeply struck by the smallness of yourself as time and space mingle overwhelmingly above you. But in itself the Altar of Heaven is the material embodiment of the settled, fully accepted, system of imperial power and imperial government of China—a concept which reached its peak in the Ming dynasty. More than that, the Imperial Palace and the Temple of Heaven manifest the central Chinese belief that *all* power, therefore *all* good, comes from a nonpersonal heaven and is transmitted solely through the person of the emperor, whose Mandate of Heaven lasted until such time as he faltered and was no longer worthy to carry out this vital function of intermediary. At that point a new dynasty, when it usurped actual power in China, was therefore thought to have acquired the mandate, and (regardless of how it came to power) to have been given the right to rule.

(continued from bottom of preceding page)

8. Officials in charge of the incense, east and west
9. Officials in charge of the offerings of silk, east and west
10. Officials in charge of the sacrificial vessels, east and west
11. Initial position of the reciter of prayers
12. Officials in charge of kneeling-cushions
13. Officials of the Board of Censors (a department of the imperial government)
14. *Kuang lu* or officials charged with presenting meat and drink to the emperor, east
15. Officials in charge of placing the shrines
16. Officials of the Board of Rites (custodians of the orthodox manner of conducting any imperial function or ceremony)
17. Emperor, Platform B, south
18. On either side of the emperor, his assistants (the Prompter and the Sacrificial Court)
19. More officials in charge of kneeling-cushions (as at 12)
20. More officials of the Board of Censors (as at 13)
21. Shrine of the Sun, Platform B, east
22. Shrine of the North Star
23. Shrine of the Five Planets
24. Shrine of the Twenty-eight Constellations

25. Shrine of the Myriad Stars
26. Shrine of the Moon, Platform B, west
27. Shrine of the Clouds
28. Shrine of the Rain
29. Shrine of the Winds
30. Shrine of Thunder
31. Princes, Platform C, south
32. Censors (as at 13), ground level and Platform C, east and west
33. Officials of the Board of Rites (as at 16)
34. Ushers
35. Director of Ceremonies, Platform C, southeast
36. Subordinate attendants who sacrifice to secondary deities, ground level, south
37. Dukes
38. Musicians and dancers, east and west of south gate
39. Minor assistants at the sacrifice
40. Singers
41. Officials in charge of the Sacrifice of Silks (by burning)
42–44. *Liao* or large earthenware jars in which the silks were burned, each attended by an assistant
45. The furnace, of brick with steps leading to it, where the bull was sacrificed in flames
46. Minor officials witnessing the burning of the sacrifice

There, on the round white marble of the altar, the emperor sacrificed to heaven as the smoke from a burning bull calf rose with the white smoke of incense from the palisades of outlandish implements into the Peking sky; and all around, in closed ranks, his functionaries in their flamboyant robes stood in utter silence. It is a place, as an architect, unable to explain his feelings, has said, where only a poet can convey the sensation of being raised out of the common world.

The altar forms the southern end of the Temple of Heaven complex. Northward from it a wide stone-paved causeway, raised to mid-tree level, connects with a circular walled enclosure inside which is a completely circular building. Here the sacred tablets were kept. Here, nowadays, Peking lovers have discovered that the circular enclosure is a whispering wall. Then the causeway runs northward again, enclosed by the dark foliage of firs, to the Hall of Prayer for Harvests. Once more a square sea of cobbles bears its round marble island, the podium of a round building whose nobility is unmatched, poised in space with its triple roof of Prussian-blue tiles surmounted by a gold lotus bud.

The majesty, the very Chinese majesty, of the imperial palaces is in itself a great achievement; but perhaps, and many people have felt this, the transcendental purity which radiates from the Temple of Heaven is an even greater one. With extreme simplicity the two concepts of heaven and earth, the circle and the square, have been used by the Ming architects with tremendous skill and in a way which, though solemn, avoids any feeling of sanctimoniousness. The pattern of Peking, the imperial palaces, and the Temple of Heaven must always stand as the most coherent and sublime statement of the Chinese essence of the Ming.

8. The Last Dynasty

The Manchus, a Tungus people related to the Nuchen Tartars who had conquered China in the twelfth century and ruled as the Chin dynasty, took over China almost by accident. For many years they had lived in close proximity to the Great Wall, a conglomeration of clans not unlike the Scots, hunters amid the vast forests of fir and larch and pine. In the early seventeenth century they had been formed into one kingdom by a leader named Nurachi. But their attempts at conquest proved abortive, until, in a series of improbable events reminiscent of many a story in Chinese opera, they achieved the Dragon Throne of Peking and China in 1644, styling their dynasty the Ch'ing. In the switch from Ming to Ch'ing the Manchu leaders were among the most surprised of all the participants. But they were quick enough, and had the military and administrative ability, to seize their chance when it came.

While the last Ming emperor was attempting to save his honor in the face of his ancestors by a family blood bath and by his own suicide, the rebel Li Tzu-ch'eng, as we have seen earlier (p. 112), entered Peking. He was, we are told, riding a piebald horse. Like all Chinese usurpers to that date, Li was a true rebel, not a revolutionary: his intention was not to change things but simply to put himself in power. The chronicles tell how this superstitious man, coming to the south gate of the palace (called at that time the Gate of Heaven's Grace), shot an arrow at the character for heaven painted over the gateway, convinced that if it hit the mark, this would be a sign that heaven approved his pretensions to the throne. The arrow struck just below the character. But, despite the foreboding omen, it was too late to turn back. Attended by the turncoat eunuchs and officials, Li was soon installed on the Dragon Throne. And his armies, true to form, indulged in a carnival of slaughter in Peking. For a few days the capital once more experienced a reign of terror.

The Chinese as a whole would have found no difficulty in accepting Li's new dynasty—as indeed they accepted the Manchus who followed on the heels of the rebel general. Misruled for long years by the corrupt governments of the last few Ming emperors, they were ripe for change. But meanwhile a Chinese army under General Wu, which had been engaged in repelling Manchu attacks at the seaward end of the Great Wall, remained loyal to the Ming dynasty. As ever in Chinese history, there is a romantic story to explain the reasons. It is said that Li Tzu-ch'eng took into his harem in Peking a girl of fabled attractions who had been the concubine of the stalwart General Wu. Hearing this, Wu demanded her return, but was refused. Enraged, he declared himself the avenger of the fallen Ming and opened the Great Wall, making a pact with his erstwhile opponents, the Manchus. Political and personal morality in these times was of no higher an order than that in Renaissance Italy or in Greece of classical times, and it

AN IMPERIAL MESSENGER. *In Manchu days an efficient and surprisingly fast system of post stations and relays kept Peking in close contact with all parts of the empire. Here a horseman bearing on his back an imperial edict in the form of a scroll approaches a waiting relay.*

would not be surprising to find that General Wu's fateful action was in fact motivated by nothing more than this loss of a favorite courtesan.*

The combined Chinese and Manchu armies then descended on Peking and easily drove out the rebel general who had just made himself emperor, but not before he had had time to loot much of the imperial treasure and set fire to part of the palaces. The lovesick—and naïve—General Wu thought without doubt that he had succeeded in restoring the Ming. But he soon discovered that the Manchus—happily and almost bloodlessly ensconced in the capital they had not dared hope they could conquer—had other ideas. They were in Peking to stay. Without delay they set their first emperor on the throne. General Wu, for his part, was forced to accept the situation and spent the rest of his long life alternately fighting for and against the Manchus in the south.

Had Wu stayed at his post at the Great Wall and accepted the Chinese rebel general as emperor, it is probable the Manchus would never have taken China. But, for the second time in its history, China fell to a foreign dynasty. The first, the Mongols, had built Peking. Now the second, the Manchus—and, as it turned out, the last of all the dynasties—set about repairing, enlarging, and rebuilding the sublime fabric left by the Ming.

Despite the fact that the Manchus chose the propitious name Ch'ing, meaning "pure," for their dynasty, they nevertheless got off to a bad start. The first emperor was a psychopathic youth, soon under the spell of the old Ming eunuchs at court. He was succeeded by a child of eight and a regency, a combination notorious as the weakest link in the chain of hereditary succession. "Few could foresee," as Fitzgerald remarks, "that the child who now succeeded was to be the saviour of the dynasty, the great K'ang-hsi." By accident China was about to enter on one of her happier and more settled periods. For a hundred and fifty years under a trio of able emperors, of whom K'ang-hsi was the first, something of the old greatness of China was to reassert itself—before the final decline of the dynastic system.

At the tender age of fifteen, on the death of the regent, K'ang-hsi assumed full control of government in 1669. During the remaining fifty-three years of his reign he pacified all

* Owen Lattimore thinks not. He suggests (*Inner Asian Frontiers of China*, p. 133) that General Wu's allegiance was fundamentally to the Manchus.

FATHER MATTEO RIPA. *It is to such Jesuit priests that we are indebted for many detailed descriptions of the Manchu court. The rather narrow nature evidenced in Father Ripa's writings is amply outweighed by the interesting glimpses he gives of the emperor K'ang-hsi at work and play.*

China, expanded its area, and signed the first Sino-Russian treaty. His forces also succeeded at last in taking back Formosa, where the famed Koxinga, son of a Chinese pirate-adventurer and a Japanese mother and the last of the Ming vassals to hold out against the Manchus, had established the final base for his considerable maritime power in his long years of resistance against the new dynasty. Thus, under K'ang-hsi the empire blossomed surprisingly and Peking recovered its former sparkle.

Jesuit priests living in Peking and favored by K'ang-hsi have left descriptions of the emperor. "His figure was taller than the average and well proportioned, his features well formed and full, his eyes lively and more open than is common among the Chinese [he was, of course, a Manchu, not a Chinese], his forehead large, his nose slightly aquiline, his mouth generous, his manner was mild and gracious, yet so grand and majestic that he might readily be distinguished among his numerous court."* The Chinese chronicles largely agree with this apparently flattering description, but add that his face was pitted with smallpox, emphasize his frugality, and praise him for his piety toward his grandmother. He was, besides, a considerable scholar and patron of the more conservative arts and doctrinaire philosophy.

To this picture of the great man, a little-known Jesuit priest, Father Ripa, adds many intimate details. Attending on the emperor at a country house three miles from Peking, the father remarks: "His Majesty . . . every day sent me a horse to ride; but as it was vicious and untamed, I left it for my attendant so as not to expose my life to danger, and made use of another which I kept at my own expense. In addition to this, I was obliged to find myself in clothing and other necessaries out of the annual allowance of forty pounds which I received. . . ."

Father Ripa quite plainly felt that the emperor was mean with money. But it is obvious that most people stood greatly in awe of K'ang-hsi, whose caustic tongue was perhaps the mildest of his expressions of displeasure. Father Ripa recounts how K'ang-hsi ordered another Jesuit, Don Pedrini, to "come and lodge in the house . . . for the purpose of tuning the cymbals and spinets which his Majesty had in great numbers in all his palaces. When it was stated that Pedrini did not understand the language, he replied that . . . cymbals were tuned with the hands, and not with the tongue. . . ."

* Quoted by René Grousset from Jesuit reports.

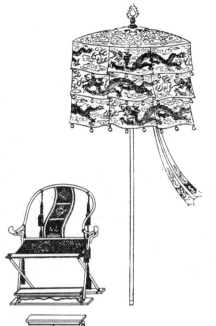

THE TRAPPINGS OF ROYALTY. *As these woodcuts from a Ch'ing-period book indicate, the Manchu court was a continual pageant of sumptuousness down to the last lavish detail. The palanquin below was only for informal use, much smaller than the palanquin of state seen in the fold-out, but it was far from beggarly: "Covered with yellow silk embroidered with gold clouds and dragons. Height, slightly over six feet. Roof ornamented with gilded carving topped by a gold knob encrusted with gems. Fitted with carrying poles for sixteen men. Inside, space for a gold Dragon Throne. Door curtain of silk or muslin according to the season. Side windows covered by glass in winter and blue muslin in summer."*

Parasols were carried in imperial processions more as symbols of majesty than for utilitarian purpose. Made of yellow silk, that shown here (but one of many types) was embroidered with a design of nine imperial dragons.

The intricately carved folding chair was the emperor's portable throne. Little wonder that the baggage train of an imperial procession was so huge when all the articles to be used by an emperor on a trip had to be carried along.

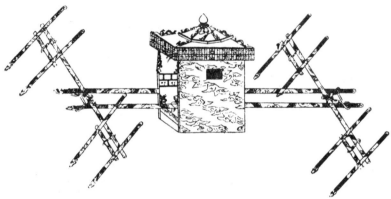

(8)   (9)

An Imperial Procession

The style and manner of imperial processions entering and leaving the Forbidden City and passing through the streets of Peking varied greatly from reign to reign and dynasty to dynasty, depending on the whim of the emperor concerned. On the fold-out we see, in considerable detail, a procession of the great Manchu emperor Ch'ien-lung. (Reproduced from Conquêtes des Chinois, *an undated volume of engravings published at Paris in the 18th century, and based upon a hand-scroll drawing by an 18th-century Chinese court painter.) The background of low* hutung *houses is typical of what may be seen even today in the capital. The days of photography had not yet arrived, but the artists who recorded scenes such as this filled in the colors with detailed descriptions beneath their pictures. The description accompanying this engraving begins as follows:*

"According to custom, it is with the greatest pomp that the emperor of China leaves his palace. Apart from the corps of guards lining the route, every so often along the way stakes are put up on which arms are placed on a sort of rack, and in front of which soldiers—like the rest of the populace—kneel on the road. Not only are the streets cleaned with extraordinary care, but they are decorated here and there with triumphal arches and with booths garnished with rich cloth, with vases of flowers, perfume boxes, and with buffets loaded with fruit. The triumphal arches are speedily constructed of wooden uprights painted and varnished, and carry crown-pieces in the form of canopies of many-colored cloth with fringes, and pennants bearing inscriptions. . . ."

The descriptions of the procession given at the left are based upon this same flowery report.

"The Emperor supposed himself to be an excellent musician and a still better mathematician; but though he had a taste for the sciences and other acquirements in general, he knew nothing of music and scarcely understood the first elements of mathematics. There was a cymbal or a spinet in almost every apartment, but neither he nor his ladies could play upon them: sometimes indeed with one of his fingers he touched a note, which was enough, according to the extravagant flattery practised at the court of China, to throw the bystanders into ecstasies of admiration. . . . I must say that I was not a little surprised to find how K'ang-hsi, who was really a man of enlarged understanding, believed all the exaggerated praises of his courtiers, and was childishly vain."

Father Ripa is obviously torn between admiration for the kingly qualities of the emperor and the odd foibles of so great a man. One more of the Jesuit's stories gives what is probably a unique glimpse behind the almost impenetrable curtain that hid imperial domestic life from public view. At Jehol, one of the country palaces in the mountains northeast of Peking, Dr. Volta, a priest and physician accompanying a Russian embassy to the Chinese court, was commanded to appear before K'ang-hsi. Father Ripa accompanied him. On being asked to take the imperial pulse, Dr. Volta remarked that it was essential to feel it on several occasions before stating his opinion of the emperor's health. And so it came about that, the same evening, the Jesuit and the doctor once more attended in the private apartments of the palace. "I observed on this occasion that his Majesty's bed was wide enough to contain five or six persons, and had no sheets. The upper part of the mattress, as well as the under part of the quilt, was lined with lambs'-skin, and the emperor slept between these, without wearing any night-clothes. As it seldom happens that an emperor is seen in bed by strangers, he said to us, 'You are foreigners, and yet you see me in bed.' We replied that we had that honor because his Majesty treated us as his sons; whereupon he added, 'I consider you as members of my own house and very near relatives.' "

Even in the midst of the heavy luxury and elegance of the Chinese court the Manchu tribal life of the mountains was not far away. The emperor's sleeping in sheepskins, as did his ancestors in their tents in the cold north, recalls the short time it had taken to make imperial stuff out of barbarous chieftains.

Both in Peking and at Jehol K'ang-hsi was surrounded by his women, Chinese and Manchu. Father Ripa was given a cottage in the gardens of the Jehol palace, and through the holes in its paper windows he "saw the emperor employed in reading or writing, while these wretched women remained sitting upon cushions, silent as novices." While fishing on an artificial lake "his Majesty would then sit in a superb little boat with five or six concubines at his feet, some Tartar [Manchu] and others Chinese; all dressed in their national costumes. The boat was always followed by many others, all loaded with ladies. . . . On reaching the spot where . . . he entered the room in which he gave audience, he left the concubines behind, in charge of eunuchs. I saw him several times about the gardens, but never on foot. He was always carried in a sedan chair, surrounded by a crowd of concubines, all walking and smiling. . . . Sometimes he sat upon a high seat . . . and suddenly threw among his ladies . . . artificial snakes, toads, and other loathsome animals, in order to enjoy the pleasure of seeing them scamper away with their crippled feet. . . . He urged on the poor lame creatures with noisy exclamations until some of them fell to the ground, when he indulged in a loud and hearty laugh."

Chinese women, but never Manchu, had for long been forced to have their feet bound, starting in early infancy, to such an extent that a girl whose feet were more than the regulation "three-inch golden lily" in size stood less chance of marriage than others whose feet conformed to this excruciating maximum length. Poetry and prose alike are full of reference to the enhanced sexual attraction of girls whose walk, because of the foot deformity, was likened to the swaying of a willow in a gentle breeze—the same mincing glide which the actor Mei Lan-fang so perfectly imitated on the stage in Chinese opera. To us, as to Father Ripa, bound feet are hard to associate with sexual attraction. But, pondering on the fluctuating size of the female bosom in the West in the last few centuries, when positive deformity at either extreme of size has generally been admired, we may come nearer to understanding the historic attractions of bound feet.*

Like most new dynasties, the Ch'ing under K'ang-hsi swept away the worst of the corruption which had blackened the name of its predecessor. In Peking great changes took place. It was at first intended to reserve the Inner City for Manchus alone, and each of "eight banners"—as the eight tribes of the Manchu nation were called—was apportioned a section of the city in which to live. The remaining officials and brigades of the Manchu army were distributed throughout the provinces of China so that there was, in theory, a Manchu official for every Chinese of rank, the Manchu naturally having the final word in all decisions. In fact there were not enough Manchus to go round, so that Chinese were welcomed in official positions provided they showed their loyalty to the dynasty. This, for the most part, the Chinese found no difficulty in doing. A long history of sudden switches in authority had made them a nation of accepters who knuckled down without much trouble, gradually worming a way into fresh power as the higher echelons of government weakened with the advancing years of a dynasty.

But once more, in the reign of K'ang-hsi, a dynasty sowed the seeds of its own decay. The imperial examinations which had been held for hundreds of years to select candidates

* In the late eighteenth century the Englishman Lord Macartney, sent by George III as ambassador extraordinary to the Chinese court, expressed a similar view in *An Embassy to China:* "I by no means want to apologise for the Chinese custom of squeezing their women's petitoes into the shoes of an infant, which I think an infernal distortion. . . . A reverend apostolic missionary at Peking assured me that in love affairs the glimpse of a little fairy foot was to a Chinese a most powerful provocative. Perhaps we are not quite free from a little folly of the same kind ourselves. . . . It is not a great many years ago that in England thread-paper waists, steel stays, and tight lacing were in high fashion, and the ladies' shapes were so tapered down from the bosom to the hips that there was some danger of breaking off in the middle at any exertion."

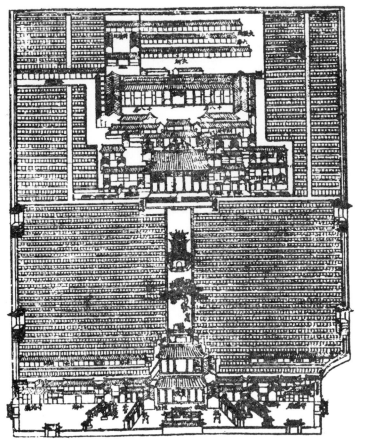

THE IMPERIAL EXAMINATION HALLS. *This walled enclosure was situated near the east wall of the Inner City and contained several hundred tiny cells, in each of which a candidate for office in the Chinese civil service was locked for three days while he completed his answers to the questions set. An elaborate system of watchtowers and patrols insured against communication with the outside. The whole structure was demolished by allied Western armies when they entered Peking in 1860.*

for all official posts were so rearranged that Manchus were almost sure of qualifying, while Chinese were selected in such small numbers, and with such discrimination against southerners, that deep resentment was induced among the literate classes. It is nevertheless worth noting here that even the Manchus never abandoned the examinations, and in fact continued to rely upon them for the selection of lower-echelon Chinese administrators. Thus China's well-known civil-service system, which had played such a formative role in the national life ever since the T'ang dynasty or, in a less developed form, since Han days in the first century B.C., survived into the twentieth century.

The south, the granary and therefore the source of most revenue and food for the north and for Peking in particular, derived little benefit from its labors. The product was spent in Peking. Huge new palaces and temples were built or rebuilt, and the whole Manchu nation, expressly forbidden to engage in trade or profitable work, was fed on the "tribute rice" ferried north to Peking on the Grand Canal. Manchus were also forbidden to intermarry with Chinese. Both the civil and military sectors of the ruling class gradually degenerated, "condemned to drone-like inactivity" as the historian Fitzgerald aptly puts it.

But in the reign of K'ang-hsi and his two successors the steady weakening of the regime was not as yet apparent. The atmosphere of government in K'ang-hsi's reign is summed up by the Jesuit father Gerbillon in describing the emperor at the head of his troops during a campaign in Mongolia: ". . . the perfect order that was maintained, the frugal existence of the sovereign and his entourage, and his solicitude for his troops. . . . The march across a country which had always been poor . . . imposed terrible hardships on the army. The emperor took his share of these, and scornfully rejected the entreaties of the mandarins who besought him to expose himself no longer. His vigorous attitude gave new courage to the troops."* All of which is a very different story from that of cringing late-Ming emperors who did not know and seldom cared what were the conditions of the army or people under their orders. K'ang-hsi seems to have reveled in his forced marches at the head of his armies, for he writes from the far northwest regions to his son: "The hares of the Ordos region have an exquisite flavor; everything here has more savor than the best that Peking can provide."*

After a long reign the emperor died of a chill caught while hunting, leaving the throne to his fourth son, Yung-cheng (reigned 1723–35), a somewhat narrow-minded man who did nothing to undo his father's work, but instigated little himself. While conditions in China were generally improved and the appearance of life in the capital was prosperous, it is not hard to penetrate beneath the gilded surface of events and personalities to the realities of the life of the people. In Peking there never was the division into poor and wealthy sectors of the city which is familiar to us in most Western towns. Great houses, looking, as we saw earlier, very similar to small ones, jostled each other and also the dwellings of the poor, in the same street; gorgeous palanquins borne by a dozen or more sweating coolies labored along streets innocent of paving and thick in dust or mud according to the season. While the route into Peking was literally hung for miles with silks as an emperor returned in state to the Forbidden City the castaway children of the poor rotted in the ditches.

Father Ripa again is an eloquent and straightforward guide to what official histories fail to mention at all: "There is nothing unusual in seeing children thus abandoned; it occurs daily throughout this vast empire. When mothers are poor, and have large families, or observe any . . . indication of an illness likely to become troublesome or expensive, they cast away the little creature without remorse. . . . The poor infants are secretly thrown into a river, or left near the public road, in the hope that some passenger may take pity on them and carry them home. . . . Not far from the walls of Peking I myself saw one infant under the paws of a dog, and another between the teeth of a hog." It is not difficult to surmise from such statements the general condition of the people whose life and labor contributed to the unsurpassed grandeur of great men described by the chronicles and by visiting ambassadors to the magnificent court of China.

Yung-cheng, in turn, was succeeded by his fourth son, a young man of twenty-four, the emperor Ch'ien-lung (reigned 1736–96). From the several hundreds of Chinese emperors—including many greater ones such as Ch'in Shih-huang-ti and Yung-lo—Kublai Khan and Ch'ien-lung are probably the only ones familiar to the average person in the West; the first through the romantic pages of Marco Polo, and the other through the variety of European contacts which were beginning to be made with China in the Ch'ing era. Our ignorance of the real civilization of China remained more or less complete

* Quoted by René Grousset.

CH'IEN-LUNG WRITING IN AUTUM-NAL SCENERY. *The Manchus had been in Peking for not quite a hundred years when Ch'ien-lung came to the throne, but already they were complete Chinese gentlemen. Ch'ien-lung himself, in addition to being a ruler of considerable ability, was also a scholar, poet, painter, calligrapher, and distinguished patron of the arts, in the best Chinese tradition. That he fancied himself in the role is made clear by this contemporary portrait.*

until the latter part of the nineteenth century, and our attempts to understand it did not really begin until well on in the twentieth.

The Chinese, for their part, showed an even more resolute disinclination to recognize the West, and have only within the last twenty years or so attempted any serious understanding of our civilization. There could hardly be a better memorial to this blindness, and at the same a better pointer to the settled pomp and circumstance of the court at Peking at the zenith of the Ch'ing dynasty, than a letter written by the emperor Ch'ien-lung to George III of England. This long, haughty, condescending epistle reveals the extravagant comedy of an attitude brought about by centuries of isolationist thought in China. But in reading it one ought to bear in mind that there exist letters sent to Ch'ien-lung by envoys from England which exhibit an exactly similar lack of understanding stemming from an exactly similar isolationism vis-à-vis China:*

"You, O King, who live beyond the many seas, urged on by your humble desire to partake in the benefits of our civilization, have sent a mission respectfully bringing your memorial. Your envoy has traversed the seas and paid his respects at my Court on my birthday anniversary. To show your devotion, you have also sent offerings of your country's products.

"I have perused your memorial. The earnest terms in which it is couched point to a respectful humility on your part, which is most praiseworthy. . . .

"As to your entreaty to send one of your nationals to be accredited to my Celestial Court . . . this request is contrary to all usage of my dynasty and cannot possibly be entertained."

The emperor proceeds to tell why permanent envoys, and trade with China on a more general scale, cannot be considered. "If," he continues, "you should protest that our Celestial dynasty fills you with the desire to acquire our civilization, I must tell you

* The translation is adapted from Backhouse and Bland.

CH'IEN-LUNG'S EMPRESS. *The consort of the great Ch'ing emperor was no exception to the rule that, with notable exceptions, Chinese empresses remained very much in the background. In this formal court portrait she is shown wearing robes as sumptuous as those the emperor himself donned when he was not playing the artist. (See p. 186 for a description of another empress's adornments.)*

that our ceremonies and code of laws differ so utterly from your own that . . . you could not possibly transplant our manners and customs to your alien soil. . . .

"Swaying the wide world, I have one single aim: to maintain a perfect governance. . . . I set no value on strange or ingenious objects and have no use for your country's manufactures. . . . . It behoves you, O King, to respect my wishes and to show even greater devotion and loyalty in future, so that by perpetual submission to our Throne you may secure peace and prosperity for your country hereafter. . . . I confer upon you valuable presents in excess of the number usually bestowed on such occasions, including silks and curios, a list of which is enclosed. Reverently receive them and take note of my tender goodwill toward you!"

The reactions of George III of England, if he ever read the letter, are unfortunately not recorded. He could hardly have been mollified by sentences in a further letter from the same source which states that Ch'ien-lung does not forget "the lonely remoteness of your island, cut off from the world by intervening wastes of sea." Addressed to the king of the world's greatest seafaring power, this is both funny and tragic.

Despite the general peace in China during the reign of Ch'ien-lung, and despite his reasonably strong government of the country, under which the population rapidly expanded, the emperor was himself the dupe of high Peking officials in his later years. History in China repeats itself with much greater precision than elsewhere in the world and to find an exact parallel we need look no further back than the previous dynasty when the eunuch Liu Chin (page 104) made a Ming emperor his dupe. Ch'ien-lung's prime minister, a man called Ho-shen, wielded power almost as great as that of the emperor himself. Once a guard at the palace gate, his evil influence in state affairs ran deep and was apparently unknown to the emperor. Of Ho-shen the British envoy Lord Macartney remarks: "I could not help admiring the address with which the Minister parried all my attempts to speak to him on the business of the day, and how artfully he evaded every opportunity that offered for any particular conversation with me. . . ."

But the ambassador did not suspect that it was to a large extent Ho-shen's reports on the British mission which influenced the emperor to send them home with nothing more substantial than those haughty letters already quoted. On the death of his master, Ho-shen was arrested and committed suicide. His treasure, filched from many sources, was valued at a staggering sum equivalent to more than two hundred million U.S. dollars.

But such was the internal strength of the massive Chinese empire that it continued to bulldoze its way into the nineteenth century with arrogant disregard for the wishes and attainments of the rest of the world. Peking, indeed all of China except a few enlightened Chinese, remained totally ignorant of the fact that it was now Western and not Chinese civilization which was the dominant force in the world at large, and that the long supremacy of China in Asia was now a myth, very soon to be discredited.

The surplus energies of the emperors K'ang-hsi and Ch'ien-lung found an outlet, among many other pleasure pursuits, in rebuilding the palaces and constructing temples in and about Peking. In the suburbs to the northwest of Peking they built what has been called a "sort of Chinese Versailles" known as the Summer Palace. With its dozens of pavilions and temples, its artificial hillocks and lakes, its contrived rustic scenery so dear to the Chinese heart, it must have been a delightful retreat. Nothing now remains of this pleasure garden of the imperial fancy, built at such colossal expense and with such ingenuity, except the broken walls and mounds of brick left by Western armies when, on the orders of a British envoy, Lord Elgin, they destroyed the place in 1860. This act of vandalism, unjustifiable in any way, occurred as a reprisal for loss of British lives just forty years after Lord Elgin's father had rescued for posterity the incomparable marbles of the Parthenon in Athens and transported them to safety in London, where they still remain. And only sixty years or so had elapsed since the great Ch'ien-lung had addressed his proud missives to a British king who he thought was a petty vassal on some unimportant island. The Chinese still closed their eyes to the outside world, pretending it did not exist.

Yet history was approaching the point when that turbulent but continuous civilization which had endured and flourished in China for a couple of millennia, and in Peking for almost exactly six centuries, began to have doubts about its own omnipotence. The intervention of allied armies of the Western powers in 1840 to force the Chinese to accept the opium trade, from which grand profits were made, and the second intervention in 1860 to enforce ratification of the Treaty of Tientsin and later to quell the T'ai-p'ing Rebellion within China, have no reasonable excuse in terms of modern thought. But the arrogance of nineteenth-century Western statesmen—comparable only to the arrogance of dynastic Chinese—lent a crusading spirit to the wars against China, a country which at that time the West considered as a mere backward territory in need of Occidental civilization and manufactured goods. The object of these wars was, quite starkly, the expansion of Western trading facilities, although at the time the "honor" of Britain, France, or the United States was frequently put forward as the reason. The Manchu dynasty tottered, alternately forced into submission and the granting of facilities which impoverished China, and then bolstered up by Western force against the rebellions of its own subjects. After the destruction of the Summer Palace in 1860, imperial power became a mere fiction. Peking, to the complete surprise of the Chinese, fell easily to a smallish force of Western soldiers. The emperor fled from the back door of the Summer Palace as the armies entered to loot and burn at the front.

With Peking in British and French hands, the Chinese were in no position to do anything but accept the terms dictated by the powers in the Treaty of Tientsin, ratified in 1860. Among these was the establishment of what Ch'ien-lung had refused Lord Macartney eighty years previously—a permanent British embassy in Peking. A legation quarter, just over the road from the front gate of the imperial palaces, was reserved for British and other embassies. Another apparently trivial sign of Manchu capitulation to the Western powers was the permission granted—for the first time to any civilian whatsoever in the history of Peking—for diplomats and their wives to promenade on the wall of the Inner City which adjoined the Legation Quarter. For the Chinese this was a profound break with tradition.

The Manchu emperor in those fateful days of 1860 was Hsien-feng, a dissolute man of thirty whose scandalous partiality was for an entourage of Chinese concubines, willing, so it was said, to comply with his more surprising sexual fancies. Scandalous was a word applied to his debauches, not on account of their character, however, but because the ladies were Chinese—by law forbidden to all Manchus. Since this law was often flouted with impunity by emperors, and lesser personages as well, doubtless it was Hsien-feng's obvious *preference* for Chinese girls that actually outraged opinion. He also had two consorts. One of these, a luscious young Manchu beauty called Yehonala, was later to rule China until the end of the dynasty and the coming of the Republic as the terrible Empress Dowager. When the emperor fled from Peking to Jehol so precipitately in 1860, Yehonala accompanied him. The annals of the dynasty record with their usual decorum simply that the emperor departed on an "autumn tour of inspection." But when the army reached his private quarters in the Summer Palace they found his belongings strewn about the rooms just as he had left them in his hasty retreat. For Yehonala it was her first flight from the capital, but not her last.

With the death of the emperor in 1861, his consort Yehonala, known to history as the Empress Dowager—or sometimes more familiarly as Old Buddha—assumed control of state affairs. Before the T'ai-p'ing Rebellion, Yehonala had risen from concubine to become Hsien-feng's favorite and, after the death of the old dowager empress, was made Empress of the Western Palace, sharing honors with his other consort, the Empress of the Eastern Palace. From that time forward she had access to all state documents seen by the emperor, and in due course it became almost obligatory to consult her before decisions were reached. It was she who, while the emperor was dying at Jehol, prevented

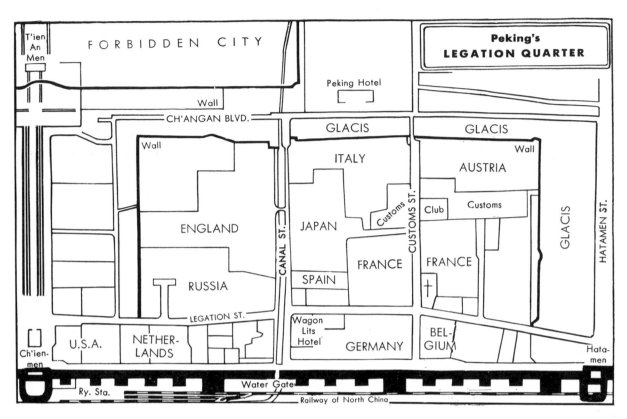

THE LEGATION QUARTER. *Established at gun point in 1860, within a few decades Peking's diplomatic enclave, the Legation Quarter, was to rival the Forbidden City as the focal point of power in the Chinese state. This map, from a Thomas Cook's guide of the early 1900's, shows the national divisions of the quarter at its heyday.*

the imperial seals from being affixed to a decree appointing regents whom she did not wish to see in office after the emperor's death; and it was she who instead trumped up the document proclaiming herself and the Empress of the Eastern Palace regents during the minority of her son T'ung-chih. Although she was only a coregent, hers was the dominating voice at court, and after her son's death in 1875 she was able to maintain her dominance by installing a nephew of her late husband's on the throne. This was the child Kuang-hsu, who was the ninth and last ruling emperor of the Ch'ing dynasty. But even when he came of age, it was the Empress Dowager who, sometimes by guile and once even by imprisoning the emperor in a portion of the palace, continued ruling China, using the young emperor as a simple mouthpiece for her wishes. Perhaps, to be quite fair to Yehonala, the retention of the reins of power was necessary to her, since there were certainly several factions at court only too anxious to relegate her to obscurity, if not actually to assassinate her, to gain that power for themselves.

Until her death and the end of the dynastic system there is no other name worth mentioning in the same bracket as hers. The career of this execrable woman is a succession of intrigues, murders, and follies hardly equaled even in the tortured history of imperial courts at Peking. Her character is a mixture of ruthless strength, inflexible and cunning will, and a complete lack of understanding of the state of her realm and what might have been done to save the last remnants of the dynastic system she wished to perpetuate.

In the midst of the most obvious decay and bankruptcy afflicting the whole of China she stomped on her way in an illusion of absolute power, torturing, murdering, intriguing

-—dominating a trembling court by force of sheer terror. Having once been driven out of the old Summer Palace, she built another nearby, at colossal expense. With a popular revolt on her hands (the so-called Boxer Rebellion) she at first attempted to quell it, then joined forces with it in an attempt to drive the foreigners from China. While this was in itself an admirable idea, it was one impossible to achieve since the Chinese armies were not only unpaid, and therefore rebellious, but unequipped to meet the force which the Western powers eventually sent in 1900 to relieve the siege of the Legation Quarter. Such was her illusion of power that even during this siege she is said to have commanded a temporary cease-fire because the noise of the artillery disturbed an outing she was taking on the lakes in the Imperial City.

The Legation Quarter was relieved by allied armies after a siege of fifty-five days, and Yehonala took flight for a second time. With her at dawn on August 15, 1900, went the puppet of an emperor and many of the members of the court, but not before Yehonala had ordered the murder of the emperor's Pearl Concubine, whom she disliked, by throwing her down a well in the palace grounds.

The flight of the empress, as retailed with more verve than accuracy in a book written some years later by Wu Yung, the district magistrate of a small town seventy miles north of Peking, has a ludicrous quality about it. Neither she nor the ladies of the court seem to have realized that traveling clothes were necessary, and they fled in Peking carts clad in filmy garments of great luxury. Somewhere along the way sedan chairs were found for the empress and her virtual prisoner the emperor, and the sorry cortege straggled into the magistrate's little town, hungry and in desperate straits. It was pouring rain as the magistrate received them in his official robes at the wayside. When he saw the conveyances of the "Two Palaces," as he calls the empress and emperor, approaching, he removed his overcoat and the oilcloth with which he had covered his tasseled hat and knelt in the mud, calling out his name and rank. When the Two Palaces were installed in the exceedingly humble accommodation he had prepared for them, he was conducted to the presence and found Yehonala dressed in a countrywoman's cotton clothes with her hair done in a knot. She informed him they had traveled many hundreds of miles (quite untrue) with nothing to eat or drink (which was nearly true since the inhabitants of the villages en route had fled). The good magistrate hastened to send her the porridge he had had prepared. It was all there was available. Trembling at having offered such poor fare to the Two Palaces, he stood outside the door of their room. With tremendous relief he records that he "heard the sound of swift eating, and of porridge being drunk with inhaling of breaths, as if the food were good." Soon the ravenous Empress Dowager asked for eggs. He found some, cooking them himself and handing them in through the curtain of the apartment. Shortly a eunuch emerged. "The Old Buddha enjoyed the eggs very much. Of the five you sent she ate three, the remaining two she gave to the Lord of Ten Thousand Years [the emperor]. The light was shed on no-one else." The eunuch, incidentally, was one of the great gourmets of Peking and probably said this with considerable feeling.

The magistrate now felt more secure. A little later his spirits rose even further as the empress begged for some clothes to wear. Recalling that Yehonala was reputed never to wear the same robe twice, and greatly moved by her plight, he found an old coat that had belonged to his mother, and some of his own clothes for the emperor. Later, he says, they "were both wearing the clothes I had sent, and I saw that dignity had returned in some degree to their appearance. . . . They no longer looked like dejected jackals."

Far from wishing permanently to alienate the ruler of China and thereby cause the collapse of the dynastic system, the Western powers now used their energies to bolster it up. This was to their advantage in gaining further trade and diplomatic concessions. Peking itself, in the months of anarchy which followed the allied army's occupation, was looted and defaced—not only by officers and soldiers from the West, but by Chinese who remained in the city for this purpose. Most of the population had fled, the streets were strewn with corpses of people murdered in an orgy of paying off old scores. With traditional common sense many Chinese now made little flags, replicas of the national flags of the conquering troops, and wore them on their clothes in the effort to escape trouble. In Chinese thought there is nothing despicable about such an action, for, with a long history of unpredictable incursions and contending factions liable to descend on them at any time, Chinese had evolved the philosophy that to accept outwardly was the wisest move.

Proposals put forward at a meeting of the allies to raze the imperial palace to the ground were rejected. A victory parade was arranged instead and traversed the streets of Peking to the considerable amusement of the Chinese.* The British minister, a gaunt figure with handle-bar mustaches, wore a "grey suit of tennis clothes and a rakish panama slouch hat." The representative of France was attired "in a garb which combined the requirements of the Bois de Boulogne on a Sunday with the conveniences of tropical attire." The American minister chose "white cottons and military gaiters." The Russian band at the saluting base made a dreadful mess of the Japanese anthem and was still wading through the "Marseillaise" as the Italian contingent marched by. When this comic-opera spectacle was over, the diplomats were escorted round the imperial palaces by eunuchs and openly stuffed their pockets with its more portable treasures as they passed through.

The panic-stricken flight of the court from Peking in 1900 ended a year later, after a peace treaty had been signed, with the near-triumphal return of the Empress Dowager to the capital. From Sian near the Yellow River, where she had passed most of her exile in increasing state, her entourage of thousands eventually embarked on a British railway

* One of the few journalists to witness this procession was the Englishman Henry Savage Landor, from whose book the following quotations come.

138 THE SECOND PEKING

train for the last lap of the journey to Peking. Four more freight trains were filled with baggage, treasure, and archives. It was the first journey of a Chinese sovereign in a train. Everyone, princes of the blood, courtiers, servants, mules, and cooks boarded this train to Peking. The imperial compartments were furnished in yellow silk and replete with thrones, curios, opium pipes, and other items for the comfort and prestige of Yehonala and her puppet emperor. The train reached Peking at the terminal which had just been built within the walls, separated from the Forbidden City itself only by the width of the Legation Quarter, and the imperial procession moved north along the broad street to Ch'ienmen, the south gate of Peking, where the empress and party got down to sacrifice at the small shrine always used for this purpose on homecoming.

On top of the high city wall facing her, under the remnants of the gate tower which had accidentally been burned in the siege of the legations, stood all the foreigners in Peking, eager to see the return of the astonishing old woman who had caused all the trouble. As she alighted from her palanquin the Empress Dowager looked up at the fire-blackened wall and saw the rows of foreigners standing on top. She refused to move for several minutes, surveying them with obvious interest. Then she walked toward the shrine. But before entering she stopped again and, in one of the very few instances of graciousness ever recorded of her life, she made several little bows to the foreign community.

So Peking once more took up a semblance of its old life. The tower of Ch'ienmen was rebuilt, the first installments of crippling reparations to the Western powers were paid by the Chinese. The empress spent most of her time at the Summer Palace, where she sailed in great state on the lake and appears to have hugely enjoyed at least part of her last years in this multimillion-dollar paradise which she had built to suit her whims.

But the end was not far off. China, however many decrees Yehonala might put forth in the name of the emperor, was in the hands of the diplomats of the Legation Quarter, in all but name. In 1908 the Empress Dowager died and the final unedifying century of the Ch'ing dynasty's rule guttered out with her last breaths. Vicious and pitiless to the end, Yehonala had the emperor murdered on the day before her death. He was succeeded, under a regency, by his nephew P'u Yi, then a child of not quite three, whose nominal reign ended in 1912 with the proclamation of the Republic. An old man with a checkered history, P'u Yi is still alive today.

The last imperial drama was now ended. The last simulacrum of former ages of greatness was dissolved in a brief speech by Dr. Sun Yat-sen, a man who, for the first time in Chinese history, did not on coming to power wish to found a new imperial line. It might be thought that at this point China would have managed to tear herself away from the middle ages and set a firm foot in the twentieth century. But, unfortunately, the forces of tradition were too strong. The time was not yet ripe.

The Dynastic Setting ▶

Over this carved marble slope leading up to the doors of the Hall of Supreme Harmony in the Forbidden City the emperor was carried in his palanquin on state occasions. The bearers ascended by steps at either side. Two dragons of the five-clawed variety reserved as imperial appurtenances seem hypnotized by the "night-shining pearl" between them. The pearl formed part of all imperial coats of arms from the Han dynasty on, and according to one story, was the reward given to an emperor by a snake whose life he had saved. The stylized clouds indicate the heavenly nature of the dragons.

Thanks to long-established conventions in make-up, the Peking opera audience knows exactly what sort of person is represented by each actor. The character in the full-page photo is known at a glance for a villain. The small photos show the leading character in one of the most popular Peking operas, Pilgrimage to the West, *the story of the heavenly Monkey King who, in a fit of pique, steals the sacred peaches reserved for the Heavenly Queen's birthday. He is assailed by the armies of the Dragon King and the gods of Thunder and Lightning, but his magic wand defeats them all in a long, boisterous, and often comic performance. Here, the actor who is to play the Monkey King applies his make-up with Chinese writing brush and liquid color, tracing the "night-shining pearl" on his forehead. On stage, the Monkey King appears, wand in hand, wearing a combination of regal and monkey costume.*

63 ▲

64 ▼

65 ▲

T'ien-ning Pagoda (63), built in Liao times on the site of an even older monastery, is one of the few surviving landmarks from pre-Mongol Peking. From the earliest days of the city, camel trains were a familiar sight as they entered the city with food and coal and other merchandise from far and near. Only in the last ten years have they given way to motorized transport. Here they are rounding a corner of Peking's outer wall. In an aerial photo taken in 1945, the straight south-north axis of Peking lies revealed like the spine of a huge fish. At the branching of the street in the foreground is the guardhouse of a now-vanished semicircular wall which protected Ch'ienmen, the front gate of Peking, beyond. Ch'ienmen, with its pavilion on top of the south wall of the Inner City, is now flanked by two streets passing into the city through arches cut in the wall. Running due north, these streets lead toward the Gate of Heavenly Peace guarding the Imperial City, top center. The long open space bordered by low buildings has now been immensely enlarged and the Great Hall and the Museum (Photos 111 and 121) placed at either side. Beyond the Gate of Heavenly Peace, the roofs of the Forbidden City continue northward, with Coal Hill beyond them and the White Dagoba a light spot to the left.

Photo 64 by Hedda Morrison, 65 by Dmitri Kessel

66 ▲ *From the parapet of Wumen, gateway to the Forbidden City, the Golden Stream in its marble trough runs across the courtyard in the shape of a giant bow, crossed by the five arrows of its bridges. Cobbled acres of courtyard lead to the*

gate-pavilion called Taihomen—the final architectural event in the stately procession of masses and spaces culminating
in the Hall of Supreme Harmony, center of the Chinese world, which lies beyond.

◄ 67

The Peking rhyme about the bow-shaped Golden Stream (see p. 114) refers to the view from the south of the previous photo, where the water is concealed deep in its trough. Here, in a side view, the languid stream appears, at the end of its journey from the Jade Spring in the Western Hills—the source of all the water in the city's moats.

Visitors to the Temple of Heaven in the Outer City descend the stairs on either side of the imperial ramp over which some of their ancestors may well have carried emperors in their palanquins on their way to commune with Heaven, the final arbiter and ultimate source of all power. Regal dragons, here as in the Forbidden City, writhe among clouds with a kind of majestic abandon—one more evidence of the richness of Ming sculpture.

An imposing bronze tortoise stands in the Imperial Palace precincts outside the pavilion in which the emperor used to confer degrees on successful candidates in the imperial examinations. Elated by achievement, and perhaps also relieved on quitting the awesome presence of the Emperor of All Under Heaven, the young men took turns at standing on their heads on the creature's back.

71 ▶

The Hall of Prayer for Harvests, northern part of the Templ of Heaven in the Outer City, stands with immense Chines dignity on three concentric stone circles fringed with th granular and sparkling white marble used so liberally in th imperial palaces. The interior consists of a single circula hall about fifty feet high, coffered and gilded. Its three roof are of Prussian-blue tile. The wide disc of the upper platform (70), from which its lacquered walls rise, is empty except fo a few urns of monumental proportions disposed around th rim. The Ming mastery of mass and space is nowhere mor striking than in the layout of this superb structure.

69 ▲

70 ▲

72 ▲

The layout of the Temple of Heaven symbolizes in architectural form the central Chinese concept of man and the universe. Set down like a mathematical theorem in its enclosure of park, the whole complex is aligned north-south. The Hall of Prayer for Harvests (73), a circle within a square, lies to the north and is joined to the smaller Temple of the Ruler of the Universe, also round but, significantly, lacking the square enclosure which signifies the world. This leads directly to the southern component, the Altar of Heaven (74). The concentric circles of this marble altar rise with fine precision in the middle of a huge walled square. The circles are the heavens, the square the world and China, which the Chinese deeply felt to be the "Central Country" of that world. To this geometric emptiness the emperor came each year to sacrifice to heaven. At the furnace just within the south wall (right foreground, 72) a bull calf was burned, while bolts of silk were put to the flames in the urns running diagonally right.   Photos 72–73 by Dmitri Kessel

73 ▲

74 ▼

Over the cold mountains north of the Great Wall came almost every important threat to Peking. And from this harsh terrain, dusted with snow even in late spring, come the bleak Asian winds that give Peking its continental climate. Heartless as that icy wind, the armies of Genghis Khan swept down from the

same direction on the capital. The building and frequent rebuilding of the Great Wall, together with its defense and maintenance during more than two thousand years, consumed millions of Chinese lives, gave birth to a whole segment of folklore, and more than once determined the course of Oriental history.

A closer look at the Great Wall, its eastern arm descending to the old Chuyungkuan fort (center) at the highest point of the Nan-k'ou Pass. The nearer slopes are stippled with small holes where saplings have just been planted.

The Valley of Thirteen Tombs (78), where the Ming emperors were buried. A pavilion housing a dedicatory stele, visible in the archway, marks the beginning of the ceremonial way leading beyond, past pairs of animal and human figures, to the tomb of Yung-lo, whose roof is in the distance. One of these marble figures (77) is a military official who formed, with other over-life-size sculpture, a guard of honor for dead emperors as they were borne past.

Photo 78 by Hedda Morrison

77 ▲

On the dreaming slopes of the foothills outside Peking, the tombs of the imperial Ming still stand. The yellow earth, the blue-dark hills surround their roofs of muted gold. Autumn complements the passionate red of their walls, and spring lays its foam of blossom at their feet. Below, the main hall of Emperor Yung-lo's tomb appears among trees in the distance. Right, one of the smaller tombs, built in the declining years of the Ming, has not yet been repaired and, in sad disarray, sheds the remainder of its dragon-embossed tiles on the tangled ground.

81

82 ▲

The Ming genius in building is often matched by skill in decoration. The flamboyance of the Nine Dragon Screen's ceramic bas-relief in Peihei Park (81) could have been vulgar, but is saved by its over-all rhythm and assurance. In the same way the rows of curiously shaped figurines which appear on the corners of almost all Ming and Ch'ing eaves add balance above the tiles to the riot of painted bracketing below. Ch'ing taste, though sometimes extravagant in later days, was at its best delicate and evocative. The line of galloping horses under stylized lotus buds on a stele erected by the emperor Ch'ien-lung in a temple in the Western Hills is little more than a foot long in the original.

83 ▲

84 ▲

In the Hall of Supreme Harmony the imperial throne stands hemmed in by the riches of Chinese art and craftsmanship. The hall is 200 feet long, a hundred broad, its roof rising 110 feet above the ground. The completely lacquered interior is in dark hues, enriched by the light gilding of huge carved pillars and enlivened by the crimson shafts of others. Elegant cranes, symbols of longevity, at either side of the throne make a sudden cool foil to the gold and cloisonné of pillars, urns, and screen. The cavernous surrounding dark of space is faintly colored, and must have brought into focus the magnificence of the emperor seated on the Dragon Throne.

85 ▼

86 ▲

87 ▲

88 ▲

89 ▲

would come each morning to fetch singing birds from homes and take them out in the early sun. The beggar-woman's paper with a few coins tossed on it says: "I kowtow to you for alms. Gentlemen of all conditions, show pity. For here is the poor woman Wong, invalid and destitute. Her husband has been missing for years ... and she has nothing left to pawn.... I humbly kowtow, asking your extraordinary favors...." In wedding and funeral processions the bearer of coffins, bridal sedans (89) and palanquins, of parasols and ceremonial fans, the scatterers of lucky money and beaters of gongs were professionals. Their reputation was as tawdry as the sham finery they wore.

Photos 87–89 by Hedda Morrison

90 ▶

After winter frost and snow, the sudden Peking spring thaws out roofs, and repairs
have to be complete before the equally sudden summer downpours. The small-bowled
brass pipe and the thick-soled canvas shoes are still to be seen in Peking.

The Lama Temple in the northeast corner of the Inner City has benefited from half 91
a million dollars' worth of repairs in the last decade and is now as good as new.
About a hundred monks, some old and doddering, chant Tibetan-style prayers each
day, and when the wind blows, small bells at the eaves send out a tinkling sound
along the passages and courtyards.

The Enduring Past

One of the more controversial follies of the Empress Dowager in the late nineteenth century was the building of this stone boat with its bow pointing into the lake of her Summer Palace. Its resemblance to Mississippi river boats is coincidental but underlines the essential vulgarity of her taste. The Summer Palace itself, stuffed with the last mockery of Chinese art, is superficially charming, largely because of its setting.

9. The Great Wall

He expressed particular enthusiasm with respect to visiting the wall of China. I catched it for the moment, and said I really believed I should go and see the wall of China had I not children. . . . "Sir," (said he) "by doing so, you would do what would be of importance in raising your children to eminence. There would be a lustre reflected upon them from your spirit and curiosity. They would be at all times regarded as the children of a man who had gone to view the wall of China. I am serious, Sir."
—Boswell's *Life of Samuel Johnson*

Within the walls of Peking, as we have already remarked, the imperial past, embodying aspects of a still wider Chinese past, is still to be found. Much as in Venice, whose walls are water instead of brick, the grandeur, the intimate details of Peking and Chinese society are perpetuated in the capital in architectural form —sometimes appealingly, sometimes with a kind of aristocratic curl of the historical lip.

But here the analogy falters. For the aqueous bastions of Venice sever that city more precisely from its neighboring countryside than ever did, or do now, the sturdy walls of Peking. To this latter city, as much as to the wider country of China, belongs the celebrated frontier marked by the Great Wall. And to Peking, more especially than to wider China, belong also the sequestered slopes and pine-clad valleys of the Thirteen Tombs, where all but one of the Ming emperors were buried. To the contemporary citizen of Peking, to his Ming counterpart or even further back in history, the Great Wall is part of his natural context—like the wall of a great estate. In the Western Hills, for centuries the delight of Peking people, the wealthy had their country houses set in surroundings of peculiarly Chinese beauty, amid trees and temples with softly ringing bells and the sound of water and birdsong. We have seen how the Empress Dowager rebuilt an earlier palace here. However decadent the structure may be in detail, it conformed in its placing with the historical canons of rustic retreats, where fancy takes architectural form amid the wildnerness of nature which the Chinese landscapist has first tamed and then allowed to run slightly wild.

And not far away from this Summer Palace, in the foothills lie the Ming Tombs, whose architecture far surpasses that expensive whimsy which so delighted the Empress Dowager. The tombs too are inseparably a part of Peking.

Side by side with these great architectural monuments in the environs of the city it may be interesting to place some reference to Peking opera. For the opera is the greatest single contribution of Peking to the art of China, and the only art form (apart from palace architecture) which attained its maturity in the capital. It is, moreover, one which is, even today, quite as much the context of Peking life as are the city's geograph-

MING AND CH'ING CHINA AND THE GREAT WALL. *The western limits of the Ming empire* (heavy line of dots and dashes, center) *roughly coincided with the border of the Tibetan plateau and the fringes of the western deserts, the Ming being more successful in maritime than in land campaigns. The Ch'ing empire, however, at its greatest extent embraced a much larger area* (light line of dashes) ; *the Tibetan region was finally more or less effectively incorporated into the Chinese realm, and the desert peoples were brought to heel as tributaries. Today's China has boundaries* (heavy continuous line) *which are almost exactly those of the Ch'ing, with the exception of Outer Mongolia, now a separate state called the Mongolian People's Republic. Some idea may be had from this map of how poorly located Peking was as a capital in former times when transport and communication were none too speedy: while at the same time it is obvious that it was in the ideal place to repel threats from the barbarous northern regions. The strategic genius which placed the Great Wall* (crenalated lines) *where it is—some two thousand years ago—is also evident.*

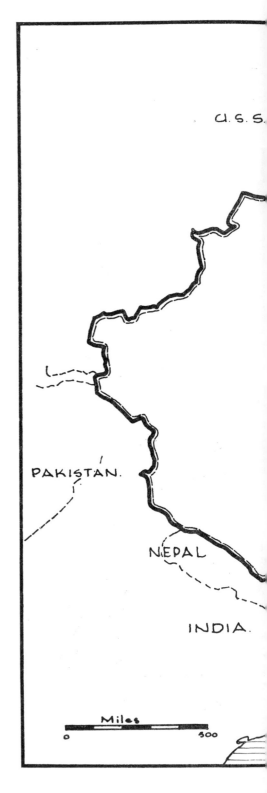

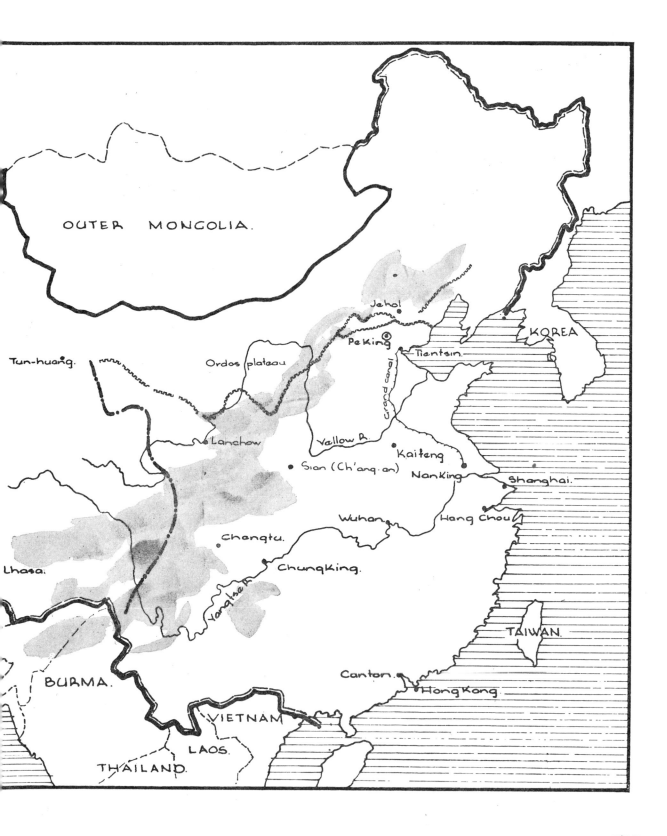

OUTER MONGOLIA.

Tun-huang.

Ordos plateau

Jehol

Peking

Tientsin.

KOREA

Grand canal

Lanchow

Yellow R.

Kaifeng

Sian (Ch'ang-an)

Nanking

Shanghai.

Wuhan.

Hang Chou

Chengtu.

Lhasa.

Chungking.

Yangtse R.

TAIWAN.

BURMA.

Canton.

Hong Kong

VIETNAM

LAOS.

THAILAND.

ical and monumental surroundings. If one were required to convey quickly to some stranger an authentic flavor, a warm breath of Peking and its particular sophistication, a visit to Peking opera might prove the most effective way to do it.

Among Peking's manifold achievements, among its treasures past and present, we may perhaps allow these three—the Great Wall, the Ming Tombs, and Peking opera—to stand as symbols of the others. The past in Peking is even more expressly part of daily life than in most old capital cities: and before we reach the point at which, early in our century, the first clear break with that past occurs, we may perhaps dally a little with these three aspects that belong both to the past and to the present.

To arrive within sight of the Great Wall up the winding, dust-choked road from Peking via Nan-k'ou in the foothills has been a breath-taking experience ever since the Ming dynasty. The solid grey ridge of the wall has a snakelike power as it runs effortlessly up the flanks of the mountains on either side of the pass and curls over the tops against the sky. Climbing slopes of forty-five degrees and more, it surmounts all obstacles, sprouting now a guard house, now a watchtower, with casual ease.

The Ten-Thousand-Li-Long Wall, as the Chinese call it, was begun in short lengths in Chou times, and joined up in the Ch'in dynasty more than two thousand years ago. From end to end it stretches the incredible distance of 1,684 miles. Counting the loops and offshoots here and there, its total length is almost a thousand miles longer. Until the Ming dynasty most of it was tamped earth and mud brick, but during that era it was rebuilt, encased in baked brick and stone.

(As it stands, visible by astronauts in orbit, it is probably the biggest monument to forced labor in the whole world. Twenty to forty feet high in various places, its base is over thirty feet wide and the paved road on its upper surface would take two cars abreast with ease. The modern Chinese passion for statistics calculates its volume at 150 million cubic meters of earth, and the volume of the stone and brick facings amounts to another 50 million cubic meters. With watchtowers projecting on the north, or "barbarian," side every 120 feet, occasional fortresses, and a beacon tower every twenty miles, it was a conspicuous success as a defensive barrier. Only large armies could hope to storm its few gates, and by the time danger was acute the garrison could summon reinforcements to its aid.)

(The wall had another, less obvious use, perhaps partly understood by the original builders. It prevented to a large extent the mingling of the "barbarian" tribes outside with the entity of Chinese culture within its confines. It "divided the steppe from the sown" as Joseph Needham puts the case. And the flowering of the remarkable culture of Peking—so dangerously close to those barbaric northern tribes—would probably have been impossible without the cultural barrier of the Great Wall.

Sitting in the sun at the base of the wall on a day in early summer, sheltered from the penetrating chill of the wind from an Asia still cold from its continental winter, you find the stones pleasantly warm at your back. A prospect of that historic plain on which Peking stands stretches southward under the hazy skies. The sun strikes hot on the cheeks, and you take off the padded jacket with its fur collar, the round hat with the fur ear-flaps past which the sharp wind shrieked as you stood a few minutes ago on top of the wall. The grass is coarse and already drying; soon it will be uniformly brown, desiccated by sun and wind. Recently, hosts of saplings have been planted all about on the dragon-backs of the hills, each little tree in its shallow basin of earth designed to catch whatever rain may fall. From the crest of the ridge up there you noticed them first, the surface of the ground pockmarked in regular patterns like the skin of a golf ball.

In the V-shaped pass, at the gate of the wall—the gate through which have poured such multitudes of camels and men, such stirring hosts of armed legions, of ferocious generals, of captive slaves from conquered barbarian tribes—there still comes and goes a brisk traffic. But now it is composed of trucks, of buses sparkling in the clear, sharp air. The camels, the aggressive armies of old, have vanished. True, there are still trains of donkeys and mules, loaded with firewood gathered by the local people from the meager land around; there are still handcarts, each pulled by several dust-drenched peasants in their faded-blue padded clothes. These are timeless sights: the peasants' clothes, you will certainly recall, are similar in almost every detail to those in paintings and drawings and bas-reliefs reaching back over two thousand years and more of Chinese art. The wall through whose gate they come is familiar too—little different from the representations of it in Ming times, still topped with crenelations of the bluish brick described accurately by Lord Macartney in the eighteenth century.

From here spreads out one of the Eight Great Views of Peking, described in Ming days and referred to in poetry and prose ever afterward by enthusiastic partisans of this great capital and garrison town. Even in this early summer season, this is surely the coldest view of the eight, the snow still forming thin straggling stars, capping the hills and fingering down the ravines. But of those Eight Great Views (the others are all nearer, or actually within, Peking) this is undoubtedly the most instinct with Chinese labor, and with Chinese breadth of vision. The wall is not so much beautiful as startling. Relaxing against its flank, you are the merest dot on a strong line of stone running from the sea in the east, far into the deserts and mountains of the outpost west, where, at the place named the Jade Gate, the confines of China proper traditionally ended and the traveler passed timorously out into the inchoate wastes of Central Asia, a land not wholly subject to, nor ordered by, the Chinese system.

In contrast to the Chinese traveler's fears at passing beyond the protective Chinese embrace of the Great Wall is his dauntless certainty in the overwhelming importance of his own civilization, the ancient temerity of a people who basically constructed the wall over two thousand years ago. For here is no spendthrift monument to the vanity of dead

"September, 2, 1793. . . . At 2 a.m. the heart-stirring drum and ear-piercing fife roused all from their beds to prepare for the journey to Tartary. It was determined that Mr. Hickey, artist . . . and myself should remain at Pekin. This to me was a most severe decision, and to have been within fifty miles of the famous Great Wall, that stupendous monument of human labour, and not to have seen that which might have been the boast of a man's grandson, as Dr. Johnson has said, I have to regret for ever. That the artists should be dismissed to remain at Pekin during this most interesting journey of the embassy, is not easily to be accounted for. . . ."

AN ENGLISH ARTIST'S LAMENT. *Outstanding among early Western depictions of China are the many engravings of sketches by William Alexander, one of the two artists who accompanied the Macartney embassy to Peking in the late 18th century, several of which are reproduced elsewhere in this book. We can only guess what romantic flights the Great Wall would have drawn from his pen had Lord Macartney taken him along.*

kings such as we see in the pyramids of Egypt; here is no palace, even, to apotheosize a living monarch or to house the accouterments of a god. Here, instead, is a unique construction of mankind: a wall built to protect and to mark off his civilization from the chaos of the outer world. It is not sufficient to suppose the Great Wall was built with only military reasons in mind. The impulse, while certainly defensive in fact, was something much deeper in spirit.

Again we come to the concept of the Chinese and their way of life in what they called the Middle or Central Kingdom, as the unique civilization of the whole world. From the first unification of the country under Ch'in Shih-huang-ti, when the wall as one continuous barrier was conceived and the earlier Chou-dynasty sections were joined together, the Chinese have never for a moment doubted this view. It was a concept at once monolithic and monotheistic, with themselves, headed by the emperor and down to the lowliest coolie, as the sole recipients of the sole divine universe. From time to time the wall may have assumed lesser importance—as in the Yuan dynasty, when the Mongols, with their original homeland outside the wall, hardly had need of its protection, physical or cultural (which may have been the reason Marco Polo ignored it). But the wall never became obsolete. Even the first course on which it was built was little altered throughout the succeeding dynasties, for the simple reason that the ancient Ch'in rulers had constructed the great barrier in both the militarily and the psychologically correct place.

Among the innumerable influences of the wall on Chinese life and thought was the shock administered to the nation by the expenditure of men in its building. In human terms the construction of the Great Wall was an event which Chinese memory never forgot. Like a terrible wound, it left its scar—not the physical scar of the wall itself as it ripples across the body of China, but the psychological scar remembered in folk tale and folk poetry. There are laments and ballads without number throughout all North China which tell the story of the wall's building, of the vast human sacrifice entailed and the misery of those who had their menfolk taken from them.

One such poem, "The Ballad of Meng Chiang-nu," takes many forms in different places. The version which follows was discovered by the eminent sinologist Dr. Joseph Needham in a temple at Lanchow, a town near the western end of the wall in the province of Kansu.* The poem certainly does not date from the first building of the wall, not at least in its written form, which is much later.

The ballad begins by describing how Meng Chiang-nu grew up and was married to "the gentle youth Fan San-lang" when they were both sixteen.

> Half a month had hardly gone before the tyrant-emperor
> Ch'in Shih-huang-ti began to build the Great Wall.
> Her husband's name was picked, so he took in his hands
> The carrying-pole and the rope and baskets.
>
> Thus husband and wife were torn apart and scattered,
> The mandarin ducks separated and sundered.
> He spoke sorrowful words, making ready to go,
> While Meng Chiang-nu watched him from the gate.
>
> He turned his head, looking back longingly,
> Lingering, loth to leave little Meng Chiang-nu. . . .

Her husband sets out, asking her to look after his parents, with whom they live, and Meng Chiang-nu weeps bitterly. By the sixth month he has not returned. Through summer and into the winter frosts she waits at home, sewing padded clothes for her husband.

One night she has a dream in which her husband's spirit visits her, weeping and telling her he has fallen from exhaustion into the wall and been buried inside it. He asks her to bring back his bones: "In this life I shall not now be able to return so far." Until dawn she cries, and next day persuades his parents to allow her to go to the Great Wall far away.

> "If I am able there to see his face,
> We will both return to the family and countryside.
> We shall gather in the high hall and wait upon you merrily,
> But if it be that his face I see not,
>
> I shall die in the wilderness, and not return home." . . .

Then she takes out the padded clothes, the leggings and shoes, and sets off. She does not know the way, but with the miraculous help of the Goddess of Mercy she reaches her destination.

---

* The translation, with some changes in punctuation and orthography, is by Dr. Needham (*Sinologica*, Vol. I, 1948) and is used by his permission. The reader may like to compare this version of the ballad with another, found in the Buddhist caves at Tun-huang at the far western end of the Great Wall and charmingly translated in Arthur Waley's *Ballads and Stories from Tun-huang*.

Suddenly she opened her eyes and wept with amaze
To see the Great Wall extended before her;
The width of the wall was several times ten feet,
To east and west you could never see the end of it.

In her mind she wondered where he could be
And how she could have reached this waste so weird. . . . .

While she was a-walking, she lifted up her head and looked
And saw a field full of folk building at the wall.
Approaching them fearfully, she opened her mouth and asked,
"You big brothers, please lend me your ears."

The workers are moved by her story, remembering their own wives and brothers. They say her husband was working on the wall at Tungkung:

"Every man suffered there a thousand hardships,
And we heard he died by the Great Wall in that place.
Good sister-in-law, if more you would know,
Follow along the wall and enquire of our mates."

Meng Chiang-nu faints. As she recovers she utters such a cry that the Jade Emperor himself, lord of the physical world and savior of men, is disturbed. His attendant tells him how the young husband

"At the Great Wall . . . met with danger,
So that his bones and body are buried therein.
Meng Chiang-nu has come thousands of li with clothes,
And now she is crying herself to death at the Great Wall."

The Jade Emperor summons the company of the gods, who, "with good omens and clouds like drapery . . . descended from heaven's courts."

Soon they reached the Great Wall in tramping and bustle,
Soon there sounded in the sky a thunderous noise;
For the space of several li the sides of the wall were opened,
Exposing the white bones of Fan San-lang.

Meng Chiang-nu, bending her head, looked at them closely,
Corpses and bones aglare under the blue sky.
Meng Chiang-nu pondered in her heart
Which of these could be her husband's bones.

> Again she bent her head and deeply thought.
> What harm would it be to bite the middle finger?
> If any bones be those of her dear husband,
> The fresh blood would certainly soak and seep into them.
>
> But if they be not truly his bones,
> The blood would not enter, but run down to the ground. . . .

Immediately Meng Chiang-nu applies the test of blood, which soaks into the bones, showing that they are her husband's.

> . . : Then Meng Chiang-nu felt an aching in her heart.
> Embracing the dead bones, she cried bitter tears,
>
> Wept that she could not more see her husband—
> No more would they enter together the bedchamber.
> "How pitiful, how pitiful, you that were a scholar,
> That the tyrant-emperor should send you to build the wall."

She gathers up the bones and starts for home:

> Now hardly was she started on her long journey
> Than the wicked Ch'in Shih-huang-ti came by that way,
> With officials and soldiers, noble and numberless,
> With spears, pikes, and swords like a forest of hemp.

The emperor forces her to tell her story.

> . . . The wicked Emperor, having listened to all,
> Said: "Maiden, now may your heart be at peace.
>
> Your face seems to me comely and beautiful;
> Follow the Lonely One to the court and be made a lady of Chao Yang.
> But should you disobey my imperial words,
> How can you bear the crime of Crying Down the Great Wall?"

He calls the axe-bearer to be ready to strike off her head. Meng Chiang-nu ponders what to do since, if she dies, she will be unable to take her husband's bones home. Eventually the emperor asks her simply to embroider a gown for him, and then she may go home. But the loyal widow of the wall is not satisfied: she asks for three favors before she enters his court:

> . . . First, bury my husband in state,
> With jade and gold, as if he were a prince.

Second, let all the state officials mourn, both civil and military,
And let your Majesty, My Lord, carry a hempen stick.
And third, that the burial be nowhere else
But upon the shores of the Eastern Sea."

The emperor agrees.

So everything was ordered quickly and well.
The bearers of the coffin marched and marched,
Moving by day and resting by night,
Until they reached the coast of the Eastern Sea.

Then, putting down the coffin, they started their labor
In a place of mountains and water, true and fitting.
The bier stood ready, the coffin by the tomb,
And Meng Chiang-nu waiting by the cliff temple.

Finally she knelt down on the ground,
Prayed to her husband Fan San-lang:
"Wait for me in the other world,
So we may come before the king of that place together."

. . . She turned to the Enlightened One, speaking as follows:
"Your maidservant Meng Chiang-nu is under a vow.

How can I obey you, O evil king?"
Covering up her face with her skirt of black silk
And lifting up her two feet, she leapt into the sea.
As for the wicked emperor, he could not stop her.

10. The Valley of Tombs

The valley is a place of ancient beauty. Buildings of brick and stone and old wood, their roofs dropping yellow tiles, mingle with the trees, with somber pines and blossoming branches in spring, and with the autumn's russets and golds. At that time the dying summer matches perfectly the decay of Ming glory, and the gentle Peking sky hangs softly over the whole natural amphitheater of the valley. Yung-lo could hardly have chosen a more magnificent setting, one more fitting for the repose of emperors of the most Chinese of all the dynasties. But for the thirteen imperial tombs with their buildings and the mounds, under each of which the secret passages of the burial chambers lie concealed, the valley must have looked much the same in his days five hundred years ago as it does now. The suburbs of Peking, then as now, were still far away over the plain. The dusty ground, a dark and passionate red after rain showers, paling in the hot sun, and rising in puffs of cloud with every breeze, is still resistant to agriculture. Thin rows of root crops are planted in spring, and the patient countrypeople extort their harvest from a reluctant soil. Persimmons hang like shiny orange lanterns from the trees when the fall strips their branches of leaves. Peasants sweep up the leaves for kindling with bamboo rakes and gather dead twigs in baskets whose design is as old as the oldest Chinese bas-reliefs. A few youngsters can still be seen at suitable seasons searching by fallen walls for wild flowers and herbs and roots which they gather and dry, later to sell them to the Chinese medicine shops in the alleys of Peking. Here and there a donkey jogs along dreaming amid the trees, weighed down with heavy panniers, a bundled figure too big for him sitting on top.

In the tomb complexes themselves the stones and bricks, the formal curvature of the roofs, the sculpture of dragon and phoenix on the inclined stone ramps over which the sarcophagi of emperors went to their last resting places, have all blended into the surroundings under the soothing hand of time. But the effect is not only the work of time: it is the genius of the Chinese, and almost only the Chinese from among the peoples of the world, that when they built in a landscape they added objects which positively enhanced the natural surroundings. Their tombs, their temples, and their pagodas are invented nature, different in appearance from natural objects but not—it often seems— different in kind. (If one doubts this, a pagoda built in the 1950's not far away from the Ming tombs demonstrates the point.) The elusive harmony toward which so many architects in other countries have striven seems almost the birthright of the Chinese builder. Perhaps it is a product—like much of their reflective poetry about living in the country— of that balance between the complementary principles of life after which they strove unsuccessfully in their government and in formal philosophy, but which, in their architecture, they managed to achieve in actual contact with the land. The Valley of the Thirteen

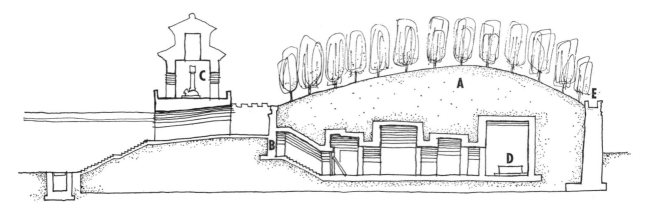

SECTION THROUGH A TYPICAL MING TOMB. *The burial mound of earth* (A) *is covered with trees under whose roots stone vaults lead one after the other from the sealed entry* (B). *A small pavilion* (C) *shelters the emperor's stele recording his name and deeds. The coffin of the emperor, and generally those of his empress or empresses, lie on a low stone platform* (D) *in the vault farthest from the entry. The burial mound often has a narrow walk encircling it* (E).

Tombs, as it is called in Chinese, is full of structures large and small, grand and less grand. But in the way that a huge tree or an outcropping rock belongs to its setting, the buildings where the dead Ming emperors and their empresses and favorite concubines lie entombed belong to the valley: the original impulse which built those tombs was such that they do not obtrude more than the tree or the rock.

Although the Ming tombs are actually only twenty miles northwest of Peking, as much a part of the city as its palaces where the emperors lived in splendor similar to that recently discovered in their vaults in the foothills, when actually at the site, one feels far away, almost in another world. As the road from Peking nears the valley it straightens out, and a white marble *p'ai-lou,* the most beautiful example of this type of ceremonial gateway in all China, straddles the road with its five square portals, giving warning that this is no ordinary route. Half a mile farther on, the warning is repeated by the Great Red Gate, through whose central arch almost the whole valley with its backdrop of rugged peaks spreads out ahead. On each spur of hill coming down from the mountains like the toes of a Ming lion, the roof of a tomb building overtops the trees. At the Great Red Gate the funerary processions of old stopped, vehicles and horses were left behind, and the cortege continued on foot along "The Spirit's Road to the Combined Mausolea." Dividing to left and right at a pavilion which shelters the largest stone tortoise in China, on whose carapace stands a ponderous memorial tablet, the procession joined again at the Triumphal Way, where twenty-four marble animals and twelve marble men line the route in solemn pairs.

Originally this road was flanked by trees and set in a landscape garden, but the trees disappeared after the fall of the Ming, chopped down for firewood by the peasants, so that the two rows of figures stood isolated and startling on the plain with only blue haze between them and the mountains. They stood thus for the three centuries of Ch'ing rule and after until, in 1958, the present government planted saplings at their backs and herbaceous gardens at their feet and made the place quite cozy, thereby destroying the excellence of a scene which nature and the peasants and the Ming had contrived.

The figures themselves are marvelously well preserved. Two pairs of lions, two of sturdy Mongolian horses, two of camels (on whose backs doting Peking parents place their children to be photographed), two pairs of griffins, two of *ki-lin* or unicorns, and

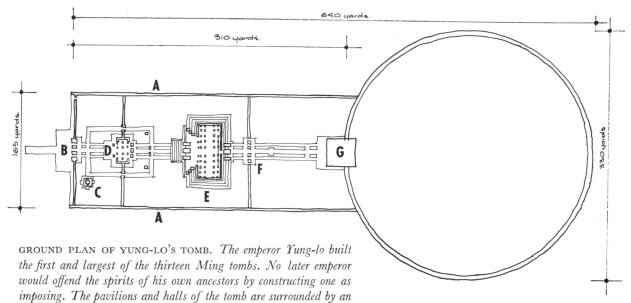

GROUND PLAN OF YUNG-LO'S TOMB. *The emperor Yung-lo built the first and largest of the thirteen Ming tombs. No later emperor would offend the spirits of his own ancestors by constructing one as imposing. The pavilions and halls of the tomb are surrounded by an outer wall (AA), and the entrance is at B. Yung-lo's stele is placed rather unconventionally, off-center, in the small pavilion (C) in the first courtyard. Beyond the larger pavilion (D) is the very large and handsome Sacrificial Hall (E), larger than the Hall of Supreme Harmony in the Forbidden City. Farther on, through another ornamental gate (F), a small square building (G) marks the rim of the circular burial mound with its copse of dark trees covering the surface. The dimensions shown give some idea of the labor, money, and forethought that must have been expended on what Yung-lo thought a fitting resting place for a Ming emperor.*

two of massive and sweet-faced elephants line the paved way. They are followed by pairs of civil officials in robes, military officials with fierce expressions and outmoded armor, and officers of merit bearing tablets. Beyond these figures is the Dragon and Phoenix Gate, through whose portal the vast tomb of Yung-lo appears in all its Ming majesty of red wall and multiple roofs.

Yung-lo's tomb is the largest of the thirteen disposed about the valley wherever the auspices proved favorable. Inside its square, walled enclosure the sacrificial hall in the courtyard of trees is larger than the biggest audience hall of the Peking palaces, and based like them on a triple terrace of white marble gloriously carved. Its several dozens of bare wooden columns supporting the tiled roof are more than thirty feet high, more than a yard in diameter. Each is cut from a single trunk of *nanmu* tree brought at incalculable expense and with what must have been the greatest difficulty five hundred years ago from the far south, or perhaps from Burma. The ceiling is worked in relief with lacquered dragons. The length and breadth of this triumph of Ming architecture, richly decorated and totally empty, make it about half the size of Cologne Cathedral (the largest cathedral in Europe). Made entirely of wood, it was the largest building in China until the twentieth century's steel and concrete made obsolete the techniques of Chinese architecture which had prevailed for more than two thousand years.

Behind it, past a building empty but for the cinnabar tablet inscribed with the emperor's posthumous title, a mound one kilometer in circumference rises in the shape of an upturned rice bowl. Like the emperor's private apartments in the palace, which were no different from the ordinary *hutung* house of his subjects except in their size, his burial tumulus is the same as their little burial humps of earth dotting the fields of the valley around, only much bigger.

Beneath the coarse grass and fine trees springing from Yung-lo's mound, the stone grave chamber is sunk far under the earth, containing his coffin decorated with Buddhist

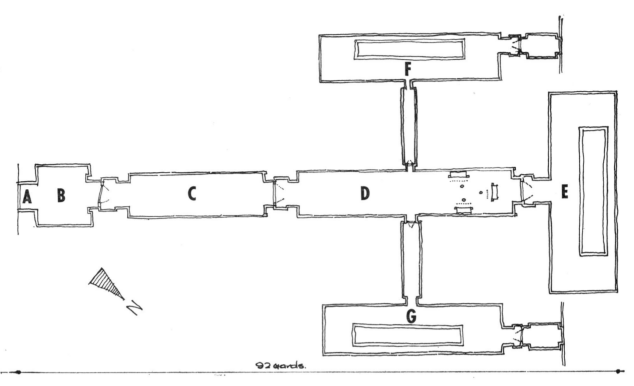

THE ELABORATE WAN-LI BURIAL VAULTS. *This entire complex was completely hidden underground. From the bricked-up entry* (A) *the first two vaults* (B, C) *were discovered to be empty though the tomb had not previously been entered. The Sacrificial Chamber* (D) *contained three marble thrones and various altarpieces, while the innermost Burial Chamber* (E), *measuring 66 by 29 feet, contained the coffins of the emperor and his two empresses lying side by side on a low stone platform. The three sets of locked marble doors are at the positions indicated. The antechambers at F and G were also empty.*

sutras and piled around with the treasures he needed to maintain in the afterlife the state and the pomp of that dazzling court at Peking over the plain.

In the 1920's travelers described the dilapidation of the thirteen tombs, where beams had given way, and caretakers, their wages unpaid, made a living by selling drinks and prodding down souvenir tiles from the edges of the falling roofs. In the 1960's there are still some minor tombs in that state. But those of Yung-lo and several other emperors have recently been repaired and put in better order than they have been for the past several hundred years. The restoration is thoughtful and scholarly. The clock has been put back in architectural time with skill and understanding so that Yung-lo himself might well be pleased if he could come back and see the tomb which he built in his lifetime.

Many of the tombs have been breached and their contents stolen in the long years since their occupants were laid to rest there. But not far from the tomb of Yung-lo another tomb has not only been repaired but its hitherto undiscovered vault opened, revealing the astonishing luxury of the Chinese court in the times of the emperor Wan-li (1573–1620). The story of the opening of the Wan-li vault, well told by Victor Purcell, recalls in its excitement the discovery forty years ago of Tutankhamen's tomb in Egypt.

In May, 1956, a team from the Peking Institute of Archaeology began work on the south side of the tumulus, finding to their surprise a tablet inscribed: "This stone is 16 *chang* [160 Chinese feet] from the scaling wall of the funeral chamber at a depth of 3.5 *chang.*" In the words of the team's director, Dr. Hsia Nai, it was "the kind of hint archaeologists dream of." Sixteen days later they came by careful excavation to the wall built after the emperor's body and effects had been sealed in the inner chambers. There was no trace of tampering. A few days later some of its bricks were dislodged and the leader

DOOR-LOCKING MECHANISM OF THE WAN-LI TOMB. *This sketch shows the interior view of a pair of the doors in the Wan-li tomb. The doors are made of veined marble with knobs carved in bas-relief at regular intervals. Here, the left door is closed, with its marble beam in its locked position, while the right door is still slightly ajar, as it must have been when the last funerary attendant slipped out after the imperial remains had been ensconced within. Each heavy marble beam was rounded at its lower end and set in a rounded socket in the floor with a small block of stone to keep it in place. When the top end of the beam rested on the inside of the still-open door, this floor arrangement kept it from sliding sideways across the door; but, as the door was slowly pulled closed from the outside, the upper end of the beam slid down and fell into a prepared hollow in the inside surface of the door. This hollow was cut in such a way that pressure from outside the door would only be transmitted to the beam, which was thereby wedged more firmly into the sockets at either end. The method of opening, discovered by the archaeologists, was to insert a strong but flexible steel band beneath the door and allow it to curl up against the underside of the beam until the top end of the beam was pushed out of its hollow in the surface of the door, in the same way as it originally entered. The ponderous marble doors then swung open easily on their bronze pivots.*

poked his electric torch through the hole into the space beyond. What he saw was an empty room at whose far end stood a carved gateway and closed doors of white marble. This was the first of three antechambers, each longer than the preceding one. The marble doors were the first of three pairs, the leaves of each carved from single massive blocks and set in bronze pivots. All the doors had a simple and ingenious mechanism whereby, after they were shut by the members of the funeral cortege on their exit from the tomb, they supposedly could not be opened from the outside again.

This set a major problem for the archaeologists who, after studying similar mechanisms in other tombs whose doors had been smashed by grave robbers, eventually devised an equally simple and still more ingenious means of shifting the interior buttresses so that the doors would open; which they did without effort on their three-hundred-year-old hinges. The second antechamber was empty like the first. But the third, 105 feet long by 20 feet wide, contained a token of the treasures still to come. There, before the next pair of marble doors, stood three white marble thrones, the central one for the emperor, carved with dragons and clouds, and the other two for his two empresses, carved with phoenixes. In front of them were arrayed many altarpieces and sets of Ming blue-and-white porcelain tubs a couple of feet high still containing the sesame oil and wicks of the "everlasting lamps," which had burned out, perhaps for lack of oxygen.

Then the great moment arrived as the last pair of doors swung open to reveal the burial chamber itself. By now the archaeologists were certain that the tomb had not been robbed, but they were hardly prepared for the profusion of treasure which it contained. Confronting them in the large room of grey limestone, its stones so well fitted that it was perfectly dry, stood three enormous red-lacquered coffins, their color obviously as brilliant as the day they were placed there more than three hundred years before. Inside lay the emperor Wan-li and his two empresses. All around, a vast array of treasures littered the floor. The porcelain alone formed a collection to dazzle the eyes of any museum director in the world. But there was much more—lacquer boxes, figurines, pewter, women's head-dresses decorated with phoenixes in gold and jewels, strings of jade pendants, jade belts, seals, and thousands of other objects.

The coffin of the second empress was opened first. She lay under a silk shroud, a shriveled figure clad in a long gown, stockings, and shoes. On her head was a complicated crownlike structure of gold and silver and jewels; in her hair, jade and precious stones; and in her ears, pendants of white jade shaped like the hare with the mortar and pestle who is the denizen of the moon and maker of the Chinese elixir of life. The eyes of these tiny jade animals were of red garnets less than one millimeter across. One had fallen out, and to find it took the archaeologists many hours. The furnishings of the first empress's coffin were similar but richer.

Now came the climax of the work, the moment when the great sarcophagus of Wan-li was prized open. Inside was a cache of incredible and unexpected beauty. Beneath the heavy silk shroud, brocaded with longevity ideograms, the remains of the emperor, his beard and hair well preserved, lay with his crown of gold mesh as fine as gauze bearing two rampant dragons chasing the flaming pearl originally symbolic of Buddhist truth. Under him were dozens of bolts of the finest silk, in themselves the most splendid collection of Ming fabrics in existence. All around were piled hundreds of objects of great luxury including a spare "dragon robe."

In this profusion of riches Wan-li was buried toward the end of the rule of the Great Ming. He was a young man of twenty-two when he began to build this tomb at a cost of eight million ounces of silver. Six years later when it was finished a morbid fancy made him give a large party in the vault. And on his death, thirty years later still, the tomb was named Ting Ling, the Royal Tomb of Security. Nowadays it is open to the public and Wan-li's fabulous treasure glitters in a museum built in the grounds amid the pine trees which he planted so long ago.

11. Peking Opera

There is one art, among the rich aggregation to be seen in Peking, whose home (if not its origins) lies within those stout walls. This is the opera. Whether you attach it to its birthplace in T'ang-dynasty Ch'ang-an far south near the Yellow River, or think of it in its satirical ebullience of Yuan times, or as it was seen under the great Ch'ien-lung of the Ch'ing dynasty—the classical manifestations of Chinese opera are now the performances in Peking.

The opera in China is at least as popular as opera in Italy. Today there are about twenty-five theaters in Peking—and about the same number of cinemas. On any night of the week many if not most of these theaters will be playing opera and it is generally quite difficult to get tickets. For a performance with great names in the cast the box offices are besieged as soon as they open, and trade unions and factories make block bookings.

Ever since Peking was built by the Mongols, opera has been very much a people's art, patronized from time to time by the nobility, but maturing in the seven centuries since the Yuan dynasty in contact with the average man and his family. The name of an artist such as the late Mei Lan-fang, male interpreter of young-heroine roles for half a century, is as much a household word in Peking and throughout China as that of the current TV or movie favorite in the West. In the mid-twentieth century it may seem surprising to find the theater running neck and neck in popularity with the screen. In China it is partly due to the small number of indigenous Chinese films made. But it is also a result of the popularity of Chinese opera in its own right.

With willful obscurantism Chinese literature always refers to opera performers as "sons of the Pear Garden." The fact would hardly be worth a mention if it did not take us back to the beginnings of Chinese opera in the T'ang dynasty under the patron of drama, the emperor Ming Huang (713–56), who is credited with having started a dramatic academy in the pear garden of his palace. This T'ang drama was purely a court function in which two characters played short scenes. Not until the capital had been moved to Peking under the Mongols did dramatic art emerge in something like its present form. In that period of alien rule the new form of Chinese art was born, almost, it seems, from popular reaction to the Mongol overlords. The dramatists of the time were traditional Chinese scholars frustrated by their relegation to minor positions under the Mongols. All of them whose names have come down to us were Chinese, as also are the themes of the many extant librettos of the time.

The new form, provoked by the stultifying effects of Mongol disregard for Chinese literary culture at the beginning of the dynasty, unfortunately never found a Chinese Shakespeare. The plots are simple dramatizations of popular tales, or historical incidents, and generally end on some moral note. Virtue is for the most part triumphant, although

OPERA MAKE-UP. *Tradition prescribes a specific pattern of make-up for each principal character in Peking opera. Monochrome reproduction can only hint at the powerful effect of the many colors used.*

its triumph may sometimes be attained by strangely bloodthirsty means. Yet the lack of a brilliant playwright has not prevented Chinese opera from expressing ideas central to Chinese thought.

In Chinese language one goes to "hear" and not to "see" opera. The conditions both for performers and audience nowadays are excellent—a great change from prerevolutionary times when, according to Lin Yutang, the theaters were "deplorable compared with modern establishments. Mei Lan-fang and other great singers used to perform, not in a great opera house but in a small theater inside Tungan Bazaar . . . where the benches were rickety, ventilation was nil and breathing almost impossible. But the surroundings did not seem to matter. There was noise and laughter in the audience; refreshments were served, and ushers, more strictly waiters, sent wrung-out hot towels flying in the air over the heads of the audience." This is now as unthinkable as it would be at Milan's La Scala.

Mei Lan-fang, who died only recently, was reared in such conditions, as were the rest of the older generation of players still on the Chinese stage. Of all interpreters of female roles Mei Lan-fang was undoubtedly the greatest since men began to play female parts in the middle of the thirteenth century. Toward the end of his long life he was in retirement, but on important occasions he still appeared, even in his late sixties, in his former parts—all teen-age girls in the harrowing dramas of court intrigue and thwarted love so dear to the Chinese opera-goer's heart. As late as 1959, about two years before his death, his gift and his superb command of the psychology of the roles still carried him through triumphantly. It was impossible to credit that this epitome of shy girlhood on the stage, singing in accents of love or grief, was in fact an ageing man—or indeed a man at all; only now and then one recalled with a conscious effort that this was Mei Lan-fang. Some of those performances belong to the great moments of the Chinese drama, and are perhaps among the great moments of drama anywhere.

Like its Western equivalent, Chinese opera is an absurd confection, and a sublime one. With musical means of a very limited kind—Chinese music is melodic and nonharmonic— and without scenery, with simple and often lame plots about ancient events, with heraldic costume and facial make-up which indicates the general character of the player, it achieves its effect by means of incomparable verve and assurance. Moments of true pathos, terror, tragedy, of excitement or of sudden porcelain beauty, follow each other with ease. The audience, which knows all the stories, is captivated, yet often discriminating. One sees people sitting forward in their seats as the beginning of a well-known and difficult aria comes along; and the satisfied shouts of *Hao! Hao!* (Good! Good!) that greet a good rendition are an accurate guide to the excellence of the singing.

Nowadays the plots of some operas have had their emphasis shifted in favor of more politically approved points. In some, various cuts have been made, and the virtue which traditionally came out triumphant has been underlined and sometimes contorted to fit a new meaning. Various sections of brilliant comedy between lordly feudal aristocrats and their yokels (identifiable by white patches over their noses) were deleted after the Communist revolution as tending to denigrate the peasants (which was not really true), but have now, in saner times, been largely restored. Similarly, the Ch'ing emperor Ch'ien-lung found that certain operas expressed sentiments opposing feudal rule, and he appointed a commission in 1777 which revised or banned them. So current practice is not without that indispensable thing, historical precedent.

It is easy to break down Chinese opera into its constituent parts: arias and recitative, simple dramatic plot (often a love story or some court intrigue of dynastic times), acrobatic battles and fights, balletic movement of the characters and conscious grouping, elements of morality play, occasional social or political satire, luxurious costume, strangely naïve music and a system of voice production quite foreign to Western convention. But it is less easy to say what makes it great. The elements are all unreal. In fact no attempt at realism is made. The stylization is intense. Yet the illusion of reality is equally strong. In the same way as one unconsciously accepts that artificial window on life, the cinema screen, and the fact of seeing life through it, so in Peking opera one accepts the conventions, the bizarre make-up, the brisk cacophony of the music, and the rest of its world which is through the looking-glass but still within the norm of human experience. The sum total of those improbables adds up to a kind of reality often more persuasive than the simulation of reality in other forms of dramatic art.

The famous Yuan-period opera *Chao-shih Ku-erh-chi* (The Orphan of the Chao Family), though it is set in the distant Chou dynasty, was perhaps at first production intended as a slap in the face to the Mongol rulers and their suppression and massacre of Chinese people. The plot, which surprisingly enough captured the imagination of Voltaire and was also adapted in England several times, opens in the emperor's palace garden, where the emperor Tsing Lin, who is drunk, has taken it into his head to shoot arrows over the wall at the ordinary citizens of the town. Remembering the drunken excesses of the Mongols and their prowess at archery, it is not hard to see how this scene could be played straight and yet be a satire in the eyes of the Chinese audience of the time. The grand chancellor, Chao Teng, pleads with the emperor to desist, but only succeeds in incurring his anger. Tsing Lin, shortly after, commands a courtier to have Chao assassinated for his impertinence. The courtier, Tu An Ku, sends a young man to do the deed. The ensuing scene between the white-bearded patriot Chao and the nimble assassin, who carries a great sword, is played almost without words and completely without music. It is typical of many in other operas, when an unsuspecting victim's pacing of the stage in meditation

OPERA MAKE-UP. *Two more examples of the elaborate and stylized make-up. Despite its complexity, actors generally complete the designs with Chinese brush and liquid paint in an hour.*

compels the assassin to execute a series of great silent leaps in order to escape discovery. The acrobatics of the killer and his facial mime are always welded into a characterization so vivid that every thought and emotion passing through his head is easily followed. The youthful assassin in this particular opera, however, is in the end so impressed by the obvious virtues of the venerable Chao that he cannot bring himself to kill the old man and instead reveals what Tu An Ku has sent him to do.

Chao then confronts Tu An Ku and denounces him before the emperor Tsing Lin, unaware that the plot was originated by the monarch. Tsing Lin, being caught out, then adopts a stratagem, saying that dogs always know a wrongdoer. But before the dog is brought into the court to smell out the evil man who wanted to kill Chao, it is secretly given a piece of Chao's clothing to sniff. At the confrontation the animal of course bounds straight for Chao.

Singing in a high, breaking falsetto, his long beard trembling, his long white sleeves swirling with gestures of imperial authority, Tsing Lin announces the imperial decree. Chao and all his family are to be assassinated. The two rows of swordbearers close in, the conspirators draw back with secret smiles as the ritual murder is arranged, and Chao is led off.

But the son of the condemned Chancellor Chao is married to the emperor's sister. Although the execution order does not apply to her, it does apply to her unborn child. Other ministers, friends of Chao determined to avenge his murder, arrange for the doctor who attends her in childbirth to smuggle the infant out of the palace in his medical chest. This is an opportunity for one of the deadly serious scenes vital to the plot but played for high comedy. The doctor, in danger of his life if discovered, engages in verbal sparring matches with palace guards as he departs with the baby, baffles them with his chop logic, keeping the whole audience sitting forward in their seats with tension until finally he makes his escape.

When the courtier Tu An Ku hears that the baby was stillborn and that the doctor simply threw it away, he does not believe it. In a towering rage, with all the resource of Chinese histrionics and that almighty voice reserved for great lords, he commands that unless the Chao baby is produced in three days he will kill every child born on the same day. Gathering the corner of his brocaded robes, and with the prescribed goose-step stride on inch-thick white-soled boots, he exits with his retainers to a terrifying bombardment of Chinese gongs and cymbals.

One of Chao's friends offers to substitute his own baby, knowing it will be killed;

and this is done in a succession of short scenes. The real Chao orphan grows up, and by a series of ruses designed to keep him absolutely safe to carry on the great name of the family, he is even adopted by his father's murderer, Tu An Ku.

Without pause, but with a skill in wielding time sequence which has all the authority of long tradition, the next scene shows a time fifteen years later. The mother, Princess Chuen Yi, is weeping one day in the royal burial ground when the orphan, now a young man, passes by. She does not know him, nor he her. They fall into conversation in a charming scene—the ageing lady with her maidens surrounding her in a bevy of acute femininity, the young man frank and outgoing. When the princess learns that he, the orphan, is the son of Tu An Ku, her husband's murderer, she curses him and has him ejected from the burial ground. In a matter of seconds, such is the extraordinary capacity of Chinese dramatic art, she turns from a sweet matron discoursing politely on things in general to the screaming hysteria of a terribly wronged woman. But even in this abrupt change, the surge of revulsion she feels is perfectly transferred to the audience. This is the amazing thing about good Chinese opera. Even the most unreal moments are made to follow naturally.

The orphan returns home and tells one of the family friends what happened. He is given a long scroll painting depicting the sequence of events leading up to his present situation. Bewildered, he scans on and on along the scroll. In another wordless few minutes the whole realization of his father's murder, the substitution of the babies, the identity of the murderer (now his adopted father) crosses from him to the audience in mime and gesture with absolute clarity. By this improbable mode of narration the dramatic tension is, if anything, deepened. He vows to avenge his father.

Then, with a slight rearrangement of the meager props on stage, the final scene is set. The characters arrive with their retainers bearing swords and banners. The princess and her fluttering ladies, the two old friends of the murdered Chao, a general from the distant provinces who is loyal to the family, and Tu An Ku—all arrive and fill the stage. The general, a terrifying figure in full battle regalia, challenges Tu An Ku on the reasons for the murder of Chao years ago. Tu, with superb arrogance, remarks that Chao deserved all he got and that fortunately all the Chao family were exterminated.

The princess then sings an impassioned accusation and warns Tu An Ku that his last hour has come. Tu, looking round, sees with horror that everyone is against him, their hands on their swords, their henchmen at the ready. He appeals to his adopted son, the orphan of the Chao family. In a moment of tremendous drama, the orphan reveals his true identity and then kills Tu An Ku in revenge.

Coming out of the theater and walking home through the streets of Peking, quite likely you will hear some pedicab man whistling a tune you just heard on the stage. For opera in China is just as popular as that. As if to spite the "official" culture which for many centuries has been embodied in literature written in archaic forms and dealing with matters almost entirely outside the experience of the ordinary Chinese, even if he could read, the opera speaks a visual and emotional language which is readily comprehensible to all. Though it deals very often with great men, exalted personages, fine ladies, and court intrigues, it treats them in the summary way of folk tale, or of the popular press in the West, bringing them down to ordinary level; and it always weaves in some minor plot or string of incidents involving ordinary people who play the dominant parts. With its lilting songs, its stylized tumbling, its exciting scenes of battle interspersed with moments of sudden pathos that are engendered by events well within the experience of everyone—peasant or prince—the few formulae of Chinese opera have been tried and tested in thousands of productions during the years since the time of the Mongols in Peking. Many other types of opera have grown up in the scattered regions of China, each with its dialect, its particular forms of plot, its regional costumes. The music differs greatly in Cantonese opera of the south from that of Peking, while in Yunnan in the far southwest there are operas in which most of the characters are ghosts.

Some idea of the more intellectual capacity of opera emerges from scenes in one such ghost drama. Two ghost-women sing a dialogue lasting a good ten minutes in which they discuss, entirely without action but with astonishingly subtle mime, their loves of a former earthly existence. The voice parts are ingeniously written in musical question-and-answer form, while the orchestra acts as pacemaker, speeding and underscoring their words as the two ladies acidly recall their rivalry over the one man in their life on earth.

Everywhere in China, despite the vastly changing outlook and material circumstances of the Chinese people, opera still easily manages to satisfy the majority. The coming of radio to every hamlet, the beginnings of Western-style drama and ballet in major cities such as Peking and Shanghai, the advent of the movies—far from diminishing the appeal of opera, all these seem in fact to have put it on its mettle. The quality of performances is probably higher now than ever before, and there is something for the connoisseur of theater as well as for the average Chinese and his family in search of an evening's entertainment.

If proof of the spontaneity of popular enjoyment of opera be required, one need only add that when Peking opera comes on a visit to sophisticated Hong Kong, the home of over three million Chinese, which lies outside the orbit of mainland China, a city glutted with all the spectacle movies of the Western world, the performances are fully booked before the season begins and a lively black market in tickets flourishes.

In Italy people love their opera perhaps mainly because they find a natural emotional outlet in melodious voices. In Russia the ballet serves an apparently commensurate popular need, one more obscure and less easy to define. But in China, opera seems to have achieved the status of a national civilization-interpreter. That Chinese-ness of the Peking people, which we have already noted, is the very heart of Peking opera. The peculiar history of the Chinese is its substance; and Chinese aspirations and achievements are its tragedies, its comedies, and its felicities.

A Third Beginning

12. The Republic

Here in a small portion of the Imperial Palace the deposed Manchu Emperor lives, the lonely child called from his play to sit on the Dragon Throne, only to see his mighty empire shrink to this. In this tiny world he and his court keep up a semblance of the old regime. Edicts are issued under the old reigning title: princes make their obeisance to their monarch: eunuchs serve him in official robes. Curious this make-believe kingdom, curious and infinitely pathetic, too, this last stronghold of mystery in once mysterious Peking!

—Juliet Bredon, *Peking*

During the uneasy years between the two world wars, when the great powers were slowly assuming their positions for the second, the history of China—even the chronicle of the shifts of power in Peking—is extremely complex. In many ways the drama, as it unfolds, is not much different from those political and economic dramas of former ages in China. But part of the complexity is in fact due to the abundance of documentation we have for this period. If there existed an equally detailed record of events, speeches, and commentary for the commencement of, say, the Ming dynasty, that period would doubtless reveal similar complexities. There were, however, at least two elements in the history of China during these recent years which were important and largely novel: the influence of the Western powers and of the Japanese.

Since the events of 1860 and 1900, when European armies, as distinct from merchants and missionaries, took a hand in the destinies of China—forcing acceptance of what the Chinese called "unequal treaties"—China had finally lost her old isolation from the world and become a bone of international contention. The Chinese themselves, unsure of the best attitude to take, alternately wooed and rejected the aid, advice, and moral and armed support offered from time to time by various Western nations. Aside from their inexperience in international affairs, which made the Chinese adolescents in a man's game, there was every excuse for their ineptitude in dealing with the Western powers, since the policies of these powers themselves fluctuated widely according to situations in the West and had little to do with the well-being of China herself. Moreover, China was in a position of extreme weakness. Thus various factions within China frequently took opposite attitudes to the West, and it is seldom in these years that we find China as a whole united on any line of action at all.

The second new factor in China's political scene was the infiltration of the Japanese, whom, after China lost the Sino-Japanese War of 1894–95, the Chinese generals had every reason to fear. This state of affairs—to delve no deeper into it—culminated in January, 1915, in the virtual ultimatum called the Twenty-one Demands presented to Yuan Shih-k'ai, at that time virtual ruler of North China, by the Japanese minister in Peking. China was powerless to refuse the demands, by which Japan gained control of North China—and yet another "unequal treaty" came into effect.

The purely Chinese part of the political scene after the end of the last dynasty and the coming of the Republic was broadly a familiar one. The fragmentation of the country, with each part under the virtual rule of a general or warlord or political leader, was no new thing in China's long history. The starry-eyed republic of Dr. Sun Yat-sen, set up on February 12, 1912, with so much naïve hope, was inevitably too dependent on personalities with divided allegiance to be effective. On the one hand, there was the new republican form of government entirely unfamiliar to Chinese but offering opportunities to the country as a whole; and on the other, there was the reluctance of leaders and generals to sink their traditional differences in trying to make it work. Too many personal opportunities for gaining power still hung on the old way of autocratic rule.

The rule of emperors, together with the imperial system of administration, was seen by many Chinese to be bankrupt; but the uprush of republicanism—ill-digested and quite unfamiliar—was too confused to be decisive. The Chinese discovered that governments cannot simply be *made* democratic. So the republic of Sun Yat-sen was doomed from the start and soon degenerated into what was in effect very like the old interdynastic scene—rule by contending warlords, each commanding the allegiance of his own portion of the country.

In the south the powerful Kuomintang had its headquarters at Nanking. Sun Yat-sen was its titular head, but later its moving spirit was Sung Chiao-jen, who was ultimately assassinated on the orders of Yuan Shih-k'ai. Founded in 1912, the KMT, as this emerging political power group came to be called by Westerners, was broadly democratic in form. But its origins—a conspiratorial organization dating back to Manchu times—were perhaps its most difficult problem to overcome. The fatal lack of unity between this and that personality and faction weakened what might have been a strong governing force. While the outlook of the KMT as a whole was democratic, that of Yuan Shih-k'ai, who became its first president while still maintaining his control of North China from his headquarters at Peking, was blatantly one of autocracy. The exponents of these opposing tendencies viewed each other with extreme mistrust, and Yuan was in most ways a law unto himself. His army, his whole possibility of eventually gaining supreme power, was in the north, and he resisted all attempts to transfer the capital from Peking to Nanking.

The "mighty empire" of China, as Juliet Bredon describes it, was in all relevant particulars a sham almost as pathetic as the fiction of imperial power maintained until his abdication in 1912 by the child "emperor" P'u Yi, who inhabited a corner in the northeast part of the Forbidden City. This child, whom the late Empress Dowager had designated as successor to the Manchu throne only a few hours before her death in 1908, was permitted to "rule" although his acts and edicts affected no one outside the confines of his little court. Like the course of the first years of the Republic itself, the life story of P'u

YUAN SHIH-K'AI'S IMPERIAL SEALS. *Seals cut in Peking for President Yuan Shih-k'ai giving his self-assumed title as the emperor of a new Chinese dynasty.*

Yi—later to be Japan's puppet emperor of Manchukuo and, still later, to become good publicity as a humble and regenerated citizen worker of the People's Republic—is pure comic opera, degenerating now and then into farce. Plots and subplots, the inconsequential interweaving of idea, aspiration, and event form a background to the biography of P'u Yi, which McAleavy aptly called *A Dream of Tartary,* describing the sorry end of a magnificent concept—Chinese imperial rule.

Against the political background which we have so briefly outlined, the story of Peking continued. Peking, imperturbable Peking, now watched not only the anachronistic pomp of its last emperor's court continuing like a play whose audience has for the most part already gone home, but also watched the self-important comings and goings of its new lords and masters: and made ready to transfer its outward affections to whichever came out on top. There was nothing new in this attitude. It proves, if anything, that history teaches valid lessons, and that the character of a people is in large part the product of its history.

The events of those years between the fall of the last dynasty and the establishment of the Communist regime in Peking were many, and the attitudes taken by its citizens, Chinese of many shades of opinion, and European residents too, were equally varied. The Chinese, perhaps more realistic in outlook on the subject of their own politics and political figures, experienced what amounted to a long and deep uncertainty on almost every level. Life was perhaps no more difficult—at least until the Japanese arrived in force and knocked the remnants of stability out of the economy—than under the last Manchus, but the feeling that one could not know what the next day might bring made for an atmosphere in which hectic pleasure-seeking and dire speculation vied for dominance. Nowhere in China, least of all in Peking, was this a time of achievement. Each new crisis, when it passed, left a deeper unease.

The outbreak of the first world war in 1914 resulted in Japan's becoming an ally of Britain and an enemy of Germany; and the Tokyo government seized the chance to annex those parts of the Shantung Peninsula which had been a German concession. And after the capitulation of Yuan Shih-k'ai to the Twenty-one Demands it was obvious to most people that the only alternatives facing China were either war with Japan or acceptance of even further humiliating treaties. Yuan himself, a relic of late Manchu times, in which he had played a highly enigmatic role, seems to have felt that the Japanese would help him in his final folly.

Perhaps the most curious of the strange events in Peking during all this epoch was Yuan's assumption of the title of emperor, a step taken on the advice of his American adviser, Professor Goodnow. With all the pomp and ceremony of a dynastic ruler, Yuan went in state to the Temple of Heaven and there performed the ceremonies as founder of a new dynasty. But the act was wholly out of gear with the times, for, even if in a muddled way, the country had by then finally turned its back on the old system. It was

SCENES OF RURAL LIFE. *Showing a peasant returning home with firewood and a fisherman with his seines and small boat, these two stone rubbings, together with those on the following six pages, come from a series of stone bas-reliefs probably dating from the T'ang dynasty. They all deal with the peasant life common to the vast majority of Chinese, then as now, and are apt reminders that, throughout the ages, the glory and might of Peking have had their roots deep in the earth of China, have in the final analysis been made possible by the Chinese peasant and the products of his labors. Depicting with a pleasing and direct simplicity the cycle of seasons and their special tasks, these unsophisticated carvings achieve their effects with remarkable economy. The unknown sculptor's observation of the rural scene is acute and his line both supple and subtle. Until a few years ago most of the activities shown were still a common sight in the countryside, and many of the implements are still in use.*

not long before the farce of his "reign" fell through and was abandoned. Not much remained of Yuan's briefly held empire except vast quantities of porcelain made to commemorate the abortive dynasty of Hung Hsien, as he had named it.

Less comical, less bathetic, was another unlikely scene in Peking when a huge group of coolies was collected in the capital and sent to excavate trenches on the Western Front in Europe. Their fate, like that of similar groups more than two thousand years before who were pressed into service in building the Great Wall, must have seemed to them as cruel and as unmerited as that of their ancestors in the hands of Ch'in Shih-huang-ti.

When the first world war was won, the Allied victory was celebrated in Peking—the old Ming courtyards and the imperial palaces crammed with thousands of soldiers and dignitaries for a ceremony which, to most Chinese, must have seemed irrelevant indeed.

About this time Peking housed a young man who worked in the university library. He lived, like many another intellectual or student, in great poverty, fell in love with his philosophy professor's daughter, and wandered about the city with an observant and utterly Chinese eye. Twenty years afterward he recalled those times: "I saw the white plum-blossom flower while the ice still held over the North Lake. I saw the willows over the lake with the ice crystals hanging from them and remembered the description of the scene by the T'ang poet Ts'en Ts'an, who wrote about Peihai's winter-jewelled trees, looking like 'ten thousand peach trees blossoming.'"* From a youthful anarchist the thin half-starved peasant out of the depths of the country changed in Peking to a socialist, steeped himself in the literature and history of his country, and left the capital as unknown and unnoticed as on the day of his arrival. Many years later he was to return. His name was Mao Tse-tung.

In the years between the fall of the Ch'ing and the beginning of the Japanese war in 1937 the life of Peking, a life which Mao Tse-tung was to change more radically than anyone in all Chinese history, has been described by many people. Especially after the first world war, when the old values of the Western world were falling in pieces about its ears, numbers of Europeans and Americans found a haven in Peking. After the hysteria

* From Edgar Snow, *Red Star Over China.*

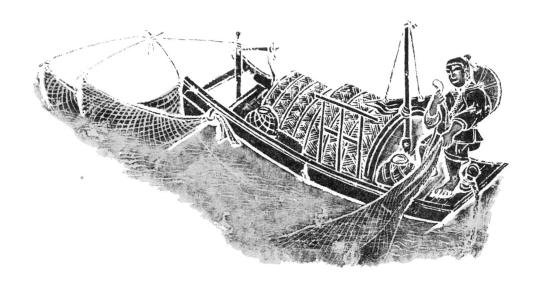

which characterizes Western accounts of the Boxer Rebellion and the Empress Dowager, the books they wrote about this ensuing period are often full of humor, of admiration for the Chinese character and way of life, and of delight in the places and faces of Peking. Quite a few expatriates were scholars well read in Chinese literature and amateurs of Chinese art. To them we owe the more perceptive records of Peking. It is they who describe the glories of Peking architecture, which the Chinese, with their traditional attitude that buildings are replaceable, neglected until many a Ming structure disappeared. From them too we hear of the growing political ferment in the minds of Peking students as Western ideas of democracy, socialism, and communism began to be printed in Chinese and read by an omnivorous youthful population.

"But beneath their urbanity and good humour," writes Harold Acton of his Chinese friends of those days, "[they] were haunted by the writing on the wall. The Japanese were exploiting every scare they set afloat in their insidious war of nerves. My students [at Pei Ta University] were exasperated with the National Government's makeshift policy of appeasement, and when they vented this in public manifestations, many of them were arrested and thrown into jail. To calm them down the New Life Movement was started, and in the schools it was taken up with Salvation Army vigour. The main principle . . . was that patriotism should begin with hygiene in the home. Teach the people to be clean and tidy and punctual; no smoking on the streets; no unbuttoned coats. . . . Perky boy scouts and girl guides told elderly gentlemen to extinguish their cigarettes and scolded them for spitting. Dripping and exhausted rickshaw pullers were ordered to . . . don their jackets." Even the walls of the Imperial Palace were painted blue. But during the following rainy season both the campaign for a New Life and the blue-washed walls became bedraggled and streaked, and a movement which had at least the seeds of a regeneration came to nothing in a torrent of popular ridicule.

In 1928, with Yuan Shih-k'ai now twelve years dead, the Nationalist Government of the KMT at last succeeded in moving the capital to Nanking. Chiang Kai-shek, who had been closely associated with Sun Yat-sen since the earliest days of the KMT and had led the right wing of that party since the death of Sun in 1925, commanded the Nationalist army which brought to a successful conclusion the campaign to subdue rebellious

SPINNING

elements north of the Yangtse. He took Peking in July, 1928. Peking then became Peip'ing, meaning "northern peace," a title it was to retain until 1949, when the Communists restored its former status and name. The Communists, whom Chiang never succeeded in crushing despite many a campaign, were thereafter his major thorn in the flesh. The Chinese Communist party had, early on, formed the KMT's left wing, and it was not until after Sun Yat-sen's death that the party split, resulting in the dismissal of its Russian advisers and near disaster to the northern campaign, which had already begun.

But ours is not a political history of modern China, and we return to the Peking scene of those years. "By slow degrees," continues Acton, "the province of Hopei [in which Peking lies] was becoming a buffer state and officials more acceptable to the Japanese were elected to the local administration. Outwardly anti-Japanese feeling was repressed; inwardly it was rampant. . . . My students deemed it their duty to foment public opinion against the 'dwarf bandits' and they had a precocious talent for propaganda."

More sensitive than most Westerners in Peking to the direction of the political winds of the times, Harold Acton was by no means the only thoughtful European living in the city. L. C. Arlington, "an exceptional character whom chance had blown from California to China in 1879 after a strenuous youth as a cowboy and an argonaut," lived and wrote in Peking. His book on Chinese opera was one of the first comprehensive studies in a foreign language of that miraculous art form, and is still a classic of its kind. There were at least two women, both writing about China: Juliet Bredon, whose prose, if not her understanding of twentieth-century China, is often lyrical and evocative; and Alexandra E. Grantham, a much greater scholar, whose painstaking research in Chinese history broke much new ground. There were Edward Backhouse and J. O. P. Bland—the first a scholar and the other a skillful popular writer—whose collaboration in many books did much to make China and the Chinese way of living less mysterious and more comprehensible to the Western world. And there was Osbert Sitwell, who arrived in Peking to the mingled dismay and exhilaration of the somewhat Philistine European society.

It is to Osbert Sitwell, a mere sojourner in the capital, that we owe the only masterpiece in English on the subject of Peking. In *Escape with Me* he delineates with astonishing empathy, with sublime clarity, the quality of the city and its life in the 1930's. The

WEAVING

history of early India was written by Chinese sojourners; and in like manner Sitwell the Englishman did for Peking what no Chinese has done.

From the none too numerous men and women of perception in Peking between the wars it is perhaps invidious to select only one other. Acton describes him: "I met several Americans who surprised me with their profound intuitive understanding of Chinese art. Among these the finest connoisseur was Laurence Sickman, whose culture was entirely Chinese though he had been born in Denver, Colorado. Some of the most splendid moments of the day were when Laurence walked in with some treasure he had discovered . . . for the fantastically fortunate Kansas City Museum. I marvelled at his integrity. Anyone else with so personal a passion for those things would have appropriated them for himself, and how would Kansas City be any the wiser? . . . But after a brief honeymoon, they were sent to sleep again behind the glass cases of the gallery in Missouri."

Other Western writers, perhaps less scholarly than those we have named, fill out the picture of Peking with the sounds of its hundreds of vendors as they called their wares in the *hutung,* with description of shopping, theaters, brothels, servants, officials, food, customs, and a thousand other details. Reading such books, it is impossible not to delight, as their writers did, in the Peking of those years between the wars. At the same time it is impossible not to be horrified at the conditions of most people in the city, conditions much more horrible in human terms than those of Dickensian London.

Acton says again, after an absence from the city: " 'Joy has no *nuances.* It is only a dilation of the heart.' My return to Peking was an immense dilation. It was winter; the land was frozen; yet nothing shivered. The sun irradiated the crisp air and the sky was a cerulean glaze. The air itself was a scintillating cordial. Every other country seemed to have been defiled to some degree by human beings, but this was improved by them. The Chinese were dominant blue notes in their own landscape, a vast encampment rather than a city." And a little later, reacting to that Chinese-ness which we have already noted: "I resolved to keep aloof from Europeans who did not share my enthusiasm for China, which at the time meant the majority."

That many Westerners did not share the enthusiasm for China displayed by a few is quite true. Westerners in China between the wars enjoyed the privileges of a near-

PREPARING FIELDS
FOR PLANTING

colonialist society, protected from the people among whom they lived by the power of their respective governments operating through the legations. But to say that these people were the majority of Westerners is hardly fair. Most, it is true, understood no Chinese language, most were tinged with the feeling that they were in the end representatives of a superior race; but very many of them loved China and found a great human joy in their contacts with Chinese. If at times that joy was what we now tend to call paternalistic, since the difference in economic status between the two parties was generally so great that a Chinese-Westerner relationship inevitably took the character of master and servant, it was at heart sincere. Talking of the beggars who lived in the *hutung* where she lived for many years, Hope Danby, an Englishwoman, says: "First of all there was the Blind Beggar who was led all over Peking by a gentle-faced little girl. Almost deaf as well as blind, he would prop himself in the gate recess and stand there as immovable as a Buddha in a shrine." When she came back from the city in her rickshaw "the little girl would reach up on tiptoe and scream excitedly into the beggar's ear: 'The lady is coming—at last she has reached home.' Immediately the old man would start plucking at the single string of his fiddle—it sent strange, melancholy, nondescript tunes down the *hutung* to welcome me." This beggar was one of five to whom Hope Danby paid a regular weekly sum, for which they seem to have done their best to repay her by their welcomes and greetings as she came and went from the house.

"The fair," she writes elsewhere, "was held three times a month in the precincts of the beautiful Temple of Prosperity and Happiness . . . one of my favourite places in Peking. . . . The scene was always gay, carnival-like, and crowded with noisy, happy, jolly and excited people who were having a holiday outing and had put on their best clothes for the occasion. . . . Most of the women wore *yu-lan* buds, jade orchids, in their hair. . . . As we approached the entrance to the temple we had to push our way through groups of people blocking the pavements, who were watching shop assistants expertly tossing lengths of silk and cottons into the air and displaying them to the accompaniment of sing-song rhythms that told their lengths, merits and prices. I wished I could better understand the quick patter . . . for they were smart and witty and kept their audience in fits of laughter. . . . After we left the household section we strolled into an inner section

PLANTING RICE SHOOTS

of the grounds and exchanged greetings with some old friends who were presiding over the curio stalls. . . . I could rarely resist when a curio-dealer called out to me that he had found a wonderful piece and I must see it at once. To me, an old friend, the price would be next to nothing. . . ."

Looking back, it seems a strange time, an interval between the acts, the background filled with rumblings of warlord wars, the Kuomintang, the Communists, the creeping presence of the Japanese. Peking at the time was a bedraggled city, precariously existing in an atmosphere of change which was liable to explode at any moment. The great imperial buildings sprouted weeds. Early automobiles honked their way through camel trains, past wondering rickshaw boys, and amid the covetous glances of the concubines of rich citizens. The telephone had looped its inelegant wires across façades more used to banners. Princes of the imperial family could be seen in a Western-style store with their concubines, who picked with birdlike excitement at pots of strawberry jam and tins of English fruitcake. European women, handkerchiefs held to their long noses against the infected dust, were trundled through the streets by ragged rickshaw-pullers—home to the Legation Quarter, from which, in effect, their husbands had ruled the city for some years. The charming, diseased, and helpless girls in the brothels, the wings of dust that rose with each footstep in the dry season, the mud that clogged everyone's feet on wet days, the leprous beggars (both real and professional) moaning at every corner, the destitute who not infrequently froze to death in winter, the stink and the poverty of a Peking whose decaying but still mysterious beauty lingered on—all those aspects have their chroniclers between the first revolution and the second.

The Legation Quarter had grown into a district of central Peking, complete in itself, surrounded by an open space called the Glacis and bounded by a wall (see plan, page 136). Originally a mere handful of Western countries had established their footholds in the capital after the ratification of the Treaty of Tientsin in 1860. England, the United States (in 1862), France, and Russia were among the first to claim their new privileges. Most were quartered on or near Chiao Min Hsiang (Street of Contact with Peoples), where envoys of tributary countries such as Tibet, Korea, and Mongolia had formerly been accommodated on their visits to Peking. The irony of the situation—the Western powers

DRAWING WATER
FOR IRRIGATION

BRINGING IN
THE RICE HARVEST

had won their rights with the signature of the treaty and were nonetheless housed in an area traditionally set aside for representatives of vassal states—was perhaps not apparent to the diplomats of those days. The name of the street was later altered to Legation Street, and as the years passed and the Boxer Rebellion brought its siege to the quarter, buildings proliferated and more nations opened legations. It became, as Juliet Bredon remarks, "architecturally speaking . . . a most extraordinary mixture. Each builder . . . attempted to bring a fragment of his own country . . . so that bits of Colonial America, of Holland, of Italy and Japan stand side by side. . . ." In 1905 Congress appropriated $60,000 for a new American legation building, which was built just inside the south wall of the Inner City near Ch'ienmen. But the British stayed on in what was their first and only home in the capital—a Chinese palace formerly given to his thirty-third son by the emperor K'ang-hsi and owned by his descendants. This vast mansion with its excellent buildings and many courtyards was leased to Britain for a very small sum, and the rent was paid in silver which was conveyed each Chinese New Year in a mule cart from the legation to the Tsungli Yamen, the Chinese equivalent of a ministry of foreign affairs.

While it is tempting to linger on this period of Peking's story, to do so would be to unbalance the picture. Although it is so well documented by Europeans (and for this reason, unlike so much of Peking history, readily accessible) the tale has not yet been told in detail from the Chinese point of view, and it is in any case only the briefest episode in the long scroll of the city's history. In essentials the feeling of optimistic Chinese at the time was that while warlords may come and warlords may go, Peking would probably go on forever. And, from both European and Chinese points of view, if one shut one's eyes to the deeper implications of the political struggle waging throughout the 1930's between Communists and the Kuomintang, there was some justification for the attitude.

As if to remind everyone of her former rule, Yehonala, the late dowager empress, turned up from the grave in 1928. Buried near the emperor Ch'ien-lung in the Manchu tombs about a hundred miles from the capital, her grave was found to have been opened and plundered of its treasures. Worse still, the team of investigators found that the coffin had been emptied and Yehonala, stripped of clothes except for a pair of trousers and her stockings, had been cast out. Her mummified body lay face down on the floor

of the chamber, still excellently preserved, only the eyes sunken and dead as once they had been flashing and terrible.

There was time in Peking during this period to know that the sum of Chinese attainments on traditional lines and within the bounds of traditional thought had largely been added up. Before the first building of the city the greatest Chinese painting had been done by the Sung-dynasty masters, and although afterward much had been added in variety, little greater painting had come forth. Sculpture, reaching marvelous heights in the T'ang dynasty, had perhaps broadened and acquired more authority in Ming times, before falling into imitation of itself and endless decoration. Poetry had largely fossilized by the time of the Ming and there is hardly any of later date which adds depth or brilliance to the profound and almost inexhaustible treasury written before. The art of building reached its zenith in early Ming, and the Ch'ing did little but faithfully reproduce the old achievements—of which today we are the fortunate heirs. Perhaps the only form which remained essentially vital until the middle of Ch'ing times was ceramics—the art for which China is best known in the West.

None of the old art forms actually died out in China. All were practiced through the Republican era. But the spur, whatever it may be, that urges a people to masterpieces, to a renaissance, to a great epoch of art, seemed in China to have rusted away long since. If "official" culture, however, was in deep hibernation, the creative energies of the Chinese had not been dammed up. Again with the exception of ceramics, from Ming times these energies had been most vital in the more popular forms—in the novel and the theater. Neither of these managed to acquire the cachet of classical poetry or recondite commentaries of the past, but they were full of richly Chinese spontaneity. The petrified, sanctified old culture of China and the heresy involved in any attempt to modify it to suit the present were the main agents in forcing the growth of unorthodox cultural flowers.

In the long cosmopolitan interval between the acts in Peking, the final warning bell rang on July 7, 1937, when the Japanese launched an attack at Marco Polo Bridge a few miles southwest of the town. The precise occurrence, whether genuine or staged, that triggered off the attack will probably remain a matter for conjecture. Writers, both popular and historical, give entirely different accounts, but Harold Acton's may serve as a typical one: " . . . The Japanese could wait no longer. With their habitual disregard as to whether the pretext were plausible, they engineered an incident. One Japanese soldier happened to visit a brothel while his company was holding night manoeuvres near Peking. . . . I have seen Japanese soldiers paraded before a brothel just off Hatamen Street and ordered to fall out of their ranks by fours. Each was alloted ten minutes to satisfy his libido and would double back. . . . 'One private missing? The honour of Dai Nippon is at stake. . . .' The sleepy little walled town of Wan-p'ing [near the bridge] was attacked. . . . More scandalous! the town guards had the effrontery to defend themselves when attacked. Within twenty-four hours some 35,000 'dwarf bandits' . . . were marching toward Peking."

In the capital martial law was proclaimed and a curfew enforced. Quite pointlessly enforced, since most Peking people—with a long tradition of similar alarms vivid in the popular memory—had immediately barricaded themselves behind the spirit screens of their *hutung* houses. While Japanese aircraft droned over the city, trenches were dug at street corners and sandbags piled up. The closure of the city gates sent food prices rocketing; and rumor, the false messenger of fear, darted through the town. Thousands of people crammed into whatever train was leaving the railway station, even clinging to the roofs of the cars, while those lucky enough to get inside were periodically splashed with urine emanating from windows further up. The legations were almost as crowded with their nationals, the Wagon Lits Hotel contained hundreds of wealthy Chinese, with their wives, concubines, and smaller treasures, as they awaited the chance to escape from Peking.

But more revealing of the vitality of Chinese people than the fears of the rich were those same students of Acton's whose ingenuity with the English language we have already noted. The university of Pei Ta, founded almost exactly forty years ago by a decree unique in dynastic annals, was moving out of Peking, southward to Ch'ang-sha in Hunan province. The students, saying goodbye to their tutor at the start of the sad journey, "were nervously calm, their faces set in an expression of fixed resolution. . . . Their eyes glittered like black steel with an excitement which was otherwise suppressed . . . they were inwardly relieved that matters had reached a climax. China's humiliation had been their humiliation: now they were going to cut it like a cancer out of their system. Even the most delicate of them, who had thought me eccentric for walking when I could use a rickshaw, were now prepared to trudge for months on end. Their smiles were radiant. . . . I could not share their optimism. They were thinking in terms of geography and manpower, of China's four hundred and fifty million against Japan's seventy million. And they were remembering China's historical assimilation of her conquerors. They had forgotten the machine."

In the deserted streets of Peking even the hawkers were for once silent. And outside the walls the independent Chinese general Sung Cheh-yuan, with an almost unarmed rabble of troops, was putting up a pathetic little show of resistance against the planes, machine guns, and bombs of the Japanese.

Peking fell. It was to remain in Japanese hands for the next eight years. Early in their occupation they staged a parade to impress the Chinese. But few Chinese witnessed it, having prudently stayed at home. Before the Marco Polo Bridge incident and the military occupation, there had been about four or five thousand Japanese in the city. Now their numbers increased with the arrival of every train. "They are like the seeds from the shade trees in the courtyard, falling into every crack and corner of the city," said a Chinese as their numbers reached a hundred thousand or so.

The city altered considerably under occupation. Many a house acquired a Japanese look with false front, and the streets "soon smelled with that peculiar odor of dried fish, pickled turnip, and damp straw which is inseparable from a port like Yokohama or Kobe." In many a quiet *hutung,* brothels and saloons were opened, to the horror of the old residents, and these, with their mock-Japanese façades, carried signs: Tokyo Beer Parlor, The Five Delights, The Palace Fairies. Korean prostitutes, imported by the conquerors, passed on their errands amid the garbage and the stench of those formerly innocent little lanes. And those Westerners who had loved Japan and the Japanese were astonished and dismayed at the terrible atrocities committed on a defenseless people at this time.

The proudly proclaimed Co-prosperity Sphere of the Japanese propagandists consisted quite starkly in the rape of China. Ancient figureheads from among the Chinese were dragged from retirement and, together with ghoulish members from the gangster cliques of the 1920's, set up as a provisional government. Others refused to take part in the shameful farce of puppet government and steadfastly remained in obscurity despite all Japanese blandishments.

That summer after the Marco Polo Bridge incident and the fall of Peking, it rained and rained "as if the heavens were weeping"; and in the evenings when the rain ceased, "like the bloodshot eye of a fabulous bird the sun vanished behind the Western Hills in flames. . . . The Forbidden City appeared to be on fire, the red walls scarlet, the gold roofs shooting out beams in an endless expanse of smouldering embers. . . ." And the sound of distant guns rumbled like the growls of animals in the distant haze.

With the outbreak of World War II, Japan became the enemy of the Western allies as well as of the Chinese. A bitter internal struggle for dominance of China was being waged at the same time. The outcome, victory for the Communists under Mao Tse-tung and the unification of all China, was not certain until 1949, four years after the Japanese war ended.

The City Today ▶

In the Peking Workers' Stadium in the east suburb 93 ▶
of the city, completed just in time for the Republic's
tenth anniversary in 1959, a capacity crowd of eighty
thousand watches a soccer match between China and
Hungary.

94 ▲

Athletes from the southern province of Kweichow entering the circular Workers' Stadium.

95 ▲

96 ▶

On Ch'angan Boulevard west of the Gate of Heavenly Peace, beyond transport pedicabs bringing rice to central Peking, are two big new buildings. At the right is the Cultural Palace of the Nationalities, a club and recreation center for non-Chinese peoples, of whom there are many millions in China. Left, a new hotel has been built. Chinese architects, lacking experience in Western techniques, still waver between pseudo-Ming decoration and stark functionalism.

Photo by Brian Brake, © National Geographic Society

In Chungshan Park a new theater has risen amid the old rock gardens. Shaped like a quarter segment of a circle, it is roofed but has open sides. Here several thousand listen to speeches commemorating May 4, 1919—a day remembered for its mass demonstration by Peking students against the Versailles Treaty, which perpetuated the privileges of foreign governments in China.

97
▶

98
▶

99
▶

Sprawling over a wide area west of the city, what is virtually a new town houses the technical faculties of Peking University, each with upwards of nine thousand students. Conditions are crowded, and both work and play are taken seriously, a characteristic of Chinese all over the world when given the chance to study. A student in the Geology Institute (97) studies the molecular structure of aluminum trioxide. A class in the Medical School (98) takes notes, and students share a newspaper between lectures. Two geology students eat their lunch in the college restaurant. Nearly all students in Peking are on government grants. Entry is strictly on merit in fiercely competitive examinations.

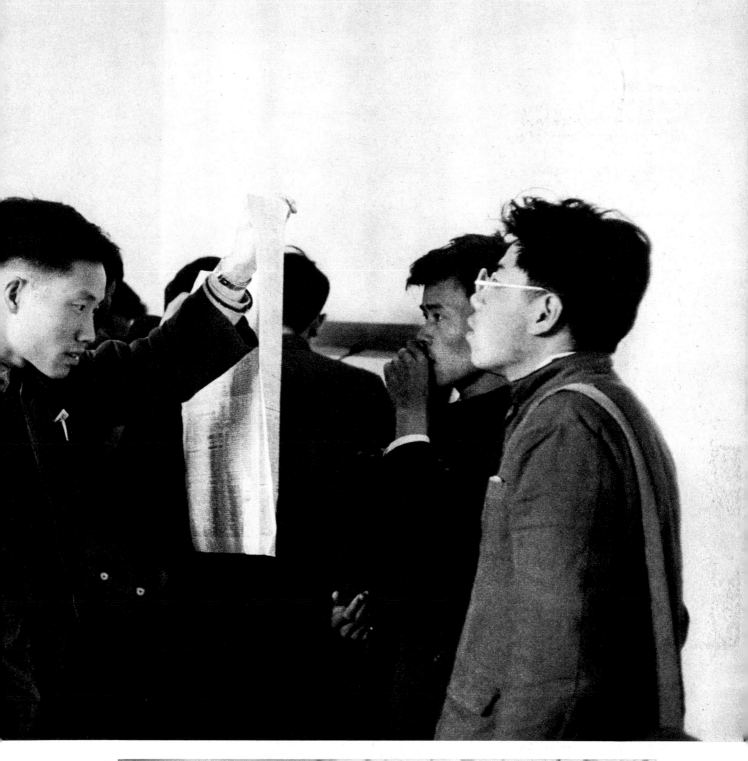

About 500 B.C. a Chinese physician postulated the circulation of the blood—twenty-two centuries before Harvey. "Sciences" of physical medicine, massage, and acupuncture, among others, developed early and continue to today. In a hutung *a local practitioner (101) on crutches massages a patient with his feet; the wall notice quotes from an early Chinese medical book describing the treatment. A child with polio (102) has acupuncture treatment, and the old man is being treated for facial paralysis. A postgraduate class in acupuncture (104) in the Institute of Traditional Medicine uses a Sung-dynasty bronze teaching aid.*

101 ▲

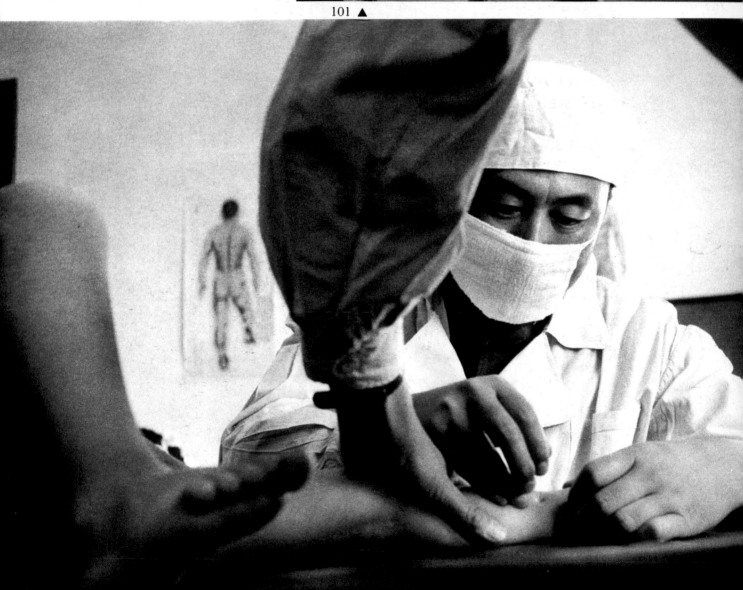

105 ▲

107 ▲

106 ▲

Among building priorities since the revolution, schools have come high on the list. Today well over a million Peking children go to school—virtually every child of school age. But construction has been unable to keep pace with the influx of pupils and many a school, like the kindergarten below, is housed in a converted Ming or Ch'ing house whose charms are manifest but whose adaptability for educational purposes is slight. Kindergarten children arrive before breakfast and do a little limbering up before their day of educational play. Primary school children (105) draw the strokes of a Chinese character in the air as a memory aid, and a girl writes the translation in Chinese characters of a phrase written in the new Romanization of the language. It means "glittering like crystal."

Three typical street scenes. On autumn days apples and persimmons are sold from street stalls (108) outside one of Peking's west gates (in the background). A pedicab driver and his son at the entrance to Chungshan Park are buying candies. And—a familiar sight in the early morning—a bicycle-driven "bus" (110) waits to collect children from their homes and take them to kindergarten. The old man with the pipe is the driver.

109 ▲

110 ▼

Westward along Ch'angan Boulevard the ancient and modern confront each other. At the top right the two old gates—Heavenly Peace and Wumen—now survey gigantic new neighbors across the widened street and inflated square. The Museum and, beyond

it, the Hall of the People—each a quarter of a mile long—replace old single-storey buildings. In the Peking haze further along, the towers of a new Post and Telegraph Building and the even newer Cultural Palace of the Nationalities dominate the skyline.

112 ▲

113 ▲

Shopping in a Peking department store is enjoyed by customers of all ages.

Chao, the pedicab driver of 109, with his family in the courtyard of the hutung *house they share with another family. The boy in a cap is a neighbor's son. The older man and woman, center, are Chao's parents. His wife, right, holds their youngest child. The courtyard, with its clutter of potted plants, its paper windows and small trees, is typical of many thousands of others in the old streets of Peking.*

114 ▼

Two old ladies in traditional clothes admire the hall and escalator of the new Peking railway station. Their feet, though not very small, were bound in infancy. Both carry walking sticks to assist balance.

Since the revolution Peking has had many new and foreign experiences, of which the Museum, displaying the whole span of Chinese history, and the Planetarium, which deprives the heavens of their traditional mystery while substituting a new scientific riddle, are two of the most surprising in the context. Two friends pause in front of a chart dealing with grain production in Ming days, while another young man (118) puzzles over a model of an ancient rocket-type flying machine powered by the Chinese invention of gunpowder. A girl attendant in the planetarium focuses a projector to show sunspots on a screen, and a crowd (119) listens to a lecture on the planets.

118 ▲

119 ▼

The T'ang horses and figurine and a modern copy of a Sung armillary sphere are housed in the Museum. This new building, if not avant-garde architecturally, shows a striving after twentieth-century idiom evolved far outside China. The tall chaste columns of its portico are the severest piece of building in Peking. In the distance lie the Monument to the People's Heroes and the Hall of the People, which forms the western side of the square.

120 ▲

121 ▲

The pride Chinese take in the revelation that they can make "foreign machines" for themselves is as large as it is natural. A visit to a technical exhibition is as a popular as a night at Peking opera. At an exhibition of Chinese industry, Tibetans (123) gaze wonderingly at an object which revolves but is not a prayer wheel; a girl explains an operating light in a display of Chinese-made surgical equipment; a pair of mechanical hands used in dealing with dangerous substances delights both adults

and children. *A young surveyor with a Chinese-made theodolite works under the roof of a partly built factory. The long plaits most Chinese girls favor before marriage give them a curiously nineteenth-century look, which is entirely canceled out by their assured technical skills. The enthusiasm of Chinese youth in learning scientific subjects is the exact equivalent of the delight in mechanical and electronic devices shown by teenagers elsewhere.*

126 ▲

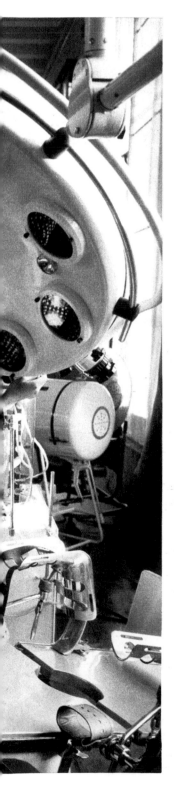

125 ▲

128 ▲

At the permanent agricultural exhibition, just outside the northwest corner of Peking, earnest peasant leaders from the provinces absorb facts and figures and new methods which will help them in crop production. Behind them are showcases topped by decorative sheaves of grain. A life-size straw lion in the spirit of Ming monsters of imperial days guards the entry to the exhibition.

◀ 127 *Under the prodigal blossoming of young trees in Purple Bamboo Park, two students spend a Sunday morning at leisure. This park outside the west wall, unlike most in Peking, is not a former imperial pleasure ground, but was made recently on the site of a municipal garbage dump.*

129 ▶

When state visitors drive into town from the airport, the Peking people turn out in thousands to clap and cheer. Here is a typical group, one that could be duplicated a thousand times along the route. A man and his wife are anxious to show their plump boy the faces of the Chinese leaders and foreign dignitaries.

The scene from the sidewalk in front of the Gate of Heavenly Peace as one of the first sections of the annual May Day parade goes by. School children let loose thousands of balloons, which soar upward in changing patterns into the Peking sky. At the left is part of the new Museum. In the center background the roof of the old Post Office is topped by a turret. The tall stele is the Monument to the People's Heroes, beyond which the massive roofs of Ch'ienmen, Peking's front gate, serve as a reminder of imperial times.

中華人民共和國万歲
世界人民大团結万歲
北京市教育局
地質部大地測量工作
逐年增长圖表
1949-1956
完成大型水库8座
正在施工水库3座

◀ 132 *The May Day parade seen from the south side of Ch'angan Boulevard. Hung with lanterns and a huge portrait of Mao Tse-tung, the Gate of Heavenly Peace bears on its parapet all the leaders of today's China as it stands rather sedately in new surroundings. The long dynastic dream of China, of Peking—which the gate seems to symbolize—is demonstrably ended. A new era has begun. Flanking the gate are two enclosures containing more foreigners than previously ever gathered in peace in the capital, while along the avenue there flows a three-hour tide of Peking people.*

133 ▲

The night of May Day in T'ien An Men Square. The Peking sky in split and shattered by a dazzling three-hour firework display. Important buildings are picked out in lights and even the old Post Office, center, appears beyond the smoke of gunpowder. In the constantly changing colored light a million people crowd the square, dance, listen to bands, watch acrobats and jugglers, stroll around in the roar of explosions and hi-fi music from the powerful loudspeakers on every lamp post.

134 ▲

*Under the Red Star on the ceiling of the Hall of the People guests
from practically every country in the world applaud the speakers. Most
of the ten thousand seats are fitted with a shelf for writing notes, and
with a row of ten buttons and an earphone, giving a choice of ten
simultaneous translations of speeches. TV cameras protrude over the
balcony, and the whole auditorium can be brightly lit for movie work.*

13. The People's Republic

On January 31, 1949, Communist troops occupied Peking. On March 25th Mao Tse-tung entered the city. On October 1st, from the balcony of the Gate of Heavenly Peace, he proclaimed the setting up of the People's Republic of China. On the old red-walled gateway, under the roof of imperial yellow, above the arches through which so many holders of the Mandate of Heaven had passed, Mao Tse-tung, Chairman of the new republic, stood and watched as thousands of Peking people filed into the square. The open space had been newly enlarged to form a parade ground of vast proportions; but beyond stood Ch'ienmen, the old front gate, still the highest and biggest building anywhere near. On every side spread out the low grey-roofed houses of Peking with here and there a yellow roof marking some place of former imperial connections. A chilly wind was blowing from the western deserts, as it so often does in Peking, and the Chairman, dressed in battle-worn clothes similar to those in which he had entered the city months before, seemed cold and tired. His face expressed nothing. To the unfamiliar chorus of *Mao Tse-tung wan sui! Mao Tse-tung wan sui!* (May Mao Tse-tung live ten thousand years!) the Chairman was seen to nod his head.

No emperor had conducted such a campaign as had Mao and his armies; and none, not even the military genius Genghis Khan, had so completely conquered China. None had ever held such a demonstration to proclaim the inauguration of a dynasty, and none had ever spoken to hundreds of thousands of his subjects from the Gate of Heavenly Peace—or from anywhere else, for that matter. The spectacle which Peking witnessed on that October day, though the Peking people did not know it then, was the first of many more.

There was sudden quiet, a hush that spread over the packed square as a flag, rolled into a tight bundle, crept up a tall new pole. Reaching the top of the mast, it burst open, an enormous area of red cloth at least thirty feet wide and bearing five yellow stars. The guns of the twentieth century split the chilly air in salute and the assembled thousands sang the anthem that had become familiar in the past fifteen years to everyone on both sides of a bloody civil war now coming to an end. The words are in the old tradition of Western national songs—valiant, heroic, positive, reminiscent of "Rule Britannia":

> Arise, you who refuse to be slaves!
> With our flesh and blood
> Let us build our new Great Wall. . . .

When the singing died down the low voice of Mao with its countrified Hunanese accent began: "The Central Governing Council of the People's Government of China today assumes power in Peking. . . ."

SEALS OF MAO TSE-TUNG. *A pair of seals carved in 1957 for Chairman Mao by a renowned Peking seal-maker. It is not only by the carving and design of the impressions themselves (the two lower squares) that seals are judged, but also by the embellishments of the upper parts. Here the sides of the seals are incised with one of Mao's most famous poem, "Snow." This highly condensed, terse, allusive utterance all but defies translation. The first stanza, of which the near seal bears four lines, recounts the beauties and vastness of China, while the second laments the lack of culture and intelligence of several past emperors, finishing with the three lines on the far seal: "Now they are all past! Only in this present age will great men grow." The seals have carved lions at their tops.*

At this precise moment in Peking the twentieth century began, very tardily, with the long struggle of Chinese dynastic history past, and with the unknowable struggles of a new system only just beginning. All the efforts of Sun Yat-sen, the Kuomintang, and others whose attempts since the fall of the Ch'ing had been directed more or less toward a new outlook, had ended in the old frustrations of warlord supremacy. Now it was the turn of another leader, another set of ideas. Everyone acknowledged that the obdurate medievalism of the past in China had received its deathblow at the end of the last dynasty, but the world's most populous country had still hovered uncertainly on the brink of that hard reality called the present. With the coming of the Communists, for better or for worse, China at last took the plunge.

For Peking—both the city and the people—the near future held what were at that time unimaginable changes. The fifteen years since that October day have changed the life and fabric of the city more than the five centuries of its existence since Yung-lo built the second Peking. No other capital in history has undergone virtual metamorphosis from the medieval to the modern in so brief a time: and there is now no other capital of size and importance left to repeat the performance.

There can be no question that, before the new regime took over, the situation of people in China was desperate. In Peking, and throughout the country, progressive devaluation of the currency made life for the majority of people outside the wealthy and privileged classes one long struggle against actual starvation. Those terrible years of economic depression in the West found their much harsher reflection in China—harsher because the Chinese, still living in a semifeudal subsistence economy, were extremely poor even before the ravages of Japanese war and occupation, together with civil war between the Communists and the Kuomintang, overlaid all life with the long nightmare whose end did not come until 1949. Every book written between the wars, by Westerners and Chinese alike, describing one or other aspect of life in the towns and countryside, holds its painful quota of human misery. Between one quarter and one third of the total population— the estimates vary within these limits—was teetering on the razor edge of starvation. Every bad harvest—and there is a proverb in some parts of China which says, "Three summers, one crop"—brought death (at its kindest) or semistarvation (at its worst) to hundreds of thousands, sometimes to millions. Each overflow of the great rivers, whose beds have long ago risen above the level of the plains and whose dikes precariously confine the water, brought a similar tragedy to a like number of resourceless peasants. These, in basic fact, were the odds in the life-stakes in China, and had been for a very long time. The conditions had been similar at the end of many previous dynasties—perhaps less terrible because the population of China was then less enormous; and at the commencement of several dynasties something had been done to alleviate the situation. In all dynasties, as we have already noted, there was a feeling that things would be different under the new regime, and generally, in different degrees, they were.

The Communist regime, in this respect, was no different from others before it. Its task, considering the number of people it had to deal with, was even greater than that of any other dynasty. Its avowed aim of giving every Chinese a reasonable livelihood within measurable time was even higher than those of former dynasties. It must be admitted that real, crushing, killing famine and the chronic ill health resulting from widespread malnutrition have, in the past fifteen years since the Communists took over, vanished from China. To live in Peking, to travel the length and breadth of China, is to see this for oneself. The traditional Chinese delight in children is everywhere visible in fat, healthy children dressed in grotesque pinafores reminiscent of our nineteenth-century forebears, massed in kindergartens and thousands upon thousands of schools.

This, then, is the most striking change to be found in Peking today—the absence of stark, physical misery. Further than that into the jungle of important but sometimes wearisome and always perplexing controversy about modern China—a debate which revolves around the Western concept of individual freedom—it is not the purpose of this book to venture. We are mainly concerned with Peking, the historical city about which there is so much to tell in order to bring its long and illustrious story up to the present day; and about which, as about China in general, it is much too soon to make judgments. Fifteen years after the inception of a new regime in China was always far too soon to tell what was happening, or what might be about to happen. There were, in fact, many "dynasties" that did not last fifteen years, but which nonetheless set out with hopes and promises just as high as those of others which entrenched themselves for hundreds of years. The present regime is perhaps no exception to the rule of history. But for the time being we cannot be sure.

Let us look, then, without attempting judgments, at some other aspects of the new

DOOR GODS. *On the eve of Chinese New Year, which generally falls in February or early March, householders paste up on their doors a pair of traditional prints showing one or other of the many varieties of protecting spirits. As always in China, stories of the origin of the custom are legion, but one example (left) will serve to show their general purport. It is said that Emperor T'ai Tsung of the T'ang dynasty imagined that he heard demons rampaging in his bedroom. Ch'in and Hu, the ministers of state, were told by his physician that the emperor's pulse was fast and that he was fevered; and they offered to sit up all night to watch*

Peking now rising in the midst of the old. That remote city, as it seemed in the beginning of this book, sheltered within its square wall, nestling on either side of the south-north axis and the sacred adjunct of the Temple of Heaven, expressed with majestic simplicity the quality of dynastic rule in China. There was about it a grandeur, if also a certain smugness in its own perfection. The culture of China and its architectural artifacts have suffered, as we have seen, from a narcissistic tendency. Now the mirror of the ancient pool is disturbed; the ancient beauty of the reflection is mixed with other images. The new city is less easy to grasp, just as its new ideology is more devious, and at the same time utterly opposed to the old. The dictates of the twentieth century, so recently heard in Peking, have no simple theme, and the structures they call forth do not naturally form a simple pattern. The new city of Peking, the third of the cities in our tale, is rising both inside and outside the old one, and its main axis, unconsciously reflecting the diametric opposition of the new ideas to the old, runs not south-north but east-west.

Outside the east wall, parts of which still stand, the prospect is filled with huge factories begriming the pearly air of Peking with fumes as they manufacture artificial fabrics, power lathes, and chemicals. Huge new apartment blocks rise on ground where the hundreds of cells of the old examination halls once stood (see plan, page 130), where the candidates for governmental office were sealed in for three days and two nights writing essays in archaic form on archaic subjects. It is amusing to recall how each entrant had to exchange his own clothes for those provided by the examining body in case he had concealed any aid to his memory, and how the cells were furnished with only a stool, a table, and the paper, brushes, ink-stone, ink-stick, and water which are the materials for calligraphy. For no reason whatever might the door of any cell be opened until the examination papers had been collected. The strain of some candidates proved too great and it was not unusual for one or another to relapse into madness, to die of sheer exhaustion, or even to commit suicide. Even in the case of death, the rules precluded the unsealing of the cell, and a hole had to be cut in its wall in order to remove the unfortunate candidate's body. Yet, inhuman and stereotyped as they were, the examinations were a Chinese contribution to civilization which in the West we did not manage to institute in the matter

over their sovereign. Posting themselves fully armed outside the palace gate, they kept vigil, and the emperor slept well. After many nights of this the emperor took pity on the faithful ministers and ordered his court painter to paint their portraits in full martial array on the palace doors instead. The emperor's health was fully restored, and the custom has prevailed ever since.

The other cut (right) shows the God of Good Business, who sometimes figures on doors at the same time. It is customary in China to settle all business debts before the New Year.

of gaining governmental office until about the time the Chinese examinations ceased after a history of well over a thousand years.

On the parapet of the east wall itself stands another reminder of Chinese contributions to knowledge and reason in human progress—the observatory built there by Jesuit monks in the Ming dynasty to replace the former indigenous one. Nowadays the old bronze orbs and astrolabes, dwarfed by factories, contemplate the result of that scientific revolution of which they were the precursors.

Inside, in the east city, the tangle of *hutung* still occupies most space, but the stench and the garbage of old have gone, and the inhabitants have learned to sweep the beaten-earth surfaces every day. Beyond the doorways of the houses spirit-screens are still there, but the only detectable spirits in an age of vanishing superstition are sounds of music and speech from radios in windows giving onto the courtyards. The prints of Kitchen Gods and of the Goddess of Mercy which used to decorate the doors and rooms in their season have changed into highly colored portraits of Chairman Mao and members of the Communist Party Central Committee. But there are still pictures of Peking opera stars and specimens of a type of art dear to Chinese throughout the land—colored drawings of overly fat babies with expressions of constipated content on their dimpled faces.

The worst overcrowding in those *hutung* houses has recently been relieved by moving some of the tenants whose families were largest to new apartments built elsewhere. The accommodation in these new blocks is simple in the extreme, from a Western point of view. But a pedicab driver and his wife and children—to take a fairly typical example—whose *hutung* house was demolished because of its age and decrepitude, expressed the most lively satisfaction with their new and, as they put it, "modern" living quarters. They liked particularly the running water inside the house, the concrete walls which did not ooze a constant trickle of old Peking dust, the built-in cooking facilities instead of the usual pottery stove fired with charcoal which stands, generally, in the courtyard of a *hutung* house under the shelter of the overhanging roof. They liked too the fact that a shopping center was nearby and that in it they could buy most things they wanted at any time, instead of the old system of scattered shops each dealing in one or two commodities, and the itinerant vendors with whom they had to haggle endlessly. Quite contrary to our Western feelings that the charm of their former *hutung* house might possibly be a factor they would miss, they, like Chinese down the centuries, showed little feeling for old architecture and treated it as expendable. When it was old you simply built a new place. It is for this reason that almost no structure in all China is older than the T'ang dynasty, and there are very few of even that date—certainly no house of any kind.

In the air above those east-city *hutung,* where once the cries of vendors echoed all day and most of the night, the roof of the new Peking railway station now rises. On its façade the two characters for Peking splash their decorative strokes, but with them are Roman letters for the same words. School children now learn romanized Chinese even before they tackle the old characters. By comparison with the congested old railway station which used to lie just outside Ch'ienmen, the new one is a palace. Its courtyard is clear of the rickshaws, mules, stalls, and patient multitudes who used to make themselves as comfortable as they could on their trunks and bedding rolls outside the old station; inside the new building are waiting rooms for several thousand people, others for playing cards, a huge restaurant, closed-circuit television information service, a nursery for small babies —as well as the usual amenities of a big terminal. If the architecture is grandiose, it is at least fairly functional. And the populace of China which passes through the station finds such new things as escalators irresistibly attractive. Old ladies with bound feet can be seen any day enjoying a ride up and down.

But, useful and practical as the station is—and that description may stand for all the other new buildings in Peking—there is in it no proportion, only a fumbling attempt at architecture. The genius of the Ming, whose constructional statements stand all around you in Peking, has vanished as completely as that of Georgian architects in England vanished and was replaced by grandiosity and cliché. To see the disappearance of a style so great, as one does in Peking, is sad indeed. But it is hardly surprising. The condensed historical process by which the medieval is turning into the modern in a couple of decades or so has required the adoption, suddenly, of building techniques which are absolutely foreign to the Chinese. It was, if you reflect a moment, only after fifty years or so of experience in those same modern materials, such as reinforced concrete, that the West began to form a new and contemporary style and once more to make buildings worthy of its own intrinsic genius. One can hardly doubt that in the future the manifest genius of the Chinese people, which has given us some of the most superlative buildings in existence, will once again come out with a new and utterly Chinese architectural statement.

Walking west along Ch'angan Boulevard, the wide and somehow barren new avenue leading toward the center of Peking, new buildings thicken on both sides. The old Peking Hotel has grown a new wing much bigger than itself, and down to the right, on what used to be Morrison Street and is still a main shopping street, a big department store

MODERN SPORTS. *A series of postage stamps highly popular with a nation whose youth has taken to sports with an enthusiasm understandable only in light of the complete absence of organized games before the 20th century. The capacity to work in teams has always been a salient characteristic of the Chinese, and now the sporting instinct is emerging as its counterpart. The old bearded man in one stamp is performing a variety of t'ai chi ch'uan with a long sword. (Redrawn for reproduction.)*

The stamps shown here and on the following pages are all recent issues of the People's Republic. Though not always great examples of graphic design, such postage stamps are nevertheless interesting as indications of the activities, people, objects, and events which a government chooses to commemorate.

causes intense surprise to countryfolk up on a visit to the capital. Toward the palaces new street lamps sprout huge clusters of opalescent globes and built-in loudspeakers from which on holidays recorded music of immense volume swirls above the imperial roofs. But on holidays too you may still hear a musical whistling sound. It comes from flocks of tame pigeons with whistles tied to their tails. The custom is as old as the taming of pigeons, and still delights the Chinese—as does the flying of kites. And in the early hours of a fine morning you can still see old men strolling toward the palaces, carrying bird cages which they uncover as the sun gets up. They sit on the wall of the moat, bathed in the yellow sun, their faces expressionless and contemplative as their small birds sing to the warmth of another Peking day.

The breadth of this east-west street sweeps on past the Gate of Heavenly Peace, which now fronts what must be one of the biggest public squares in the world. For the tenth anniversary of the revolution the square was further enlarged, a big museum built on one side and the Great Hall of the People on the other. Each of these buildings is about a quarter of a mile long, both were constructed in ten months, both are objects of considerable pride to Peking people. The museum contains a chronologically arranged display of objects that gives a panoramic view of Chinese history. Even to walk around it takes an hour, but an exciting hour in which the astonishing continuity of Chinese civilization marches on through thousands of exhibits. The whole genius of a closely integrated culture is set out in those galleries, from its beginnings to the present day, in terms which the average person can grasp.

Somewhere along this wide new street occurred an incident, typical of one aspect of the new Peking and the alteration in traditional Chinese values which has taken place. An officer of the Chinese army was riding his bicycle at top speed along the road, completely disregarding the pedestrians who were crossing at one place. At the intersection nearby, there stood a policewoman controlling the traffic and urging the pedestrians, in the usual manner, not to stray all over the road. (The Chinese have yet to cultivate

COMMUNE ACTIVITIES. *Stamps from a set idealizing life in the communes. Left to right: recreation, a public-health worker, technical training, and consumer goods.*

any traffic sense.) Turning her megaphone on the officer, she shouted: "Comrade Officer! Dismount at once! Dismount at once!" Obediently, the officer got off his bicycle, and the policewoman crossed over to where he was. A small crowd gathered round.

"Comrade!" she addressed him. "How can you, an officer of our glorious army, a man expected to protect the lives of Chinese people—how can you dare to endanger the safety of those pedestrians in such a rash manner? If we had not seen it we could hardly have believed it. We look up to the army as saviors and protectors, and you, Comrade Officer, you who ought to know better, are so antisocial as to ride your bicycle at full tilt through the people in the most reckless way, risking the lives of women and children! . . ."

The officer, eyes downcast throughout this harangue, suddenly burst into tears. Quickly he seized his bicycle, mounted, and rode off at top speed down the boulevard. In China, where, traditionally, women were subject to male authority, where army men had the overweening authority we associate with the Prussian tradition, and where "face" was more important than almost anything else, this story is revealing. But in fact the officer, despite being a product of the new regime, lost so much face in public that he could not stand it and ran off ignominiously.

A ten-minute stroll across the square outside the museum, past the obelisk Monument to the People's Heroes with its calligraphy by Mao Tse-tung, brings you to the Great Hall of the People, grandiose, immaculate, architecturally out of date, but capable of seating ten thousand under its single unsupported roof. The entrance hall of the building is a hundred yards long, a shining lake of polished marble, and its chandeliers are apparently innumerable. The banqueting hall can seat five thousand in great comfort and is a place of memorable meals in which the virtuosity of Chinese cuisine is often demonstrated to have lost none of its subtlety or variety. Here have taken place such amusing (and nowadays somewhat ironic) incidents as that in which Mao Tse-tung spent many minutes good-humoredly teaching a rather clumsy Khrushchev the elements of chopstick technique. Here too, with the entirely novel puritanism which has swept over Chinese life since 1949, one's hosts at each of the large round tables for a dozen guests tend to regale one with somewhat platitudinous stories and anecdotes of deep banality, as dishes fit for emperors succeed one another with relentless culinary resource. It is still true that there are only two great cuisines in the world. The first is French and the other is undoubtedly Chinese. Whatever may be thought of the style of the Great Hall as a whole it is certainly big by any standard. And before it was built, in this country of almost seven hundred million people, there was no public hall with a capacity of more than a thousand.

Pausing a moment on this impressive point, one recalls the other, the new Chinese puritanism. A Western visitor to Peking, feeling perhaps that a daily diet of discovery in the fields of technical advance and ideological change is eventually a little dyspeptic in its effects, took his Chinese interpreter to see a Chinese movie. The story of the film dealt with incidents in the civil war, and the interpreter faithfully translated all dialogue. But at one point when the Kuomintang armies were depicted entering a village and, in the course of their search for food and money, pushing some young women into a barn, dialogue was absent from the sound track. After some minutes the interpreter turned to the Western guest and said: "You understand, perhaps, that the soldiers—the young women—that they have been deflowered." "You mean they've been raped," replied the amused Westerner. The interpreter was then so overcome that it was some time before he recovered sufficiently to continue his translation of the ensuing dialogue.

The story is worth telling if only because its atmosphere, the puritanism which has little precedent in Chinese history or common outlook, is a factor which is very obtrusive in Peking today. There are, however, recent signs that the rigidity of the attitude is lessening as the first sweep of the regime's new broom is followed by a more sensible outlook on life.

Westward along the boulevard, new, raw concrete rises on all sides—the Post and Telegraph Building, Peking Radio Station, the Palace of Nationalities. Some have curly Chinese roofs perched on top of multistorey façades, some have dragons and Ming clouds moulded in concrete, others attempt a more contemporary look. And far away past the great west gate of old Peking the former dusty and squalid suburb has vanished and a concrete jungle of new buildings has mushroomed in its place. Here lie the new university —each of whose many faculties has upwards of ten or twelve thousand students—and another industrial complex. Here too are a planetarium, a zoo, and other strangers to the Peking scene.

In a decade and a half the old has been thoroughly penetrated by the new; the formal perfection of the square plan and its subtle spine of imperial buildings are now embedded in a much bigger city constructed with entirely different objects in view. The buildings are totally different from the old ones because it is as impossible to adapt traditional architecture to multistorey forms as it would be to adapt that of the Parthenon in Greece. The two walks in modern Peking—the dynastic walk already described, and the new one across the breadth of the city—give a fair impression of China's capital, a place where the slow alteration that time produces in any city in the world has been greatly speeded up. Much of the old has gone, but at the same time so much of the new—even if it is less charming—was long overdue. Life in Peking, inseparable from the old structure of the city, has changed too. To describe the alteration in one is to outline the change in the other. The old triple arches of wood and colored tiles that straddled streets have gone with the long gown worn by the men—for the reason that both were impractical in modern times. The multiplicity of restaurants, many with a history of hundreds of years, has dwindled to a few, and the hundreds of curio shops are now represented by a handful which sell, for the most part, the imitations of antiques for which the Chinese have long

MEI LAN-FANG. *Two stamps commemorating the great Peking-opera star, who died in 1961. The portrait is a good likeness of him in middle age, while the other shows him in one of his favorite roles, that of a young heroine in a romantic opera.*

been famous. Gone too are the costly and clamorous bridal and funeral processions which used to wend their way through the streets to the delight of the populace. They have vanished as completely as the lepers, beggars, prostitutes, and houses of pleasure. The rickshaws have turned into pedicabs, the palanquins into taxis; the Legation Quarter is no longer in Ming palaces but in its new accommodation outside the city. Sections of the old walls and all the old gates are still there, the gates circled by new roads so that their central archways might just as well be closed forever.

In the parks of the imperial palaces where the artificial lakes lie and where many emperors formerly took their country pleasure in the center of the city, where they constructed a rustic playground and peopled it with concubines, the people of Peking have long been able to stroll. And now many hundreds each weekend or holiday drink their tea in pavilions meant for kings. In the palaces themselves the peeling paint and falling tiles have been restored, some of their treasures have been reinstated, and for a few cents you can wander through courtyards and pavilions enjoying the splendor of other times. And to go home you can take a bus which is un-Oriental in its cleanliness, its punctuality. (Mussolini, of course, also made trains run on time; no special moral need be drawn.) The dilapidated museum city of Peking has gone for good. In its place is a city compounded of the old with brash areas of the new. Yet this is not unpleasant, not even prosaic as it might have been. Peking is an exciting city because of its intense activity, apart from any other reason. Having said that, the phrase must be justified and amplified. *What* is exciting in Peking, what is the nature of the intense activity?

There is a paragraph in the writings of the Polish composer Witold Lutoslawski that, applied to the revolution in music which has taken place in the West in the last fifty years or so, seems to sum up the nature of what is happening in Peking, and in China as a whole. "The language of the classics, which has taken shape down the centuries and is the result of the endeavors of . . . generations of composers, is like some mighty building whose existence seems assured for all eternity."* In terms of Peking for "classics" we might read Chinese life and its classical buildings, which seemed assured of continuing for all eternity. "There are cultures," Lutoslawski continues, "especially in Asia, which follow the same pattern of . . . conventions over thousands of years. Such could never be the case in our own culture in view of the peculiar restlessness and nervous energy that reside in the European character. The European, it would seem, is happier when he is striving after some goal than when he has attained it; he prefers the process of perfecting something to perfection itself, and the exploring of new possibilities gives him more satisfaction than the subsequent exploitation of them."

* This and following quotations from Witold Lutoslawski come from the unpublished text of a lecture and were privately communicated to the author.

GIANT PANDAS. *Two more recent postage stamps, showing the giant panda, several of which are to be seen at the Peking Zoo munching the bamboo shoots which form their main diet, and always surrounded by a crowd of entranced children. The panda comes from the mountains between China and Tibet.*

One feels that something like this is happening to the Chinese. After several thousand years they seem to have abandoned their pursuit of life within the traditional conventions. If we cannot accept their new ideology, we must still recognize the changes that have come about in Peking as in the rest of China. For the Chinese have begun to experience, by virtue of an essentially Western ideology and Western techniques, that "peculiar restlessness and nervous energy" which is the characteristic of our own civilization. The charming and often baffling disorder and hubbub of life with its abounding but unchanneled energies which is the basis of the Orient as opposed to the Occident has quite obviously been given a direction. In the visible context of a city which is still largely medieval the Chinese are going about their now very twentieth-century business. It is a little like finding a computer in a museum or a launching pad in a cathedral close. Both objects are at least potentially efficient, in an un-Oriental way, and their situations are peculiar, slightly shocking. Broadly, this is the quality of Peking today.

After a while in the city those first glimpses of peculiar activities—shadowboxing and the opera singers practicing their voices against walls, old men airing their birds in the sweetness of a new Peking morning—cease to be the experiences which strike you. A new set of observations presses firmly into your thoughts. Converging on the kindergartens in various parts of Peking in the early morning are fleets of strange vehicles consisting of bicycles, each trailing what looks like a small glass hothouse about eight feet square. Behind the panes are not potted plants but infants whose ages range between four and six on their way to school. Walking along one of the main shopping streets one sees a display, with completely explicit diagrams, of contraceptives—part of the drive to limit the explosive population. Outside the photographers' studios on most days there stand lines of people, mostly young men and girls, sometimes whole families of three generations, waiting to have their portraits done. The young men are often hand in hand with their girl friends—a radical change in manners from the old China when the only people who ever walked hand in hand in public were young boys (they still often do). A visit to the engineering or the medical or the geological faculties of the university brings the sight of almost as many girls as young men among the students. To us in the West nothing of this, except the window display, is unfamiliar. But in Peking, in terms of the medieval which substantially persisted till the Communists came to power, it is utterly surprising.

Among the younger people of the capital there is an almost pathological desire to be "modern," to jump the gap between the Chinese traditional way of life and their concept of twentieth-century existence. "In order to build something new," Lutoslawski goes on, talking of twentieth-century music, "it was first necessary to dismantle the vast edifice . . . namely the traditional language of the classics." This is almost exactly what is being attempted in China. The vast edifice of classical China with its ancient and (it must be admitted) hopelessly out-of-date way of life is being dismantled, and a new one built up. It is a Communist way of life which we do not share, but it would be myopic on our part not to recognize that at least parts of it are built on recognizably Chinese foundations. In Peking in the past fifteen years much has outwardly been achieved. How deep the change really goes is impossible to judge. We have seen how the Chinese traditionally conform to whatever is decreed, reserving their judgment inside themselves. We have seen that perhaps the history of a race is what forms its characteristics. But if this is true, it is certainly a very slow process. Fifteen years of totally different outlook, of a type of living not experienced before, are too pathetically little a basis on which to form opinions. One suspects that the Chinese, following well-established precedent, have reserved a number of theirs.

In essence Peking people seem to have changed very little. Like their city, they have retained their identity. The historic charms of both are now mixed with a contemporary if somewhat fumbling efficiency. Old customs are jumbled up with new celebrations. Chinese New Year, falling generally in February, with its family celebrations and its basis in superstition, is followed by May Day, when half a million citizens romp past the Gate of Heavenly Peace among balloons and missiles, with every sign of intense jollification. And after nightfall on the same day the streets of the capital are alive with people strolling and singing to the music from loudspeakers on the lamp posts. The huge new square fronting the gate fills up again with another half a million people, with amateur bands, jugglers, family parties, acrobats, and foodstalls. There is dancing, there are traditional Chinese guessing-games, and an infectious, simple enjoyment of life quite strange to modern Western experience since our lands became in most essentials one vast urban community in their sophistication. There is a guilelessness in the fun the Peking people have that night which is inescapable and wonderful to see. As if to point the near-rustic charm of the evening's pleasure, the Peking sky is slashed by the soaring beams of searchlights arranged in a circle round the city and converging in one brilliant spot of light above the square. The sturdy old Gate of Heavenly Peace is outlined (one feels even slightly outraged) by lights, and for two hours a continuous ear-splitting bombardment of fireworks (bursting bamboos, as the Chinese call them from the original method of making such delightful bangs) shatters the air and laces the sky with cascading sparks. The dolorous ghosts of the past are thus, to everyone's content, dispelled in traditional manner, whatever may be officially said about celebrating the victory of socialism. Peking people, for once, stay up very late, for the following day is another national holiday and only essential services must work.

Maybe it is this vitality of the Chinese—striking, astonishing, capable of adapting itself to almost any conditions in many parts of the world under all sorts of governments—which allows them to keep their identity: just as it is that, and maybe, the quintessence of its great buildings which allows Peking to retain its tremendously lovable quality. In

Peking it is people and their now museum-piece buildings which are the only constants in a world of galactic flux. And if we must find the clue to Peking's indefinable charms it is to this constant, the people, that we must return.

The people have a natural gaiety and a natural friendliness. They remind you of countryfolk in other lands, more simple than townspeople, more inclined to take others at face value. Like the buildings of the past, however grand and imposing, the spiritual feet of Peking people are firmly placed in the rice field. They are still near enough to the simplicities (and the poverty) of the nonindustrial past to retain much of its charm, its humor, and its unsophisticated ways. And they have (it is worth repeating) endless stores of energy, together with an intense curiosity as unabashed as it is uncalculating.

Nothing in Peking, from the foreign visitor to the newest of the new amenities, escapes this Peking curiosity. Their enjoyment of life is far from the intellectual and somewhat pensive resignation of Chinese sages and poets of the past (a characteristic, it may be noted, that belonged *exclusively* to the sages and poets). It is ebullient, unself-conscious. Like all peoples who have lived closely together with little chance of solitude, the Chinese as a general rule do not care to be alone. They love to go in great masses on picnics, on outings to the Summer Palace, to climb the Western Hills in hundreds, to build—as the Peking people did not so long ago—a new reservoir to ensure their water supply. They are individualists, without any doubt, but like most other Oriental individualists —Mongols, Thai people, Malays—they do not feel that to be units in a mass is to sacrifice their particular form of individuality. This is something which it is hard for the Westerner to understand, but something very obvious in Peking, in China, and in other countries of the Far East.

In Peking—the city that has seen the ringing changes of history for seven centuries— the revolution of 1949, which culminated within its walls, has begun to produce the third in the series of capitals on the old site. Like every other new rule in China's history, the new regime decided to alter much. But in terms of that long history, which is so intensely unitary in its Chinese-ness, the new regime has controlled the city for only a brief candle of time. Harking back to 1435 when the Peking of Yung-lo was fifteen years old, or further still to a time fifteen years after Kublai Khan had built the first Peking—we should undoubtedly have been rash to form any opinion of the Ming or of the Mongol dynasties. Whatever our initial feelings may be, historical perspective cannot be hurried. The quality, as well as the quantity, of the changes in Peking this time may prove to be more far-reaching than ever before. But one thing is certain, the third Peking is just beginning.

Bibliography

Sources of information on almost every aspect of Peking are embarrassingly numerous, especially for more recent periods, and a list that was anywhere near complete would fill a sizable booklet. The selection discussed in the following paragraphs, then, is no more than an indication to the reader who would like to follow up one or another phase of the subject in some of the more important and interesting volumes available. Full bibliographical information concerning each Western-language volume mentioned will be found at the end of this section in a consolidated alphabetical listing, which also includes the works which there has been occasion to mention, generally in brief form, in the text.

CHINESE-LANGUAGE SOURCES. There are two major Chinese compilations. The first, whose whimsical title translates as "Details Found in the Chuming Bookshop in the Intervals Between Slumbers," by Sun Ch'eng-tse, is a seventeenth-century work dealing with Peking buildings and the usages of the imperial court. The second is a collection made by Chu I-tsun, a friend of the emperor K'ang-hsi, whose title may be translated as "Ancient Tales Heard Under the Sun" (i.e., in the capital). This comprises an anthology of almost everything that has been said in Chinese literature on the history and topography of Peking. It contains a somewhat inconsequentially arranged mass of information ranging from ancient history through descriptions of palaces and parks, to poetry extracts and population estimates. Neither of these lengthy volumes has been fully translated, and the work involved would require very considerable scholarship.

HISTORY. In Western languages, despite the enormous accumulation of books dealing directly with Peking or touching on aspects of the city, there is no single volume giving a consecutive history of the capital. This must be gleaned from various general histories such as those by Clubb, Eberhard, Fitzgerald, Goodrich, Granet, and Grousset. All these histories are eminently readable and their different approaches to the subject give, between them, a reasonably full picture of Chinese (and to a lesser extent Peking) history. For the reader who wishes to know the dates of the many dynasties and the hundreds of emperors, together with the relationship between one ruler and his successors, and all the relevant Chinese characters, Moule's is the clearest and best guide. The anonymous *Outline History of China* gives a Communist view of the past with emphasis on the history of rebellions and on the rise of Communist power.

At the present time it is increasingly realized that the history of man's technical mastery of his environment is a vital part of general history. We are fortunate in having the fascinating volumes of Dr. Joseph Needham's *Science and Civilisation in China*. Those so far published probe deeply into this side of Chinese life through the ages. The information, hard to find elsewhere and previously little correlated, is now brought together in a manner which can only be described as masterly.

DESCRIPTION. The best all-round description of Peking is that by Juliet Bredon. The books by Arlington take a closer look and are generally more accurate. Bretschneider gives the basic research data, and the scores of illustrations in Sirén's *Walls and Gates* and *Imperial Palaces* bring the construction of the city to life. Marco Polo, Favier, De Guignes, and Du Halde give descriptions of varying interest—of people and customs and buildings—at various epochs. Lin Yutang's book is a highly personal view of Peking.

ART, ARCHITECTURE, AND OPERA. Chinese art in its many forms has engaged the attention of a large number of historians and critics. The early members of both professions should be avoided by the reader who is not a specialist, as they did not have sufficient documentation at their command and are, if interesting, highly unreliable. The two recently published volumes by Speiser and Willetts may serve as introduction to the whole bewildering kaleidoscope of over three thousand years of recognizably Chinese art. For architecture the best small book is Boyd's, while Nelson I. Wu presents another modern and interesting view of the subject. On Chinese painting perhaps the best concise book is Sirén's *The Chinese on the Art of Painting,* in which the author allows the painters themselves to speak on their aspirations and theories. Among other books worth reading, some of them dealing with minor aspects of art, are those by Priest, Prodan, Schafer, Waley, and Williams.

MISCELLANEOUS. Here the reader may take his choice from a list of works in European languages ranging in time from approximately the sixteenth century down to the present. All are interesting, a few are of literary as well as historical value. There is perhaps only one whose merit as literature singles it out from all the others—that by Osbert Sitwell; as an interpretation of Peking life prior to World War II and as a piece of creative writing it is unique among the hundreds of books on Peking.

Father Ripa's *Memoirs,* though less known than the writings of other Jesuits in China, give an intimate picture of life at ordinary levels and also inside the court of the emperor K'ang-hsi. Staunton and Lord Macartney (the latter in Cranmer-Byng's excellent book) make a combination from which many interesting views of Ch'ien-lung's court emerge with peculiar brilliance, while the work by Backhouse and Bland, and also that by Collis, portray similar details on a more anecdotal level.

For the history of relations between China and the rest of the world, Hudson's volume is probably the best in a small compass. But also well worth reading is the first Needham volume, especially the section "Travel of Ideas and Techniques," which throws a great deal of light on what has been until lately a poorly illumined subject.

Landor, Fleming, Wu Yung, Grantham, and Pierre Loti may be taken as typical of writings on the Boxer Rebellion culminating in the siege of the legations at Peking in 1900, while McAleavy traces the curious history of the last child emperor of the Ch'ing.

John Blofeld gives an inside look at the lighter sides of life in the capital from brothels to picnics in the Western Hills just before World War II, while Acton paints an excellent, evocative picture of the same period. Purcell is well worth reading for his sketch of Chinese life and culture with particular reference to the last century, as well as for his description of the opening of the Wan-li tomb. The Tun Li-chen title, the tourist guide, and Waley's charming *Ballads from Tun-huang* speak for themselves. Robert Payne's biography of Mao Tse-tung is easily the best yet written, both fair and empathetic, while the background of the Communist rise in China—inseparable from the development of Mao—is presented with skill and excitement.

CONSOLIDATED LISTING
Acton, Harold: *Memoirs of an Aesthete.* Methuen, London, 1948
Arlington, L. C.: *Chinese Drama from the Earliest Times Until Today.* Kelly & Walsh, Shanghai, 1930
——: *The Story of the Peking Hutungs.* Vetch, Peking, 1931
——, and Acton, Harold: *Famous Chinese Plays.* Vetch, Peking, 1937
——, and Lewisohn, W.: *In Search of Old Peking.* Vetch, Peking, 1935
Attiret, F.: *A Particular Account of the Emperor of China's Gardens Near Peking.* London, 1752
Backhouse, E., and Bland, J. O. P.: *Annals and Memoirs of the Court of Peking.* Houghton Mifflin, New York, 1914; Heinemann, London, 1914
Blofeld, John: *City of Lingering Splendour.* Hutchinson, London, 1961
Boyd, Andrew: *Chinese Architecture and Town Planning, 1500 B.C.–A.D. 1911.* U. of Chicago Press, 1963; Tiranti, London, 1962

Bredon, Juliet: *Peking.* Kelly & Walsh, Shanghai, 1922

Bretschneider, Emil V.: *Recherches archéologiques et historiques sur Pékin et ses environs.* Leroux, Paris, 1879

Clubb, O. Edmund: *Twentieth Century China.* Columbia U. Press, New York, 1964

Collis, Maurice: *The Great Within.* Faber, London, 1941

Cranmer-Byng, J. L. (ed.): *An Embassy to China: The Journal of Lord Macartney.* Shoe String, Connecticut, 1963; Longmans, London, 1962

Danby, Hope: *My Boy Chang.* Gollancz, London, 1955

de Guignes, Joseph: *Voyages à Pékin.* Imprimerie Impériale, Paris, 1808

du Halde, J. B.: *Description géographique, historique . . . de l'Empire de la Chine et de la Tartarie Chinoise.* Paris, 1735; Gardner, London, 1738

Eberhard, Wolfram: *A History of China.* U. of California Press, Berkeley, 1950; Routledge & Kegan Paul, London, 1950

Favier, Alphonse: *Péking: histoire et description.* Imp. des Lazaristes au Pé-t'ang, Peking, 1897

Fitzgerald, C. P.: *China: A Short Cultural History.* Cresset, London, 1954

Fleming, Peter: *The Siege at Peking.* Harper, New York, 1959; Hart-Davis, London, 1959

Goodrich, L. Carrington: *A Short History of the Chinese People.* Harper, New York, 1943; Allen & Unwin, London, 1948

Granet, Marcel (trans. by K. E. Innes and M. R. Brailsford): *Chinese Civilization.* Meridian, New York, 1958

Grantham, Alexandra E.: *Pencil Speakings from Peking.* Allen & Unwin, London, 1918

Grousset, René (trans. by A. Watson-Gandy and T. Gordon): *The Rise and Splendour of the Chinese Empire.* U. of California Press, Berkeley, 1953; Geoffrey Bles, London, 1952

Hawley, W. M. (ed.): *Chinese Folk Design.* California, 1949

Hudson, G. F.: *Europe and China.* Longmans, New York, 1931; Arnold, London, 1931

Landor, Henry S.: *China and the Allies.* 2 vols. Scribner's, New York, 1901

Lattimore, Owen: *Inner Asian Frontiers of China.* Beacon, Boston, 1962

Lin Yutang: *Imperial Peking: Seven Centuries of China.* Crown, New York, 1961

Loti, Pierre: *Les derniers jours de Pékin.* Calmann-Lévy, Paris, 1902

Macartney, Lord (see Cranmer-Byng)

McAleavy, Henry: *A Dream of Tartary.* Allen & Unwin, London, 1963

Moule, A. C.: *The Rulers of China, 221 B.C.–A.D. 1949.* Praeger, New York, 1957; Routledge & Kegan Paul, London, 1957

Needham, Joseph: *Science and Civilisation in China.* Cambridge U. Press; Vol. I, 1954; Vol. II, 1956; Vol. III, 1959; Vol. IV, 1962

Odoric of Pordenone (Odoricus, Matthiussi): *Les voyages en Asie au XIVe siècle . . . de Odorico de Pordenone.* Trans. by H. Cordier. Leroux, Paris, 1891

Outline History of China, An. Collet, London, 1959

Payne, Robert: *Portrait of a Revolutionary: Mao Tse-tung.* Abelard-Schuman, New York, 1962

Peking: A Tourist Guide. Foreign Languages Press, Peking, 1960

Pelliot, Paul: *Histoire secrète des Mongols.* Restitution of the Mongol text and translation of Chapters I to VI. Paris, 1949

Polo, Marco: *The Travels of Marco Polo.* Available in many different editions

Priest, A.: *Costumes from the Forbidden City.* Metropolitan Museum, New York, 1945

Prodan, Mario: *Chinese Art.* Pantheon, New York, 1958; Hutchinson, London, 1958

Purcell, Victor: *China.* Benn, London, 1962

Ripa, Matteo (trans. by Fortunato Prandi): *Memoirs.* Wiley, New York, 1849; Murray, London, 1855

Schafer, Edward H.: *Tu Wan's Stone Catalogue of Cloudy Forest.* U. of California Press, Berkeley, 1961; Cambridge U. Press, 1961

Sirén, Osvald: *The Chinese on the Art of Painting*. Schocken, New York, 1963
——: *The Imperial Palaces of Peking*. Van Oest, Paris, 1926
——: *The Walls and Gates of Peking*. John Lane, London, 1924
Sitwell, Sir Osbert: *Escape with Me! An Oriental Sketch-book*. Smith & Durrell, New York, 1940; Macmillan, London, 1939
Snow, Edgar: *Red Star Over China*. Random House, New York, 1938; Gollancz, London, 1937
Speiser, Werner (trans. by G. Lawrence): *China: Spirit and Society*. Art of the World Series. Methuen, London, 1960
Staunton, George L.: *An Authentic Account of an Embassy from the King of Great Britain to the Emperor of China*. 2 vols. Campbell, Philadelphia, 1797; Nicol, London, 1797
Tun Li-chen (trans. by Derk Bodde): *Annual Customs and Festivals in Peking*. Stechert, New York, 1936; Vetch, Peking, 1936
Waley, Arthur: *Ballads and Stories from Tun-huang*. Macmillan, New York, 1961; Allen & Unwin, London, 1960
——: *An Introduction to the Study of Chinese Painting*. Benn, London, 1923
Willetts, William: *Chinese Art*. 2 vols. Braziller, New York, 1958; Penguin, London, 1958
Williams, C. A. S.: *Encyclopedia of Chinese Symbolism and Art Motives*. Julian, New York, 1961
Wu, Nelson I.: *Chinese and Indian Architecture*. Braziller, New York, 1963; Prentice-Hall, London, 1963
Wu Yung: *The Flight of an Empress*. Yale U. Press, New Haven, 1963

Index

Staunton, Sir George, 44
Sui dynasty, 48, 55-56
Summer Palace (and road to), *40,* 44, *50, 53,* 134, 135, 137, 139, 171, 253; *ph. 13, 92*
Sun Yat-sen, 139, 196, 199, 200, 242
Sung Cheh-yuan (general), 206
Sung Chiao-jen, 196
Sung dynasty, 8, 48, 58, 68, 69, 70, 87, 88, 97; *ph. 35, 36, 40;* Northern, 55, 69, 70; *ph. 38;* Southern, 55, 69, 71, *72*
Su-tsung (T'ang emperor), 67

t'ai chi ch'uan; see shadowboxing
T'ai Tsu (Ch'ing emperor), 106; *ph. 49*
T'ai Tsung (Sung emperor), 69
T'ai Tsung (T'ang emperor), *244*
Taihomen, *ph. 66*
T'ai-p'ing Rebellion, 134, 135; *ph. 54*
T'ang dynasty, 38, 39, 48, *50, 51,* 54, 55, 56–57, *56,* 58, 67–68, *74,* 97, 130, 187, 198, 205, *244,* 246; *ph. 31, 33*
Taoism, 57
Ta-tu (Peking), *50,* 76, 77–92, 95
tea, 89
Temple of Agriculture, *40, 50,* 102
Temple of Five Hundred Buddhas, *89*
Temple of Heaven, *40,* 42, *50,* 102, 117–20, 197, 244; *ph. 5, 6, 68, 70–74*
Ten-Thousand-Li-Long Wall; *see* Great Wall
Thirteen Tombs, the; *see* Ming tombs
Three Kingdoms (San Kuo), 48, 54–55
Tibet, Tibetans, 39, 87, 89, 203, *251; ph. 123*
tieh (Chinese ideograph), 42
T'ien-ning Pagoda, 77; *ph. 63*
Tientsin, Treaty of, 134, 135, 203
T'oung Pao, 100
traffic, 43, 247-8
Ts'en Ts'an (T'ang poet), 198
Tsungli Yamen (Chinese office of foreign affairs), 204
Tsungwenmen; *see* Hatamen
Tu Fu, 8, 67
Tungan Bazaar, 188
T'ung-chih (Ch'ing emperor), 136
Tungchimen, *50*
Tun-huang, *76*

university, 92; *see also* Pei Ta University *and* Peking University

University of Peking; *see* Peking University

Venice, 171
Verbiest, Ferdinand (Jesuit priest), 91
Volta, Dr. (Russian physician), 128

Waley, Arthur, 177
Wang Ch'eng-en (eunuch), 111–12
Wang Ching (eunuch), 103
Wan-li (Ch'ing emperor), 111, 184, *184, 185,* 186
Warring States period, 51
Western armies, 134–35, 137, 138, 195
Western Hills, 44, *53,* 77, *89,* 171, 207, 253; *ph. 26, 27, 67, 82*
White Dagoba, 8, *38, 39, 40; ph. 8, 65;* Island of the, *see* Emerald Isle
writing, Chinese (ideographs, characters), 42, 49, 53, *83; ph. 105, 106; see also* romanization, schools
Wu, General, 121–22
Wu Liang (eunuch), 97–98
Wu Yung (magistrate), 137–38
Wumen (Meridian Gate), *40,* 114, *116; ph. 4, 7, 29, 66, 111*

Xanadu (Shang-tu), 79

Yang Kuei-fei (T'ang empress), 57, 58, 67; *ph. 39*
Yangtse River, 51, 53, 90
Yeh-lu Ch'u-ts'ai (governor of Peking), 75
Yehonala, Empress Dowager, 95–96, 106, 135–39, 171, 196, 199, 204–5; *ph. 53, 92*
Yellow River, 9, 41, 49, 51, 54, 68, 69, 71, 84, 90, 92, 96, 97, 138, 187
Yen state, 51, 54, 55
Yenching (Peking), 55
yin-yang, 7, *7,* 41
Yuan dynasty (Mongol dynasty), 37, 48, 58, 74, 76, 85, 88, 89, 90, 92, 98, 176, 187, 189, 253; *ph. 39*
Yuan Shih-k'ai, 195, 196, 197, *197,* 199
Yuchow (Peking), *50,* 55, 57, 68
Yung-cheng (Ch'ing emperor), 131
Yung-lo (Ming emperor), 86, 96–102, 106, 114, 131, 181, 183, *183,* 184, 242, 253; *ph. 48, 78, 79*
Yungtingmen (South Gate of Outer City), *40,* 42, *50*

zoo, Peking, 45, 249, *251*

The "weathermark" identifies this book as having been planned, designed, and produced at John Weatherhill, Inc., 50 Ryudo-cho, Azabu, Minato-ku, Tokyo | Book design and typography by Meredith Weatherby | Layout of photos by Brian Brake | Text composed and printed by Kenkyusha | Color plates, in six-color offset, engraved and printed by Dai Nippon | Monochrome plates, in gravure, engraved and printed by Inshokan | Line cuts and halftones engraved by Misaki | Endpapers, in offset, engraved and printed by Obun | Binding by Makoto | The text is set in 12-point Monotype Baskerville, with display type in hand-set Bulmer